John Grigsby took a degree in Prehistoric Archaeology at the University of Wales, Bangor, followed by a Masters in Celtic Mythology. This, his first book, represents the results of ten years' research into the psychology and mythology of the prehistoric Celts.

WARRIORS
OF THE
WASTELAND

A Quest for the Sacrificial
Cult behind the Grail Legends

JOHN GRIGSBY

Watkins Publishing
London

This edition published in the UK in 2003 by
Watkins Publishing, 20 Bloomsbury Street,
London, WC1B 3QA

Cover design by Echelon Design, Wimborne
Cover picture © PhotoDisk
Designed and typeset by Echelon Design, Wimborne
Printed and bound in Great Britain by NFF Production

British Library Cataloguing in Publication data available

Library of Congress Cataloging in Publication data available

ISBN 1 84293 058 3

www.watkinspublishing.com

CONTENTS

PART THREE: THE DOLOROUS STROKE

PART FOUR: THE FISHER KING

LIST OF
ILLUSTRATIONS & MAPS

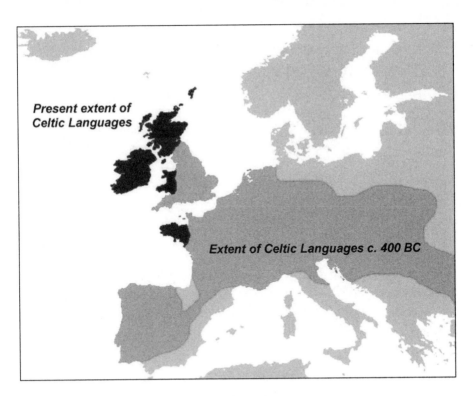

Map 1. *Extent of Celtic languages c. 400 BC and AD 2000*

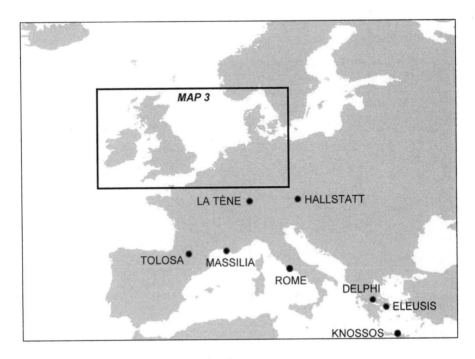

Map 2. *European place names mentioned in the text*

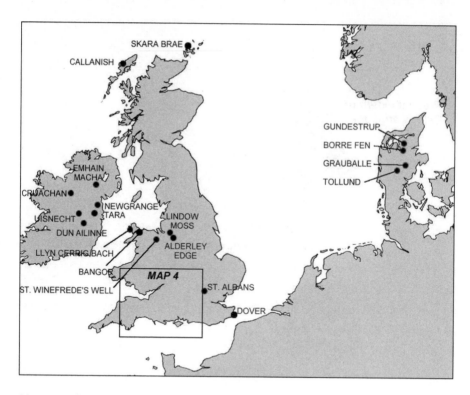

Map 3. *North-west European place names mentioned in the text*

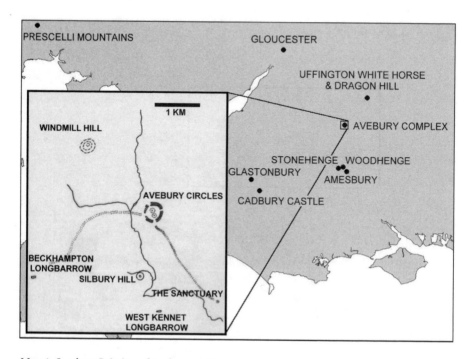

Map 4. *Southern Britain and Avebury environs*

ACKNOWLEDGEMENTS

My first words of thanks are to the numerous writers, living and departed, whose footsteps I followed through the forests of myth; this book marks the forging of my own pathway, so any flaw in my work is to be laid not at their door, but at my own.

My heartfelt thanks go out to my tutors at Bangor University: Frances Llewellyn – who may not agree with what I have written, and Dafydd Glyn Jones – the Yoda to my undisciplined Skywalker, who may.

I want to thank Colin Wilson and Mark Booth for inspiring me to put pen to paper; Frances Kelly, my agent; Michael Mann of Watkins Publishing for believing in this venture, and Florence Hamilton, my editor, without whom this book would probably be twice as long and half as readable.

The photographic section of the book could not have been completed without the help of the following: the artist and inspirational tour guide Martin Byrne (details of whose 'Sacred Ireland' tours can be found on *www.carrowkeel.com*); Peter Chow, who kindly allowed me to use his photo of Stonehenge; the staff at Dover Museum; Ulla Erikson at Silkeborg Museum and Helga Schutze at the National Museum of Denmark, Copenhagen, as well as the photography department of the British Museum. My warmest thanks go to my friend and fellow seeker, the mercurial Rob Speight, for whom photography is but one of many talents.

I would also like to mention Pam Warriner, Julie Grigsby, Joanne Jones, Mike Harcourt, Steve and Aly Young, Nick Bray, Simon Scullion and Matt Philpott, for keeping my feet on the ground. Special mention must be given to Jonathan Holden for both his superior archaeological knowledge and his many helpful suggestions, and to Martin Latham for being so understanding when my mind wasn't fully on my work. Thanks to Siri for keeping me company during the long hours of writing, and, of course, love and thanks to my long-suffering partner Heidi, who was kind enough to threaten to leave me only once during my immersion in this volume. Ultimately, though, the blame lies at the door of Paul, my twin and sternest critic, who not only provided me with photographs, but whose gift of a book on the Arthurian legends when I was 16 started this quest. Thanks Paul.

Perhaps the biggest thank-you is to my parents, who encouraged me to follow this wayward path through university and beyond and have never ceased in their support (both emotional and financial!). I dedicate this book to them.

For my parents, with love

INTRODUCTION

Perhaps it was inevitable – having been brought up on a diet of J R R Tolkien and C S Lewis and thus acquiring a love of fable and landscape – that when at the age of 16 I first encountered the legends of Arthur in the form of Marion Zimmer Bradley's novel *The Mists of Avalon*, I would be instantly smitten. From then on I devoured every book I could find on the subject – from classics like Sir Thomas Malory's epic *Le Morte d'Arthur* to modern retellings such as Mary Stewart's Merlin trilogy and T H White's *The Once and Future King*. What interested me was not so much the question of whether the existence of Arthur could be proven historically (though I thought it probable), but the discovery of something vital about my own and my country's heritage that my formal education had ignored. I had been taught about Odysseus and Hercules at school, but little mention had been made of Arthur and Sir Lancelot; I knew the tales of Jacob and Moses, but what of Sir Gawain and Guinevere? It was as if our native traditions were deemed less worthy than those of the Classical world – as if they occupied a cultural blind spot. Wishing to remedy this one-sidedness I launched myself, despite my forthcoming exams, into an extracurricular study of native myth that would change not only my choice of further education, but my whole life.

My study of native myth opened up a whole new dimension to the landscape in which I lived. I awoke to a land saturated in fable and ancient lore as rich as the 'dreamtime' of the Australian Aborigines, to whom every feature of the earth had its own story, its own mythical resonance.

In my own home town of Dover, for instance, to my surprise and joy I discovered a legend that stated that the head of King Arthur's nephew, Sir Gawain, had once been kept at Dover Castle – with its grievous wound dealt by Sir Lancelot plainly visible. According to Sir Thomas Malory, the king himself had laid the relic in the Castle chapel following Gawain's death during a battle in the harbour.[1] The printer William Caxton in his 1485 edition of Malory's epic supported the author's story by writing in his prologue that 'In the castle at Dover ye may see Gawain's skull.' Caxton, who had worked as a merchant in Bruges and so had passed through Dover on numerous occasions, was no doubt speaking from experience.

But if any such skull had existed, and I saw no reason for Malory and Caxton to lie, to my disappointment it was no longer on display – perhaps it had been taken away, hidden or even destroyed during the Reformation. Many years later, as a custodian at the castle, I could also vouch for the fact that it had not been secreted away somewhere, hidden from the prying eyes of the public. But at the time its disappearance somehow added to its mystery. Whose skull was it? Had it originally been that of a local saint – or even a martyr, given the vicious wound on its crown? Had this been the case surely he would have been remembered; his precious relics would not have become attributed to a mythical hero. And it was only when I looked deeper into the Arthurian corpus that I was to stumble on some semblance of an answer.

The legends surrounding Arthur, the quasi-historical 'Once and Future King', I soon discovered, were rooted in traditions from a time far earlier than the Dark Ages in which he was supposed to have lived. Behind the lords and ladies of the Arthurian legends lay, for the most part, the gods and goddesses of a prehistoric Iron Age people called the Celts, whose modern-day descendants – the Irish, Welsh, Scots and Bretons – still speak the ancient tongue that was used in these islands before the coming of the Romans. The witch Morgan le Fay, Arthur's half-sister, for instance, was no other than a version of the Irish war goddess Mórrígan clothed in medieval dress; and behind noble Sir Gawain lay a Welsh hero named Gwalchmai (the 'Hawk of May'), whom some saw as a solar deity because his strength waxed and waned with the sun.

The name 'Celt' (*Keltoi*) had first been applied to these people by the Greeks, who used it as a general term to define a number of tribes of north-west Europe sharing an underlying homogeneity of language, culture and, arguably, religion.[2] Archaeologists have argued that these 'barbarians' originated in the Alpine regions around 700 BC and then, catalysed into growth through trade with the civilisations of the Mediterranean, 'migrated' throughout north-west Europe and across the Channel into Britain, over-running the native population.

These prehistoric Celts exerted a great fascination for me, not least because my (English) education had seemed so dismissive or ignorant of them. British history, I had been taught, began in 55 BC with the arrival of Julius Caesar – who brought the 'light' of civilisation to this primitive land. The peoples that the Romans encountered here, according to the conventional image, were little more than savages. It seemed an embarrassingly ignoble start for Britannia that while other nations were building pyramids and debating philosophy these isles were populated by skin-wearing brutes.

This view of the 'primitiveness' of the Celts was no doubt encouraged by the fact that they entered battle naked and painted with blue dye, and collected the heads of their foes as trophies, and that their 'priests', the druids, were accused by their Roman contemporaries of performing abominable human sacrifices. Many have argued (and continue to do so) that these accusations were unfounded, being nothing more than Roman propaganda to justify the subjugation of the Celts and the annexation of their land. However, the numerous finds dating back to the Iron Age of fatally injured or dismembered human bodies and severed heads uncovered from bogs, lakes and wells in north-west Europe (such as the body of a man found in a peat bog at Lindow Moss in Cheshire in 1984, who had been killed in a bizarre triple method) seemed to prove that the Classical authors were reporting the truth.

I found it hard to believe that the people whose myths lay behind the beautiful and haunting legends of Arthur had perpetrated such horrendous crimes, but I could not refute the evidence that lay before me. Although unpalatable, this evidence of sacrificial rites did provide clues to the origin of the Dover skull. With its deep head wound, might it not have belonged to the victim of a Celtic sacrifice? Had this skull, a gory talisman facing towards the Continent, perhaps been placed there in Celtic times to protect the land from invasion? Could this ancient trophy have then been kept at the Castle (whose site was thought to have once been a Celtic hill fort), with each successive occupant unwilling to banish the uncanny relic for fear of supernatural reprisals? This was the case with many so-called 'screaming skulls' associated with old buildings.

The research that I undertook to find an answer to such questions would revolutionise my earlier view of the Iron Age Britons and their ancestors. Far from being uncivilised troglodytes the ancient prehistoric populations of these isles belonged to a unique cultural tradition that had arisen, independent of Greece and Rome, on the Atlantic coasts of Britain, France, Spain and Denmark – areas linked through maritime contact since Neolithic times. This zone was a centre of innovation and culture long before the establishment of the great city-states of the Mediterranean. The breathtaking monuments of these indigenous megalithic cultures *predated* the pyramids of Egypt, and their stone circles, once credited to the Romans or Phoenicians, showed a precise knowledge of astronomy and mechanics that shattered any belief that they had been erected by savages.

What's more, archaeologists began to argue that the Celts had not 'arrived' in Britain with their language during the Iron Age, but were the *descendants* of the indigenous population of the Atlantic coasts,[3] whose language and unique culture had developed in those regions over the thousands of years that they had been in contact with each other. Such a view explained Caesar's hitherto puzzling observation that the druidic religion had originated not on the Continent (as would be expected if the Celts had sprung up in the Alps, as previously thought), but *in Britain*, and that those wishing to learn more of this system of knowledge travelled there to study it.[4] The druids, it seemed increasingly possible, were the direct heirs to the knowledge possessed by the builders of Stonehenge.

Suddenly statements in Classical sources that referred to the druids' possession of a body of lore akin to the teachings of Pythagoras did not seem so unlikely. Was it possible that there had once been a 'light' burning in the north (before being extinguished by Rome), that there once existed the glimmerings of a civilisation to rival those of the Classical world but which had been forgotten, or deliberately repressed and eradicated from the mainstream Western view of history? It was easy to imagine how this could have occurred – history was always written by the victors, and the Celts had been on the losing side of conflicts from Roman times onwards.

The Celts may have been seen as the 'losers' of the Western world – surviving only at the very edges of the Atlantic, where the Romans, Saxons and Normans had failed to reach them – but I soon realised that their rich culture had not been as mercilessly eradicated as their victors would have had us believe. The spirit of this culture had in fact permeated the very foundations of Western civilisation – not politically or economically, but *spiritually*. The Celts' gift to the Western world was one of magic and imagination: the stories of Arthur and his court were to entrance and enthral the courts of Europe, and central to these tales was the legend of the Holy Grail.

The Grail myth was one that fascinated and confused me in equal amounts. What was this Grail that in some versions was the cup of the Last Supper and in others an emerald stone fallen from heaven? Whatever its form its function remained the same – in all myths and retellings it was something divine, something magical that touched upon the spiritual; a revelation of the Holy. Yet beneath their overtly Christian gloss these legends were hedged in strangely primal imagery; they told of magical wounds that would not heal, of enchanted vessels that dispensed whatever food was desired. In one myth, in place of the Grail there was a *severed head* borne on a bloody silver salver – a throwback to the pagan cult of the head to which Gawain's skull seemed to belong. Was it possible that a connection existed between the sacrifices of Celtic times and this medieval myth? It was this question that ultimately led to the writing of this book.

Warriors of the Wasteland is the story of my search for the forgotten rites at the heart of the Grail myth – not only a quest to uncover the lost beliefs of the Iron Age Celts and reveal what part human sacrifice played in them, but also an attempt to understand how this apparently 'civilised' prehistoric people justified the ceremonial killing of innocent men and women.

Because very few details of the pagan religions of the Iron Age Celts survive (the only contemporary sources were compiled by their Classical enemies, and their own literature was written after the demise of paganism), fundamental to the writing of this work has been my attempt to reconstruct Celtic beliefs, a feat akin to reconstructing Christianity using only broken stained-glass windows. Of course such an attempt cannot uncover the full diversity of cults that probably existed throughout the Celtic world any more than ruined church windows can provide information about Catholicism, Protestantism, evangelicalism, Greek Orthodoxy or any other faith. At its height the Celtic world (i.e. regions where a Celtic language was spoken) spread from Ireland in the west to Galacia in the east, and yet because of its later eclipse under the Roman Empire, the only vernacular Celtic literature to survive in any useable form is that of Ireland and Wales. From the outset, then, my reconstruction is necessarily limited to the Celts of the British Isles, whose rites and myths may well have differed from those of the Continent.

The reconstruction is based on Celtic myth and the latest archaeological research, but also uses comparative myths and religion, especially those of other Indo-European peoples, to fill in the gaps (much as in Steven Spielberg's film *Jurassic Park*, frog DNA is used by Ingen scientists to bridge the gaps in dinosaur DNA, thus enabling the long-dead beasts to live again). Unlike these scientists, however, my attempt at resurrection has been undertaken not for entertainment but to provide a glimpse into the world of sacrifice, into the last thoughts of the man in the Cheshire bog or the long-lost head from Dover Castle. For if we are truly to grasp the meaning of these rites we have to understand that Celtic myths were not just stories or tales for the fireside, but parts of a living religion with real value to their adherents. We therefore need to take a step into the psychology of the Celts.

And this is where previous attempts to recover the pagan religions of our ancestors have failed, for they brought with them the modern Western bias that either sees the act of sacrifice as a cruel aberration, with its victims lamentable and unwilling, or glosses over it in the hope that the omission will go unnoticed. But in my view the act of sacrifice was as pivotal to the Celtic religion as the crucifixion is to Christianity. And in neglecting it scholars have missed the very essence of Celtic paganism, for my research has uncovered that the individuals sacrificed died not as scared and unwilling offerings to hungry gods, *but as gods themselves*, acting as a bridge between the earthly world and that of the divine. The origins of these rites lay in a cult of rebirth and immortality as sophisticated as any found in the Classical world – a cult that would in time become the legend of the Grail.

John Grigsby
April 2002

Introduction

Notes

1. Malory, T (1969) p. 510.
2. The earliest mention of 'Keltoi' is in the work of the Greek geographer Hecataeus of Miletus (540–475 BC), who states that the Greek trading port of Massilia (Marseilles), from which the traveller Pytheas originated, was founded near the 'land of the Keltoi'. See Cunliffe, B (1997) pp. 2–3.
3. This argument is best put forward in Cunliffe, B (2001) pp. 293–7.
4. Caesar, *The Conquest of Gaul* Book VI p. 13.

Prologue

THE MAN
IN THE WELL

My hands and face are numb, and although I am wet-through, half-frozen, and breathless from the climb, I feel an enormous sense of exhilaration and, what's more, of homecoming. It is strange to think that the last time I scaled the Tor at Glastonbury it was midsummer, many years ago, when along with many others I made the heady climb to witness the sunset. On that occasion I was part of an eclectic congregation of travellers, some of whom with chanting and drumming were serenading the dying of the light. Today, however, I am alone. And even the sun to which those many voices were raised is absent, hidden behind the leaden sky of an English winter morning.

I seek shelter from the freezing rain in the solitary ruined tower of St Michael's Church that tops the Tor. Luckily the rain lashing against the walls in intermittent squalls is unable to penetrate the tower so the interior is mercifully dry, although dark and other-worldly.

The tower is all that remains of the 1360 church, itself the second on the site – its predecessor fell in an earthquake on the inauspicious date of 11 September 1275.[1] This act, according to the occultist Dion Fortune,[2] who once lived in a house at the foot of the Tor, signified that here the 'old gods' still held their own. In her 1934 book *Glastonbury – Avalon of the Heart*, she states that the Tor had never said 'Thou hast conquered, O Galilean.'[3] Today, I am inclined to agree. The wind is making an unearthly moaning as it whips through the doorless arches, and I have a sudden fear that lightning might strike the tower, or that I might at any moment be joined by one of Fortune's 'old gods'.

This great hill on which I am perched rises out of the Somerset levels like some colossal crouching beast or slumbering giant. Some have seen in the stepped levels that wind about this hill evidence for a vast prehistoric maze, or in its curvaceous rise the form of a recumbent goddess. Rumour has it that the Tor (a West Country word for 'hill') is hollow, filled with subterranean chasms and caves, an entrance to the underworld itself. One story tells how a Dark Age hermit, the Welsh St Collen who lived in a cell on the slopes of this strange hill, had once met the king of fairyland and leader of the Wild Hunt Gwyn ap Nudd, within the Tor.[4] St Collen dismissed the infernal king and his palace with a sprinkle of holy water (perhaps taken from the waters of Chalice Well, the chalybeate spring that bubbles up in the valley below the Tor) and found himself alone once more on the hillside. I had filled a plastic bottle with the self-same iron-rich water, and taking it now from my rucksack, I unscrew the cap with numb fingers and take a swig of its blood-tasting contents, leaving enough in the bottle to cast about me should the need arise.

It is hardly surprising that such pagan presences abound here: Glastonbury, so the legends say, was ancient 'Avalon' – the apple-isle, a pre-Christian Celtic Elysium to which the wounded Arthur had been brought to be healed by his half-sister, the bewitching Morgan le Fay.

Set in the heart of cider-country, this strange hill, once almost an island, no doubt had always struck man as somewhat other-worldly. Quite when it became associated with the apple-isle of Avalon is not clear, but a connection between Glastonbury and Morgan le Fay's earthly paradise, derived from a Celtic land of the dead, must have existed before 1191, when 'Arthur's tomb' – a hollowed-out oak coffin containing the skeleton of a man with many wounds, and a woman at his feet – was said to have been 'discovered' by monks in the grounds of Glastonbury Abbey. This 'discovery', which many take to have been a forgery cunningly crafted to boost the Abbey's finances after a disastrous fire, no doubt rested on an already-common connection between Arthur and this site. Upon the coffin, according to Gerald of Wales, was an iron cross bearing the words 'Here lies buried the renowned King Arthur, with Guinevere his second wife, in the Isle of Avalon.'[5] Modern archaeological surveys have revealed that something had definitely been unearthed where the chronicles say the tomb was discovered – so the grave itself (if not the cross) may not have been a forgery. It had perhaps contained the body of some ancient king after all, though whether of Saxon or British stock it is impossible to say. Whatever the dubious nature of the foundations of the Glastonbury legends, they undoubtedly had power. Glastonbury had fulfilled a need – and continues to do so, it seems, given the number of pilgrims who still tread its hallowed soil.

From my place of relative shelter I wander over to the eastern doorway and watch the landscape come into focus and then dissolve again into swirling cloud. From this vantage point, some 500 feet/150 metres above the surrounding levels, it is possible on a fine day to see for many miles. To the north you can sometimes glimpse the mountains of Wales, and to the south the earthen ramparts of Cadbury Castle, the Iron Age hill fort re-occupied by the native Britons after the departure of the Roman legions in AD 410 and that some believe is the famed Camelot of Arthur. I scan the horizon for this landmark, but low-lying cloud prevents any chance of a view.

I walk across the tower to the western arch and gaze out over the levels. From here, when the clouds lift, I can just see the crumbling remains of the Abbey. Despite the claim that Arthur's grave had been found here,[6] many continued to believe that Arthur was not dead but merely sleeping under Cadbury Castle's mighty defences, to awake in Britain's hour of need – a myth no doubt supported by the sense of 'personality' and 'presence' felt at places such as the Tor.

The rain ceases; exiting from the western door I glance up at the carvings above the archway. Far above me I can make out an eroded carving of St Michael, pinning down the dragon with his left foot, symbolising the victory of light over darkness, or, as many believe, the suppression of the old religion by the new. The powers of darkness, it seems, are winning the battle today, for in the stormy half-light I can barely make out the other carvings. To the left of the doorway I am just able to discern a depiction of St Bride milking her cow – commemorating, so I have read, her alleged visit to Glastonbury in AD 488[7] – and to the right of the door a curious image of an angel weighing a soul on a set of scales. Here in the dim light, on a spot many have claimed is the entrance to the other world, it is easy for such meanings to shift and change – to see in the weighing of the soul a connection with the Egyptian *Book of the Dead*, and in St Bride (as Dion Fortune states) the Egyptian cow goddess Hathor. Glastonbury can play such tricks with the unwary.

The ever present clouds that course seemingly just yards above my head are of that curious golden grey that often presages snow, and so I make the decision to risk the treacherously muddy descent before I get caught in a blizzard. I take another gulp of the icy water, and with a half-smile pour the remainder onto the grass beside me.

To avoid falling flat on my face, I take a good half-hour to retrace my steps to the bottom of the Tor, but once down I am warmed and invigorated, and only a few dozen steps from my destination – Chalice Well gardens. The promised snow has failed to materialise, the cloud has thinned a little and my mood has lifted. A handful of people are milling about the lower part of the gardens amongst the pools and waterfalls, which are stained a rust-red from the iron content in the water, but I take the path up the slope to the wellhead – the carved head of a lion from whose mouth the waters pour forth onto a circular slab of stone. I lift the glass placed there and take a sip of water – which maintains a constant temperature of 52 degrees Celsius – then replace the cup and walk up to the well itself.

The name Chalice Well is typical of the myth-making qualities of Glastonbury. In fact it derives from 'chalk-well', but the place has been called Chalice Well ever since it became associated with the Holy Grail – that mysterious cup whose story is embedded deep within Arthurian legends, and which was said to have been brought here by Joseph of Arimathea and secreted in the depths of the well by the 'Fisher King'.

Although the day is still cold, the wind has died down, and overhead patches of blue are appearing through the clouds. At my feet lies Frederick Bligh Bond's elaborate well cover, made in 1919. Bond (a contemporary of Dion Fortune) had helped excavate the ruins of the Abbey – with the help, so he claimed, of the ghost of one of the monks.[8] On the cover, rendered in black iron, is the *vesica piscis* in the form of two interlocking circles. It's a good choice of motif for this place because it symbolises the blending of opposites: pagan and Christian, this world and other world, ancient and modern, male and female, yin and yang. It sums up Glastonbury, yet also has a deeper meaning: early Christians used this ancient Pythagorean symbol as a secret sign, for within its design could be discerned a fish, which in Greek was *icthys*, a word whose letters were an acronym for 'Jesus

Christ the Son of God'. But the symbol of the fish had had a long and ancient association with the pagan religions preceding Christianity, and had played no small part in the legends of the Grail. Bending down, I lift the well cover and peer into the dark waters below, the same still depths I had peered into 13 years earlier on my first visit to Glastonbury, aged 17, half expecting to see the glimmer of a golden vessel concealed here by the Fisher King.

Within the well I can just discern the huge masonry blocks from which it is formed, oriented, according to Dion Fortune, so that the sun shines into its depths as it skirts the Tor on midsummer's day. Within the chamber is a man-sized recess in which she believes human victims had been bound in pre-Christian times – their blood mixing with the iron-stained fungus in the water and their sacred deaths lending power to the visions of the officiating druids, and later of Arthur's half-sister, Morgan le Fay.[9]

In fact this chamber and the 'man-sized' niche within it were not built until some 1,000 years after the last druid walked the land, for it was constructed in the Middle Ages when Glastonbury was a spa town rivalling the popular nearby Bath. No pagan sacrifice had ever taken place in the niche in this well, at least not in Christian times. What happened before this, however, is anyone's guess.

It would be easy to scoff at Fortune's 'error' and label her a romantic, a dreamer and self-deluded mystic, but while looking into these black depths I am aware that her vision of the man in the well lies chillingly close to the truth. After 13 years of questing, my own answer to the mystery of the Grail is inextricably bound up with such a sacrificial tradition for, as I discovered in the years following my initial visit here, bodies of sacrificed men have been unearthed from peat bogs, wells and rivers, where they had lain preserved beneath the water. In trying to decipher the meaning of their deaths I would eventually stumble upon my own elucidation of the Grail myth.

It flashes before my eyes now, my own vision of the Grail, the fruit of my long search, in a parade of startling images that take on a life of their own. In the dark before the dawn, emerging from the covering of the wood are two pallid shapes – a pair of milk-white oxen drawing what appears to be a wagon, upon which are seated a bearded young man and a smaller figure, a white-robed woman with flowers entwined around her plaited hair. Following them is a train of men and women, a dozen or so, robed in white and black – and behind them a silent crowd. The wagon stops and the man and his companion are led to a boggy clearing beside mist-covered waters. He is stripped naked save for an armband of fur, and then bound. His skin seems to writhe and move with emerald-coloured serpentine patterns – is he painted or is this just the effect of the moonlight through the branches upon his bare skin? In the half-light he looks as if snakes are coiled about his arms, chest and neck. He is offered a dish containing bread or grains, and white berries. Around him figures caper and dance to a tune that does not reach my ears. He stumbles once, twice, as if drugged. Beside him now is the woman, also naked, holding in her delicate hands a knotted length of cord, which she proceeds to slip around his neck.

The attendants of the pair form a circle around them within a rough ring of trees on the edge of the water. They begin to turn, so that it is difficult to see what is happening. As they turn it seems as if the skies above are also turning, feverishly spinning around the pole star, a place of still-ness and repose, echoed by the centre of the ring where two alone stand still. In tantalising glimpses through the encircling dancers I can just discern the greenish-white body of the man and the whiter body of the girl blur into one on the waterlogged ground. What happens next is swift and shocking. At a given signal from the girl, another figure – or is it two – enters the central space. The naked man is pulled up by his hair so that he is kneeling in the mud. There is then the flash of a falling axe, the noose slipped around his neck during the pair's union tightens sickeningly about his throat, and a crimson arc of blood shoots from a swiftly made cut to his jugular. Amid the whirring of limbs and flashes of weapons I see a spear held aloft and watch as it is thrust down between the victim's crumpling legs. Another gush of blood joins that already staining the marshy ground. The woman is led away, bedecked with garlands, sticky with his blood.

I cannot hear the keening and lamenting that follow the death strokes; black-robed women pull at their hair, rake their faces with their nails – the air seems to turn colder, the sky darker. From the victim's throat dark jets of lifeblood pulse, first strongly then limply, into a silver vessel that is passed to the spear-bearer with whoops of joy, of victory. Somewhere in the grove a fire is lit. Do the celebrants drink from the cup? I cannot see. The world seems to stop. Time seems to stop.

The Man in the Well

Sometime after – maybe an hour, maybe a lifetime, time has ceased to have meaning – a youthful figure emerges from the shadows and kneels on the muddy shoreline amongst the reeds, looking down through the mirrored surface of the water in which the naked man has been placed. I see as through the newcomer's eyes, and notice that in the black waters clouded with blood, the victim's red hair forms a strikingly vivid nimbus around the pale green of his disembodied face, which is set in a serene expression as if he were but sleeping. The newcomer is handed the silver vessel: he drinks from it and shudders as he tastes its bitter contents – blood and a fiery liquor that masks an unpalatable mix of mind-altering herbs. A cauldron is brought to him, filled with boiled fish; he takes a small morsel and chews on it. Again, time passes … he then begins to sway, to dance. He is spinning, shouting, wheeling, until his eyes go up into his head and he collapses. He falls before the dead man, crouching over the water and touching with a wand the pale lips inches below the surface, muttering over and over a voiceless question. The bloody-haired green-faced man beneath the water shifts and changes form – from man to fish and back to man again.

And then I see that below the filmy surface of the pool the lips of the dead man are moving; but is this really happening or am I just seeing what the man who has drunk the bitter drink is seeing, befuddled by the secret ingredients of the cup and beguiled by the ever changing surface of the lake? The dead mouth, it appears, is moving, forming words; and as it speaks the dead branches about the grove are moving too, twisting, budding, blossoming … And as the rising sun sends a path of shimmering gold across the lake the eyes of the dead man open … and he begins to sing.

I rouse myself from this daydream and gently close the lid of the well. My bloody vision strikes me as make-believe, as pure invention, but I know that it is not something I have just dreamed up. Thirteen years of research had led me to it, to my belief that behind the myth of the Holy Grail lies a lost rite of human sacrifice, part of an ancient mystery religion that offered to its participants a glimpse of immortality that was already thousands of years old when Caesar came to these shores. My journey has been a long one, its path strewn with both frustration and elation, but it is one that I believe to be worth telling.

And it begins with the wounding of the king.

Notes

1. Mann, Nick (1986) p. 12.
2. Née Violet Mary Firth. See Benham, P (1993) pp. 251–63.
3. Fortune, Dion (1986) p. 58.
4. Ashe, Geoffrey (1990) pp. 115, 117.
5. For a good discussion of Arthur's tomb see Ashe, Geoffrey (1957) pp. 93–8.
6. Unfortunately lost after the dissolution of the Abbey at the orders of Henry VIII.
7. Mann, Nick (1986) p. 15.
8. For a good introduction to this intriguing topic see Benham, P (1993) pp.192–238.
9. Fortune, Dion (1986) pp. 9–10.

Part One

THE WOUNDED KING

Chapter 1

THE LEGEND

The legend of the Holy Grail captured the imagination of medieval Europe like no other tale. The many variations of the tales are all based on a broadly similar theme; they tell of a wonder-working vessel which provides food and drink in abundance and is processed through a strange castle that is difficult to find. Within the castle is a king, known as the Wounded or Fisher King, grievously injured with a spear or sword – usually through the thigh – and for as long as his wound remains unhealed, the land will be laid waste. It is the purpose of the Grail knight, a spiritual warrior in this Wasteland, to find the castle and ask a specific question (sometimes 'Whom does the Grail serve', or 'What ails thee, uncle?' or even 'What is the secret of the Grail?'). Failure to do so will result in him waking the next day with the land still blighted and the castle gone. If, however, the right question is asked, the land and the king will be healed, or he will at last be allowed to die and the hero become the Grail king.

Although I had briefly encountered the myth of the Grail in Malory's *Le Morte d'Arthur* and other sources, it was not until I saw John Boorman's film *Excalibur* when I was 17 that the legend truly captured my attention. Before this, my view of the quest had been somewhat narrow and dismissive, coloured by images remembered since childhood from MGM's *Knights of the Round Table*. In this film the Grail is a floating chalice caught in a brilliant shaft of heavenly light, accompanied by the sound of wailing sopranos, and the Grail knight himself is the chaste and pious Galahad – the most boring, it has to be said, of all Arthur's knights. It is an image of saccharine holiness that seems out of place with the rest of the legend.

But in Boorman's film the hero is not Galahad but Perceval, a country bumpkin, a simpleton; and the Wasteland is explicitly linked with the health of the king in some kind of mysterious symbiotic relationship. Perceval's quest was far darker and more pagan than anything I had seen before, and was the inspiration for my own quest to uncover the secrets of this puzzling legend.

The Grail's first appearance in European literature, I soon learned, was in a work of the Frenchman Chrétien de Troyes, in 1182. The hero of this tale, the unfinished *Conte du Graal*, is Boorman's Perceval, a Welsh country lad who witnesses, while dining with the crippled Fisher King, a youth bearing a bleeding spear, and 'a damsel … fair and attractive and beautifully adorned [who] held in both hands a grail … of pure refined gold'.[1] As in Boorman's film, there is surprisingly no mention in the tale that this cup had any connection with the cup of Christ. Because Perceval fails to ask the Grail question, the land remains waste and the king unhealed.

The wounding of the king is a strange theme: in Boorman's film it is Arthur himself who lies wounded, but the wound is a psychological one, inflicted by the betrayal of his wife and best friend; but in the original Grail stories the Wounded King is the guardian of the Grail, and his wound is all too physical. In Malory, the king is called Pellean and his wound is inflicted by a sword-blow from a knight named Balin le Sauvage, an act termed the 'dolorous stroke'. In the *Parzival* of Wolfram von Eschenbach (1170–1230) this wounded king is known as Anfortas, a name meaning 'infirmity'.[2] He receives his wound in a joust with a Saracen knight, whose poisoned spear passes through the king's testicles. The wound, which could not be healed, causes him most grief at the changes of the moon. On such occasions he is taken to a lake to fish – hence his name, the Fisher King.[3] The king's injury is clearly a castration.

The fish connection is reiterated in the work of Englishman Robert de Boron's Grail romance (written around 1210), in which the Rich Fisher is named Bron or Hebron, and whose task it is to catch the fish served at the feast of the Grail. It is in de Boron's work that this mysterious grail – once a commonplace word meaning a deep, flat-bottomed dish (from the Old French *gradale*, meaning 'by degree' or 'in stages', for it was used to serve a number of courses, most commonly *fish*) – is first associated with the chalice of the Last Supper. He describes it as a chalice containing blood taken from Christ's side after the crucifixion, by Joseph of Arimathea, who according to legend then brought the cup to Glastonbury and handed its keeping to his brother-in-law, Bron.

What interested me about the Grail legends was the fact that the earliest recorded versions had totally failed to make any connection between this mysterious vessel and Christ. What had the Grail been prior to its identification with Christ's cup by de Boron? This question inevitably led to others: Who was this mysterious Wounded King and how could his health be connected to the land? How, moreover, could the land be healed by a question? What was the role of the mysterious bleeding spear? De Boron claimed it was the spear of Longinus, the blind centurion who had wounded Christ in the side on the cross. But to me the whole scene smacked of ritual – of half-forgotten rites. It intrigued me. Might the Holy Grail have had its roots in the pagan past, as did many of the characters in the Arthurian legends?

A major clue was revealed in my study of ancient Welsh literature, where I stumbled upon the tale of 'Peredur son of Efrawg' – the Celtic Perceval. In this version of the Grail myth – which seems to be either a replica of Chrétien's early tale or one based on the same source[4] – the grail houses more than blood:

> *Thereupon he could see two youths coming into the hall, and from the hall proceeding to the chamber, and with them a spear of exceeding great size, and three streams of blood along it, running from the socket to the floor … After silence for a short while, thereupon, lo, two maidens coming in, and a great salver between them, and a man's head on the salver, and blood in profusion around the head. And then all shrieked and cried out, so that it was hard for any to be in the same house as they.*[5]

The appearance of a severed head immediately brought to mind the legendary head of Sir Gawain that I had searched for in vain at Dover Castle. Faced with this horrific item Peredur says not a word, and thus the enchantment on the land stays in place. Later on, a loathsome hag, who appears in many Grail legends as the messenger of the Grail, berates him:

> *Peredur, I greet thee not, for thou dost not merit it. Blind was fate when she bestowed favour and fame on thee. When thou camest to the*

*court of the Lame King, and when thou sawest there the squire bearing
the sharpened spear, and from the tip of the spear a drop of blood, and
that running in a torrent as far as the squire's grip – and other marvels
besides thou sawest there, but thou didst not ask after their meaning
nor the cause of them. And hadst thou asked, the king would have had
health and his kingdom in peace.*[6]

Clearly Boorman's film, which links the health of the land to that of the
king, touches on an important element in the Grail myths. The idea that
land and king are one is obviously not derived from Christian thought, but
is to be found in pagan Celtic myth, such as in the tale of the Irish god king
Nuada, who is forced to abdicate after his arm is severed in battle. There
can be only one reason why a king has to be 'whole', and that is because any
infirmity is seen to bring ill luck to his kingdom. Nuada's British counterpart, some argue, is a god named Nodens, a name that can be translated as
'fisher'; he is, therefore, a maimed fisher king.[7] Only when the king is young
and healthy, it seems, would the crops grow.

But Boorman is not the only one to have made this pagan connection.
The whole Grail genre has been flooded with such vegetal interpretations
ever since the publication in 1920 of Jessie Weston's *From Ritual to
Romance*, which argues that the origin of the grail myth lies in a forgotten,
or deliberately hidden, Classical fertility rite.

Weston's thesis has, in the main, been derived from the work of the
anthropologist J G Frazer, who in his 12-volume study of ancient myth and
ritual, *The Golden Bough*, argues that all ancient religions (including Christianity) are based on rites of fertility. In Frazer's schema the figure of the god
represents the crops – he is the corn spirit who will die at the end of the
growing year so he can be reborn in the spring (the Egyptian god Osiris, who
is green, the colour of vegetation, typifies such a god). From this primary
idea Frazer argues that in order to prevent the crops withering when the
god's representative on earth, the sacred king, grows old, he is killed at the
end of a fixed term and replaced by a younger man, called the *tanist*.

The weakness in Frazer's thesis is that he could provide only one firm
example of such rites of tanistry in the ancient world. Nevertheless, his
theories had a profound effect on modern ideas about the ancient world.
Although he failed to provide concrete evidence for the literal killing of

kings by their successors, he uncovered a host of vegetal symbols at the heart of many old religions. And it was in such symbolism that Jessie Weston found her explanation of the Grail legends. The cup and the spear, she claims, are ritual objects in a Classical fertility cult, and the wounded king is the vegetation spirit that dies and is reborn. However, scholars rightly slated her thesis, as they had Frazer's, by demonstrating that there was no evidence to show that the cult she describes had ever existed in the Classical world.

In my own quest I would discover that despite flaws in their theses, both Weston and Frazer had been on the right track – that at heart the Grail legend is connected to both sacrifice and a lost mystery rite, but a rite that had originated not in the Classical world, but in the Celtic. And the first glimmerings of a clue to all of this came, ironically, from a sacrificed green man ...

Notes

1. Chrétien de Troyes (trans. D D R Owen) (1988) p. 417.
2. Campbell, Joseph (1968) p. 393.
3. Quoted in Campbell, Joseph (1968) pp. 392–3.
4. See Lacy, N (ed.) (1988) p. 424: 'Independent references show that Peredur was a figure well established in Welsh tradition, and it is possible that "Peredur" is a retelling in Welsh of material found in, or used by, Chrétien.' If it is the latter, perhaps they both utilised a single lost source, in which the Grail is a head.
5. Jones, G and Jones, T (1974) p. 192.
6. Jones, G and Jones, T (1974) p. 218.
7. Campbell, Joseph (1968) p. 409.

Chapter 2

THE GREEN MAN

When I try to cast my mind back to when I first heard about the existence of the man from the Cheshire bog, I realise that there had been something familiar about him from the start. It could not have been that I saw in him echoes of Dion Fortune's man in the well, for I had not yet visited Glastonbury, so perhaps it was that he possessed a certain fairy-tale quality, for fairy tales about him and his kind do exist. There is a Grimm brothers' tale, for instance, in which a hunter drains a dark pool in a haunted wood and finds, crouching in the slimy mud, a wild man covered in rust-red hair – a feature that lends him his name, Iron John.[1]

It can be quite disconcerting coming face to face with a figure out of a fairy tale, especially if one chances upon him suddenly, as I did, in a glass coffin in the British Museum, where this red-headed ancient man now sleeps. The Iron John of the fairy tale is taken to a castle and locked in a cage where all can marvel at him; in a similar manner modern-day archaeologists have placed the man in a humidity controlled display case, where visitors can regard him either with sick fascination or with something deeper and more appropriate for a wizened visitor from the past. My reaction was one of awe. Nothing could have prepared me for coming face to face with a pagan sacrifice.

I recall my first view of the ancient man as I stooped over his flattened corpse, which resembled a dry and twisted piece of earth-brown hide. Examining the hair of his head and beard I could see that it had been stained a fiery red by the tannin-like chemicals present in the peat bog in which he had slumbered for centuries. It was these chemicals from the soil-acids in the water that had preserved the body, reacting with the proteins in his skin and converting it into a leathery hide whilst dissolving most of the innards and bones. These remarkable remains had lain deep below the marshes of Lindow Moss near Wilmslow, Cheshire – where, local legend states, travellers would be led to a watery death by strange lights, 'boggarts' or other 'spirits'[2] – until on 1 August 1984 (an auspicious date, being the ancient Celtic festival of Lughnasadh) a pair of peat-extraction workers uncovered this 'Iron John'.

Their first glimpse of the body – now named 'Lindow II' by archaeologists – was of a leg, severed from the rest of the torso by the metal jaws of a peat-digger. Digging was halted and the police and archaeologists called, as had been the case a year and a half earlier when the same workers had discovered a severed head in the same locality. The discovery of this skull, initially thought to have been that of a woman (now classified as Lindow I) had prompted a local man to confess to the murder of his wife – rather prematurely, it turned out, for the skull was soon declared to be many hundreds of years old.[3]

When contacted that August morning the police initially thought that the leg at Lindow might belong to the decapitated head – but further excavation proved this was not the case. The body was that of a male in his late twenties, naked save for a fox-fur armband on his upper-right arm. The majority of the lower half of the corpse, however, except for the fortuitously discovered leg, was missing – having been severed, it was supposed, by earlier peat-cutting operations. And this indeed was the case, for it was found during the summer of 1988 some 50 feet/15 metres from the original find.[4] Interestingly, the genitals were never found; had they simply been lost when the body had been cut in half, or was this evidence of something more sinister? But, save for the left hand, the upper body was intact – head and all.

When I had gazed down at Lindow II over a decade ago, I had examined him closely for any signs of his murder, for he had met with a strange and violent death. Three axe blows had rained down onto his skull – two to the crown and one to the base. His neck had been broken and the cause was clear: a thrice-knotted garrotte clung tightly to his throat, still biting into the flesh. And a neat and deep incision had been made to the jugular. Following all of this he had been dumped into the black enveloping waters of the lake – not just thrown into a pool, but forcibly pushed down into its slimy depths. The question that rose in my mind was one that has puzzled archaeologists for nearly two decades. Was this man the victim of a vicious crime or something more bizarre? Was he perhaps a player in a long-forgotten druidic ritual?

Lindow II was not alone. I remember reading with astonishment that in the last 300 years peat deposits in Great Britain and Ireland had yielded the remains of over 220 such bodies. In the Lancashire and Cheshire countryside around Lindow, for instance, remains had been recorded from Birkdale, Southport ('a human skull'); Red Moss, Bolton (the skull of a female 'with a plait of thick, reddish hair'); Kentucky, near Pilling in Lancashire (a human skull with an 'abundance of auburn hair'), as well as two bodies and two male skulls from an unidentified peat moss in nearby Lancashire recorded in the nineteenth century.[5] The red-haired bog folk from Lindow should be looked at not in isolation but within a wider sacrificial schema. Indeed, it seems probable that the number of remains so far uncovered in peat cuttings is but a fraction of the total once deposited in sacred waters. How many victims have been lost to us – carried away by tides or floods, or downstream? How many are still waiting to be found?

Nor is this phenomenon restricted to the British Isles. Similar finds fill the archaeological record throughout much of north-west Europe. The seminal work on these relics is Danish archaeologist Professor Peter Vilhelm Glob's *Mosefolket* (The Bog People), first published in 1965, which I had picked up in a local bookshop not long after my visit to the British Museum. In this study Glob concludes that many of the bog bodies, which date back to the European Iron Age and early Roman periods, preserved evidence of ritual sacrifice. Could it be that the Lindow finds were of similar provenance? Professor Glob was present at the excavations of two discoveries in the Danish bogs in the early 1950s. The remains, named Tollund and Grauballe Man after the localities in which they were found, are the best-preserved human remains from world prehistory. They are in a better state of conservation than Lindow II even: their facial expressions are as clear today as at the moment of death. As Glob says of Tollund Man, who was found naked save for a belt and a leather cap:

> It is the dead man's lightly-closed eyes and half-closed lips, however, that give this unique face its distinctive expression, and call compellingly to mind the words of the world's oldest heroic epic, Gilgamesh, 'the dead and the sleeping, how they resemble one another'.[6]

The words of Glob were evocative, but what fascinated me were the pictures. Tollund Man indeed looked as if he might at any moment open his eyes; the face of Grauballe Man, however, displayed a look of terror and pain. Both men had met with violent ends: around the neck of Tollund Man lay a noose of animal sinew, 5 feet/1.5 metres in length; he had been hanged before being deposited in the bog. Grauballe Man had received a blow to the temple and another to the leg, fracturing the shin, and his throat had been viciously cut. The resulting gash, which extended from ear to ear, had completely ripped open the gullet.

Obviously both men had been executed, and there was evidence that their deaths had been sacred acts rather than some form of prehistoric capital punishment. Analysis of the stomach contents of both men revealed that they had eaten a 'last meal' consisting of a variety of cereal and wild plant grains mixed into an unappetising gruel.[7] Both meals were riddled with ergot, a toxic fungus that prospers on cereal grains in cold, damp climates[8] (a fact that would later prove to be of much interest in my research). Glob concludes that the stomach contents probably represented the diet of a people suffering from a failed harvest, and that, because there was no trace of summer fruits or greenstuffs, they had died in the winter or early spring – perhaps as sacrifices to the gods of fertility.

There was more linking these men than just a shared diet. Both men seemed to have been in fine physical condition and in their twenties. The hands of Grauballe Man (so well preserved that his fingerprints could be taken) showed no signs of calluses or wear that might be associated with manual labour or use of weapons; perhaps, Glob argues, he had been a noble-man or a priest. This was also the case with Lindow II, whose well-manicured hands and lack of muscular bulk revealed that he had never been a farmer or warrior. His last meal had also been wholly vegetarian – possibly a griddlecake or unleavened loaf, containing traces of mistletoe pollen. And to add to the list of similarities with the Danish finds, further analysis had narrowed down the date of his death to some time between the last century BC and the first two centuries AD[9] – so he was from the Iron Age, too.

Archaeologists, if not the media, were at first unwilling to jump on Glob's 'ritual' bandwagon, preferring to speak with caution, suggesting that the man might have been the victim of a robbery. The garrotte, it was argued, could have been just a necklace; the cut to the throat a post-mortem injury. It was even proposed that the blows to the head might have been caused post-mortem by a fence post or wood scavenger's pole,[10] and that the ancient peat in which the body had lain had possibly corrupted the radiocarbon date of the body, in which case the body might be much younger than previously thought.

Of course all these were valid points, but none of the scholars who made them, it seems, was aware that nearly 20 years earlier, on 18 August 1958, a discovery had been made – at a peat bog in Worsley Moss, Lancashire, just 20 miles away from Lindow – whose similarity to the Cheshire find is astounding. It was the head of a male, between 20 and 30 years of age, severed at the second vertebra by a blow from a sharp weapon; the top of the skull had collapsed under a volley of hard blows. Had perhaps the skull of Gawain once looked like this? But there were more wounds to be seen: a sharp jagged instrument had lacerated the jugular below the ear, and a garrotte of animal sinew had been tightened around the victim's neck before he had been decapitated. Radiocarbon dating suggested the skull was 1,800 years old – from the Romano-British/Late Iron Age period.[11] It might be possible to attribute the injuries on one body to a series of unlikely post-mortem events, but to find identical marks on another surely argued against accidental damage.

Three years on from the finding of Lindow II, as the debate continued to rage over his true provenance, a second torso was recovered from Lindow Moss. Discovered in some 70 fragments in a swathe of peat already extracted from the bog, this macabre jigsaw comprised remnants of a male headless body.[12] There was evidence of polydactylism – he had two thumbs on each hand (in reality, the 'second' was a stubby outgrowth on the primary thumb, but nevertheless it was something that may have marked the bearer out as 'special'). A large portion of the gut remained, enough to clarify that his last meal had consisted of hazel nuts.

This body (Lindow III) soon joined that of Lindow II in the laboratory of the British Museum, where a variety of tests was carried out. Analysis of the skin yielded particularly interesting information. The top layer, the epidermis, had been removed by the acids in the bog water, but the chemical make-up of the secondary layers revealed higher than normal proportions of copper ions. Given the high copper content of the landscape around Alderley Edge, which would have contaminated the waters around Lindow, these results were first taken to indicate that both men were local in origin. But the high levels of other mineral ions – aluminium and silicon, for instance – could not be so easily explained. Neither element was present in the locality to such a degree, nor had the elements leached into the skin following its immersion in the peat. The only reasonable explanation was that these elements had soaked through the pores following a deliberate application to the skin. The Lindow bodies had been painted.[13]

Scientists believe that hydrated aluminium silicate (found in certain clays) had been used as a base for a copper-based pigment. The colours that could be produced by such methods were dramatic: either a fierce red (in the case of an oxide) or a bright green or blue (if a carbonate). The differing amounts of minerals obtained from each of the Lindow bodies implied they had been painted differently. A fluorescent stain observed on part of the fox-fur armband worn by Lindow II indicated that he, at least, might have gone to his grave a vivid shade of *green*.

There could now be no doubt that Lindow II had been the victim of a prehistoric ritual killing. Body painting has never been noted as a habit of the populace of Cheshire in historical times, whereas it was, if Classical sources are to be believed, a common feature among the pre-Roman population of these islands – a people known as the 'Britons', a word thought to derive from the Celtic *Pretani* that meant the 'tattooed' or 'painted ones'. Caesar, who came face to face with the Britons during his putative invasions of 55 and 54 BC, says of them:

> All the Britons stain themselves with vitrum *which gives a blue colour and a wilder appearance in battle.*[14]

Contrary to popular belief, I was surprised to discover that the word *vitrum* did not refer to the woad plant, whose leaves yield minute quantities of the deep-blue dye 'ingotin'. Only in one Classical account is this *vitrum* referred to as a vegetable product. The same word, however, is used by Pliny to refer to a sky-blue *copper-based* pigment, and this must have been Caesar's meaning before it was mistranslated (as it has been since the sixteenth century). The poet Ovid supports this theory by talking of *viridis Britannos* (the 'Green Britons'); woad does not produce a green colour but copper pigments do.[15]

But who were these painted Britons, and why did they consign certain individuals to a violent death within these marshes? It was such questions that the bog victims posed.

Standing over Lindow Man, I knew that at some point I would have to break my reverie and return to everyday concerns. How did I feel looking into the face of a long-dead man? Part of me, of course, felt the visceral horror of a creature confronted with the evidence of his own mortality, but also I felt pity, and a measure of guilt: I was horrified that this man had been brutally murdered in a long-forgotten savage rite, and equally horrified that he had been disturbed from his rest – and for what? So people could stare at him for a second or two as if he were a shrunken head in a travelling show? We had learned much from the analysis of his body – when and how he had died – but were we any closer to knowing *why*?

Even as I stared at him the faint glimmer of a pattern was forming in my mind – the filmiest of webs connecting the Wounded King of the Grail legend and this ancient victim, a hint that they were one. I recalled the words of the hag berating the silent Peredur:

When thou camest to the court of the Lame King, and when thou sawest there the squire bearing the sharpened spear, and from the tip of the spear a drop of blood, and that running in a torrent as far as the squire's grip – and other marvels besides thou sawest there, but thou didst not ask after their meaning nor the cause of them. And hadst thou asked, the king would have had health and his kingdom in peace.[16]

And I suppose it was at that moment, standing before that shrivelled and lamed king, that I knew that if this Iron Age relic was not to remain mute in his glass tomb, I had to attempt to unlock the mystery and seek to answer the 'why' of his puzzling murder.

Notes

1. Grimm, W and J (1993) pp. 612–20.
2. In both meanings of the word, as one Samuel Finney writing a history of Wilmslow made clear: 'Men ... have found their last home upon this dreary place too in my memory. Nat Bell, and Radcliffe, returning home, loaded with ale, fell under the fatal burden and died before morning.' (Worthington-Barlow 1853) quoted in Turner, R C and Scaife, R G (1995) p.10.
3. Stead, Bourke, Brothwell (1986) pp. 10–11.
4. Turner, R C and Scaife, R G (1995) p. 52.
5. Turner, R C and Scaife, R G (1995) pp. 205–20.
6. Glob, P V (1988) p. 31.
7. Holden, T G, in Turner, R C and Scaife, R G (1995) pp. 76–82. For a discussion of these ritual meals see Ross, A and Robbins, D (1989) pp. 29–33.
8. Green, M (2001) pp. 88, 194.
9. To the uninitiated this process relies on the fact that each living organism contains traces of a radioactive element called carbon-14 (C14). On death the C14, which remains at a constant level throughout life, begins to 'decay' at a uniform rate known as its 'half-life'. By testing how long the C14 has been decaying in the sample one is able to pinpoint how long ago the organism died.
10. Turner, R C and Scaife, R G (1995) p.177.
11. 'Worsely Man, England' by A N Garland, in Turner, R C and Scaife, R G (1995) pp. 104–7.
12. Immediately it was asked whether the severed head of Lindow I, which had been found less than 100 yards away, had once belonged with this body. The pathologist's report stated that the head was in all probability that of a female, but as only the cranium survived this could never be more than a good guess. The matter is still unresolved.
13. See Turner, R C and Scaife, R G (1995) pp. 62–73.
14. Caesar (trans. Handford) (1982) v. 14.
15. Turner, R C and Scaife, R G (1995) pp. 70–2.
16. Jones, G and Jones, T (1974) p. 218.

Chapter 3

APPRENTICESHIP

The druids, it was reported, underwent an arduous and lengthy apprenticeship lasting some 20 years before becoming qualified priests.[1,2] My own education, studying Prehistoric British Archaeology at the University of North Wales, Bangor, took only a fifth of that time, but during this period I learnt much about these enigmatic priests and their religion that would begin to reveal clues about the Lindow murder and its connection to the Grail. Many hours I spent in lecture halls and the library, reading and researching, ever mindful of that tannin-stained man in his glass prison at the British Museum. But I never felt closer to him and the druids than on the occasions when I quit the demands of academic study and headed for Anglesey, the Druids' Isle, where their mysterious sacrificial groves had once stood.

I often walked across the bridge to Anglesey at night and gazed down at the Menai Straits, replaying in my mind the scene that must have confronted the Roman governor of Britain, Suetonius Paulinus, some 1,930 years earlier during his attack on Anglesey in AD 59. As Tacitus notes, the shore opposite his troops would have been thick with armed warriors, women in black waving flaming torches, and druids, filling the air with curses that rooted Paulinus's troops to the spot before being roused into action by his urging.[3] Their fright did not last – they crossed the straits, massacred the druids, and burned the sacred groves to the ground. It was said sacrifices were commonplace in these groves, and the future was told through examining the entrails of the victims.

It would have been easy to see in Tacitus's description an element of anti-druidic propaganda or pure fantasy, but the Roman poet Lucan,[4] in *Pharsalia*, his poetic history of the Roman Civil War, describes a similar

17

druidic grove near Massilia where 'the altars were heaped with hideous offerings and every tree was sprinkled with human gore ... Water also fell there in abundance from black springs.' It was a place, too, where even the priest feared to tread lest he chance upon the Lord of the Grove.[5]

While studying Welsh, I discovered that the name Lindow was derived from Llyn Du ('the dark pool'), suggestive indeed of the 'black springs' of Lucan's poem. Had the Lindow victims – two beheaded and one garrotted – died within the bounds of such a bloody grove at the hands of barbarous priests? The evidence was strong – for a start there was the mistletoe pollen found in the stomach of Lindow II. According to the Roman writer Pliny, mistletoe was held sacred by the druids, who on the sixth day of the moon cut it from the sacred oak with golden sickles.[6] The pollen in Lindow II's stomach, possibly from a mistletoe-based beverage, was almost a calling card for druidic involvement in his death. And the more I studied what was known of the druids' religious practices – their veneration of water and of the severed head, and their penchant for human sacrifice – the more the bog rites appeared to fit within a clear pattern, part of a clearly defined cult. But who were the druids? What is known about this ancient priesthood beyond the cliché of white-robed bearded men prancing around stone circles on the solstices?

Despite its romantic appeal the name 'druid' is not derived from the Celtic word for the oak tree, but from the Indo-European *dru-wides*, the first element meaning 'well', 'very', or 'all', and the second meaning 'vision, seeing' or 'knowledge'. 'All-seer', 'All-knower' or 'All-wise' seemed to approximate the original meaning. The druids were the 'wise ones' – 'wizards' – the ultimate origins of figures such as Merlin and Gandalf.

Celtic myths portray the druids as powerful, sinister figures – uncanny and to be feared. They could shape-shift, summon mists or use magic to help or hinder the course of a battle; they are described as being able to kill a man by satirising him in song, or to heal him with incantations. They strike a bizarre and outlandish image: standing on one leg and closing one eye to utter their dreadful curses. Such descriptions make it clear that they were less like 'priests', as I understand the term, and more like the archaic 'medicine men' or 'shamans' of more primal societies.[8] Little of the religious concepts or philosophy of these medicine men has survived; but one important matter that their Classical contemporaries made pains to

18

record was their belief in the immortality of the soul.[9] So strong was this belief that payment of debts could be carried over into the hereafter.[10]

The actual form of this cult of immortality is unclear, for whereas Caesar mentions a belief in metempsychosis (a view supported in a few Celtic myths that speak of souls entering other bodies after death),[11] other writers mention a belief in reincarnation[12] or the dead dwelling in the ancestral paradise, the other world, the 'Land beneath the waves'. If the druids truly held death to be of such little consequence it was no wonder the Celts were so feared in battle; and as propagators of this belief, the druids held ultimate power.

The importance of the druids in the Celtic world is demonstrated by the fact that they held a place in society above that of the king. No king or chief could speak at an assembly before a druid had spoken. But they were more than just sorcerers; they were also heavily involved in the running of society: they were judges and lawmen, wielding real political power. The druids were, it seems, pan-tribal, able to rise above the internal squabbling that divided the Celts; a unifying force that could foster a sense of concord among the tribes and unite them against Rome.[13] And it was this political authority that most worried the Romans and led to the forcible eradication of druidism. Its destruction was effected by a curtailment of the druids' judicial and political powers, those which clashed with the dictates of the Empire, but it seems as if the religious aspects of druidism – including the practice of sacrifice – persisted, as the Worsley and Lindow bodies, all dating to Romano-British times, make clear (though whether the priests still called themselves druids or donned some other name we may never know).

There are many other examples of sacrifice from the Roman period, when druidism had supposedly been eradicated. Within the well of a local goddess or water nymph, Coventina, at Carrawbrough, the old Roman fort of Procolitia on Hadrian's Wall, a number of bronze heads and a human skull, were found. Roman wells at Tripontium (Warwick) and Heywood (Wiltshire) contained similar gory treasures, and in an underground pool in Wookey Hole (Somerset) archaeologists uncovered 14 human heads, 13 of which were between 25 and 30 years of age, dating to the Romano-British period.

These heads in the well reminded me of the skull of Gawain at Dover and the contents of the gory salver processed before Peredur. Archaeologists explain the appearance of the heads in a slightly less prosaic form – as evidence of a Celtic 'cult of the head', which was well attested in Classical sources and archaeology. Livy mentions that the Celts fashioned skulls into vessels for feasting, and Diodorus Siculus and Strabo both record the practice of taking the head of an enemy in battle and preserving it in cedar oil, or displaying it as a trophy on the lintels of houses.[14]

However, I began to suspect that this 'cult of the head' was a more complicated affair than simply a barbaric form of trophy taking. I knew that in myth heads were often portrayed as talking, feasting and entertaining after their severance from the body. The majority of the magical heads found in Celtic romance were not those of warriors taken in battle, but those of chieftains or kings whose deaths happened in a number of bizarre and unlikely ways – deaths that set them apart from ordinary mortals, that were also linked with regeneration and/or healing. Often some kind of talismanic power was attributed to these heads – a fact echoed in legends associated with many of the skulls found in sacred Celtic wells connected with healing. For example, at Drumconda in Dublin a drink from an aged well skull was said to cure toothache, and at Tobar a'Chinn ('The Well of the Head') in Wester Ross, such a draught was effective against epilepsy. These skulls in holy waters were no spoils of war.[15]

As the most visible form of druidic ritual, the ritual deposition of humans and prestige goods within springs, wells or bodies of water would become increasingly important in my quest for the truth behind the Grail myths. The tradition itself had emerged in north-west Europe around the middle Bronze Age, when great horns (known as 'lurs'), cauldrons, shields, swords and rapiers were deliberately thrown into the waters – the offerings often deliberately broken before being deposited.[16] Perhaps, like the broken bodies of the dead, or the mutilated bodies of the sacrificial victims, the treasures, too, had to be maimed, 'killed' so that their essence, their spirit, could pass below.[17]

Water was sacred in the Celtic world; in some tales it is an entrance to the other world, a magical place inhabited by gods and departed heroes – more than an abode of the dead, but a realm to which mortals could travel and return. It was Elysium and Narnia rolled into one. Water was also in itself divine: a number of Romano-British shrines, for instance, were dedicated to goddesses of water, and many Celtic rivers owed their names to pagan water divinities.[18]

This tradition of deposition did not go unnoticed by the Classical world. The Romans recorded how after a defeat by the 'Celtic' Cimbri and Tuetones tribes at Orange in 105 BC (part of the La Tène expansion down the Po valley), the Celts offered all their booty to a river deity. The Romans nonchalantly pillaged such holy shrines, most famously that of the Volcae Tectosages of Tolosa (Toulouse), said to contain 100,000 pounds of gold and 110,000 pounds of silver. This treasure was 'reclaimed' in 106 BC by the general Caepio, who, with little foundation, declared it to be the gold of Delphi that had been plundered by a Celtic leader named Brennus in 279 BC.[19]

The two greatest druidic votive deposits in Britain both came from Wales. The earliest, Llyn Fawr (the 'big lake'), in Glamorgan, dates from the seventh century BC and contained two massive sheet-bronze cauldrons as well as axes, sickles, chariots and slave-chains.[20] The second site, a peat bog on Anglesey – Llyn Cerrig Bach (the 'Lake of little stones') – has been dated between 200 BC and AD 100. It contained torcs, swords, shields, horse gear, chariot equipment, a trumpet and cauldrons – objects that had come from far and wide, hinting that the shrine was of national (or even international) importance.[21] These objects had possibly been hurled into the glassy waters in the same way that Sir Bedevere had returned King Arthur's sword Excalibur to the Lady of the Lake. This legend seems to connect the offering of valuables to the death of a king, and it is also possible that they could have accompanied a dead person or acted as a substitute for one.

Explanations as to why such human sacrificial offerings were made are scarce. The Classical sources, which are never shy about mentioning this side of the druids' character,[22] offer few clues beyond the usual speculation. Caesar clearly believed sacrifices were propitiatory measures to win divine favour in war or to barter for health. Other sources believe the sacrifice of prisoners of war was an offering of thanks for victory in battle. Interestingly, no source mentions the offering of human victims to promote fertility, which is the view favoured by many modern authors – including P V Glob. Many sacrifices, however, are seen not as propitiatory gifts or offerings of thanks at all, but as a means of foretelling the future, as Diodorus Siculus says of the druids:

For having consecrated a man, they strike him above the diaphragm with a sacrificial knife, and when the struck man has fallen, they know destiny from his fall, from the dismemberment of his limbs, and from the flow of his blood, for they trust to ancient and time honoured observance in these things.[23]

Similarly, Tacitus, writing about the druids of Anglesey, notes that they could 'consult their deities through human entrails'. [24]

Lucan alone offers any hint of the deities to which the bog men may have been offered, mentioning the names of three gods: Teutates, Esus and Taranis.[25] A ninth-century commentator on Lucan, from Berne, Switzerland, describes the method of sacrifice sacred to each divinity: Taranis ('the thunderer') was appeased by fire, an obvious choice for a god of storm and lightning; Esus ('Lord' or 'all-competent') by hanging from trees and stabbing; and Tuetates ('god of the tribe') by drowning.[26] Had the garrotted, stabbed and drowned Lindow II been dedicated to such gods? Did he die a mysterious triple death to appease three Celtic deities, as some believe?

Could the existence of severed heads and bizarrely murdered bodies in watery graves be so easily explained away as simple offerings to hungry gods, or just the remnants of a simple act of divination? The skulls in the wells, for instance, were associated with healing; they were not dumped in the water and forgotten about, but formed an integral part of later rites. The same might be said of the Lindow bodies. It was possible that they had been specifically placed in the preservative waters of the bog so that they would not decay and could therefore be 'used' somehow at some later point. If this was so, then maybe they were not simple offerings, unblemished lambs slaughtered to placate bloodthirsty gods, after all. Maybe they were playing a role unguessed at by the Classical authors.

But what was that role? Archaeology has provided the material evidence for these deaths, and Roman sources offer a tantalising, if biased, view of why they had taken place, but to learn more of beheadings, murders and sacred occurrences beside bodies of water, it is necessary to consult the Celtic vernacular literature itself.

However, the vernacular Celtic tales have not been preserved intact or unchanged. They were recorded by Christian clerics at a time when the living religion that had informed the tales no longer existed. Although the

Celtic world they portrayed was seen, to use a phrase of St Paul's, as 'through a glass, darkly', the tales seem to offer the only real windows on that world. By attempting to see through the overlays of a later non-pagan society, I hoped I might discern elements of pre-Christian belief and so unlock some clues as to the nature of the death of the bog men.

The dark forest of Celtic myth is really made up of two great trees – Irish and Welsh literature – each of which has many splendid branches. The Irish tales are sub-grouped into four 'cycles', the first of which is the Mythological Cycle, in the main a twelfth-century manuscript titled the *Leabhar Gabhála Éireann* (the Book of the Invasions of Ireland) that tells of the peopling of Eire from the time of the flood to the coming of the Irish. It was to this group of tales that Nuada the wounded king belongs, whose place as king is to be taken by a newcomer named Lugh, a multi-skilled god who possesses a magical spear. The second cycle is the Ulster Cycle, recording the deeds of the 'Red Branch' band of warriors under King Conchobar mac Nessa of Ulster, chief amongst whom was Conchobar's nephew Cú Chulainn ('Culann's hound'), the Achilles of Irish myth, fated to die young, yet remembered for all time for his deeds of valour. This cycle's grand epic is the *Táin Bó Cuailnge* (the 'Cattle raid of Cooley'), telling of a great raid on Ulster headed by Medb ('the intoxicator'), queen of Connaught, to steal the great Bull of Cooley. The last two cycles are the Cycle of Kings and the 'Fianaigheacht'. The former comprises a handful of tales of ninth-century composition, grouped together for convenience, telling of the semi-legendary reigns of a number of historical kings of the seventh and eighth centuries. The latter is a cycle of tales surrounding the figure of Fionn mac Cumhaill (Finn mac Cool) which appeared from the twelfth century onwards, telling of the eponymous warrior, his poet son Oisín, and his *fianna* ('war band'). Fionn and his men lived in the forests like a prehistoric Robin Hood and his Merry Men, engaged in clan warfare and druidic magic.[27]

Although not as overtly pagan as the Irish tales, those from Wales are the more literary and well crafted. Aside from a number of mythological poems of dubious origin, the main material is found within a collection named *Y Mabinogi* (the Mabinogion) and the so-called triads – a collection of mnemonics grouped in threes to help a bard remember his stories. The *Mabinogion* itself was derived from three sources: the White Book of

Rhydderch, which dates to the last half of the fourteenth century; the Red Book of Hergest, written in the first quarter of the fifteenth century; and, in fragmentary form, Penairth 6, which dates to the thirteenth century, though the stories found in these manuscripts are derived from tales crafted in the mid eleventh to early twelfth centuries.[28]

The *Mabinogion* was so named by its first English translator Lady Charlotte Guest, after the finishing sentence of the tales: 'And here ends this branch (*cainc*) of the Mabinogi.' It consists of four 'branches' which form the *Mabinogion* proper: 'Pwyll Prince of Dyfed', 'Branwen daughter of Llyr', 'Manawyddan son of Llyr' and 'Math son of Mathonwy'. Seven further tales with mythological themes (including the tale of Peredur) were also included in Lady Guest's translation.

The word 'Mabinogion' had been translated as 'tales of childhood' – a meaning that has mistakenly led to its relegation to the nursery; however, these 'childhood tales' were not tales *for* childhood, but tales *of* childhood – the childhood of Celtic heroes, corresponding to the *enfances* of medieval French literature. In this instance the *enfance* is that of the hero Pryderi, the only figure to appear in all four tales. The four branches tell of Pryderi's birth, youthful exploits, and death at the hands of the enchanter Gwydion. But Pryderi's presence is more for structural purposes; his fate may well have formed the backbone of the tales, but he was never wholly at the forefront of them. Other theories see the tales as derived from Mabon, the name of a pagan Celtic god, the 'Divine Son'.[29] If pagan gods and rites truly lurked behind the characters and motifs of these medieval tales, I would do my best to uncover them. In time these two trees, the Irish and the Welsh, would form the twin supports of my theories, the solid foundation on which my ideas would be built.

What I was not to know at this stage was that also lying in the depths of the forests of myth, like Iron John in his pool, lay clues to the solution of a mystery far greater than that which I sought. I had set off in search of the fate of a sacrificed man, but would inadvertently stumble on the key to the legends of the Grail.

Apprenticeship

Notes

1. Caesar *Gallic War* V 14.
2. The name 'Bangor', I had read, meant 'wattle enclosure'. But to some this suggested that a pagan Iron Age college had once been sited here for the training of the Celtic *priesthood* (*The Druids*, Markale, J (1999) p. 21). He notes that 'Bangor' is an enclosure for a college or an assembly.
3. Tacitus *Annales* XIV 30–1.
4. b. AD 39 in Cordoba, Spain; d. AD 65, in Rome.
5. Lucan *Pharsalia* III.
6. Pliny *Natural History* XVI 249.
7. See Markale, J (1999) pp. 7–14 and Lincoln, B (1991) p. 176.
8. The druids were often compared by Classical writers with the *gymnosophists* ('naked philosophers') encountered by Alexander the Great in India – the forest dwelling Yogis and Brahmins. Such associations may not have been idle, for both cultures shared a common Indo-European background.
9. 'They wish to inculcate this as one of their leading tenets, that souls do not become extinct, but pass after death from one body to another, and they think that men by this tenet are in a great degree excited to valour, the fear of death being disregarded' (Caesar *Gallic War* XIV). Such a firm belief in an afterlife is demonstrated archaeologically in the amount of wealthy grave goods and feasting equipment buried with their dead
10. Mela *De Situ Orbis* 3.2.18–19.
11. The classic tale is 'Tochmarc Etain'; it tells of the soul of the other-worldly maiden Etain taking the form of a pool of water and a mayfly before being born again as a human.
12. Sometimes Cú Chulainn is seen as a re-incarnation of the god Lugh; and the historical Irish Mongfind (ninth century) was believed to be a reincarnation of Manannán mac Lir, the god of the Sea.
13. As was the case in the Gallic rebellion of 52 BC led by the Arvernian chieftain Vercingetorix. The fact that this uprising had begun in land of Carnutes – what Caesar calls the religious centre of pagan Gaul where the druids would meet to elect a leader – hints that it was the druids who instigated the rebellion. Similarly, in Britain druidic influence has often been seen to be behind the rebellion of Queen Boudicca (Boadicea) in AD 60, thus diverting Roman troops under Suetonius Paulinus away from the attack on the druidic stronghold of Anglesey.
14. Ronald Hutton has played the importance down, but only as a purely Celtic phenomenon. Head cults flourished worldwide throughout prehistory; however, the magical qualities ascribed to the head presented in this book go beyond simple trophy taking.
15. See Ross, A (1996) chap. 2.
16. Green, M (1986) pp. 138–9.
17. Many goods, it seems, were crafted wholly as offerings and were never intended for use in everyday life; the so called 'Waterloo' helmet and 'Battersea' shield, both elaborate works of art cast into the River Thames, which was a focal point for such offerings, would have been useless in battle. A single blow from an iron sword would have destroyed these bronze goods.
18. The Shannon is derived from Sinnend; the Dee and Don from Danu; and the Boyne is

named after the Goddess Boann. A goddess named Sequanna was worshipped at the source of the Seine, where a healing sanctuary was housed. Similarly, the Roman baths at Bath (Aquae Sulis), were constructed on the grove of the healing water divinity Sulis. Quite clearly there is an association between the healing spring and pagan sanctuaries.

19. Some scholars see the act of deposition as a way of disposing of excess riches, thus heightening and maintaining the value of goods still in circulation; while this may have indeed been a result of these rites, the actual impetus that led to the deposition of such offerings (which, we must not forget, included human beings) was far from economic in origin. If great riches were deposited it was because the act itself was of extreme importance.

20. Green, M (1986) p. 142.

21. See Lynch, F (1991).

22. Most people were aware of the so-called Wicker man, evidence of which was recently uncovered at Leonding in Austria. 'The site has been interpreted as the site of a grisly sacrificial ritual, repeated three times every two or three years, in which humans and beasts were tethered to a wooden device suspended above the pit, which was then set on fire so that the entire edifice, with its hapless victims, collapsed into the hole.' Green (2001) p. 69.

23. Diodorus Siculus (5.31.2-4).

24. One bog body discovered at Weerdinge near Bourtangemoor in the Netherlands seemed to bear out Tacitus's statement; he was discovered disembowelled with his entrails heaped upon his abdomen. Was the future revealed in the serpentine twists and turns of his innards? See Green (2001) pp. 88, 165.

25. Lucan, *Pharsalia* I, 422–65.

26. Also in Green (2001) p. 171 and Ross, A (1989) p. 47.

27. A few tales exist that defy inclusion in the four cycles yet still provide some flavour of pre-Christian thought. Chief amongst such tales are the *echtrai* – voyages into the other world by mortals, which carry down pagan traditions of such a realm. Also of great importance is the twelfth-century 'Dinnshenchas', or 'The Lore of Prominent Places', which has been called the 'mythic geography' of Ireland (Sjoestedt). This remarkable work reveals the origins and meaning of Irish place names and the formation of natural features in the actions of heroes and gods, much of which corroborates the mythic material from the sagas.

28. Ifor Williams gives a date of 1060, Saunders Lewis 1170–90, but more recently T M Charles-Edwards has come up with the probable range of 1050–1120.

29. Especially Caitlin Matthews and Eric Harp. Matthews, C (1987) pp. 1–6 provides a brief but useful introduction to the Welsh material. For a more detailed analysis of the subject see MacCana, P (1977).

Chapter 4

THE GREEN KNIGHT

One of my favourite tales of the Arthurian corpus is *Sir Gawain and the Green Knight*, a Middle English poem that had caught my imagination when, at the age of 17, I was obsessed with finding the head of this legendary Celt at Dover Castle. On re-examining the poem, I was intrigued to discover that motifs and symbols I had completely glossed over on my initial reading took on new and important meanings in the light of what I had learned in the meantime about the druids and their rites. The plot of the poem is worth telling in full:

It is during the New Year feast that the doors of Arthur's feasting hall at Camelot burst open, and in rides a giant figure astride a mighty charger, grasping a holly branch in one hand and a great axe in the other. What is most disturbing to the folk of Camelot is his otherworldly colouring: from head to foot he is a brilliant green.

The Green Knight challenges those present to strike him a blow with his axe and in return, a year and a day hence, receive a blow in return. Only Sir Gawain, Arthur's nephew, is valiant enough to comply, raising the axe and smiting the great head from the green shoulders. But to Sir Gawain's astonishment and dismay the green man does not fall, but seizes his head by the hair and re-mounts his horse. The dead eyes open and he tells Gawain to journey to the Chapel Green the next New Year and receive the return blow, as agreed.

All too soon the appointed time comes around and Gawain leaves Camelot, travelling through North Wales, past Holy Head, and on to the Wirral in search of the Green Chapel. (Now the 'Holy Head' of the poem cannot be modern Holyhead in Anglesey, for that is hundreds of miles west of Gawain's route, but must be Holy Well in Clwyd – a popular shrine dedicated to the seventh-century Saint Winefrede – or, to give her proper Welsh name, Gwenfrewi. Here, according to the legend, a local chieftain named Caradoc attempted to rape the virgin Gwenfrewi, who fled to the safety of her uncle St Beuno's church.[1] Caradoc caught up with her and beheaded her at the door. At the spot where the head of Gwenfrewi hit the ground the healing waters of Holy Well sprung forth. St Beuno took the severed head and placed it back on the body, miraculously bringing the girl back to life.[2]) The journey of Gawain past the shrine of Gwenfrewi had been included in the poem on purpose, its motif of beheading and reconstitution paralleling the fate of the Green Knight.

It is approaching Christmas, and noble Sir Gawain, having passed through the Wirral, despairs of ever finding the Chapel Green. On 24 December he finds himself in a dark valley; thrice he crosses himself, when from the mists emerges a castle.

It is not long before Sir Gawain is beside the hearth, enjoying warm soup, freshly baked loaves and fish with his host, Sir Bertilak (or Bercilak in other sources). As midnight turns and the bells toll for Christmas Day, into the hall comes Lady Bertilak, a woman, Gawain muses, more beauteous than Arthur's Guinevere, and at her side, an ugly crone. Wine flows freely and the gracious host offers his fine hood, which he fixes to his spear, as a reward to the man who would make 'the most mirth that merry yuletide', adding that he would give as good as he got.[3]

After three days of feasting Gawain makes to leave, but his host takes him aside and bids him not to depart so soon. Gawain tells his host of his deadly tryst, and of his need to discover the whereabouts of the Chapel Green, but his host informs him that the chapel is but two miles from the castle and Gawain can stay until the morning of his meeting. Gawain accepts. A glint comes into Bertilak's eyes, for he has an idea for another game: he will go hunting in the next few days, but

Gawain, he orders, is to stay at home and rest. And at the end of every day, each must tell the other everything he has 'won' during that day.

Over the next few days, as Sir Bertilak hunts game in the forest Gawain is the prey of the pursuing lady. On the first morning, after a hot pursuit, Bertilak nets a magnificent hind, while Gawain, still in his bed, is accosted by the sporting Lady Bertilak, who mischievously threatens to bind him to it like an enemy caught unawares in battle. She makes it clear to Gawain that not only is her lord away, but most of the castle folk are abed. She offers herself to him, but Gawain parries her advances with wit and humour, declining without offending. However, on leaving, the temptress chides him for not offering her a courtly kiss, and he concedes. That evening in the hall the exchange is made – Gawain receives the hind and his host a chaste kiss. On asking where he got such a gift, Gawain answers that such a divulgence was not part of the contract, and his host laughingly concedes.

The second day passes much as the first, though the lady is more pressing, and Gawain, though still defensive, is obviously enamoured and less fired up with chivalrous restraint. In the forests about the castle, Bertilak kills a boar single-handedly in the midst of a river with his sword, while within Gawain's chamber the lady similarly captures her quarry on the mouth – twice. (The audience were no doubt aware that a 'river' was a crude euphemism for the rut in a bed caused by lovemaking.)

The last day of the pact arrives; it is New Year's Eve, the last full day of Gawain's young life. Bertilak is hunting early, as is his wife, hair down and decorated, her back and breasts revealed in a low-cut dress. She greets Gawain with a kiss, the first of three, and he is suffused with rapture – even the poet admits that if it weren't for the Holy Virgin looking out for her knight, 'peril would have impended'. But rebuff her he does, just; but he does accept a love token from her, a girdle of green silk from around her smooth waist, a 'love-lace' with an astounding magical property: the man who wears it cannot be harmed.

Such a garment might be his redemption. That night, as before, he gives his lord three kisses, but of the girdle he says nothing; after all, he can hardly make a gift of it and then ask for it back. Bertilak apologises for his own gift – the hunt was a paltry affair and all he has to offer his guest is a pelt of rust-red fox fur, rank and flea bitten.

After a poor night's sleep Gawain awakes early and dons his armour, beneath which he wears the green silk girdle, wrapped twice about his loins. A guide shows him the way to his destination, advising him to flee if he can. Gawain, however, declines, and through the mist that lies in swathes over the snowy ground follows the path down by the river. Out of the haze looms the shadow of a great mound that is described as a cave, before which Gawain baulks with sudden fear: it is the Chapel Green.

At this point he hears the dreadful sound of the sharpening of a giant blade. And a green form emerges from the mist, vaulting over the stream on the haft of his mighty axe. Welcoming his guest, the Green Knight wastes no time and bids Gawain to remove his helmet and bow his head. Gawain, acting as if unafraid, kneels down and reveals his neck, but as the blade comes down he flinches from the first blow. The Green Knight chides him sternly. Ashamed, Gawain asks to be struck again, and in reply the knight feints a stroke. Seeing that Gawain holds resolute for this second mock blow, he deems him ready to play again. The Green Knight begins to wax lyrical, but Gawain, now convinced, despite the girdle, that he is about to die, snaps at him to get on with the strike – which he does. The enormous blade slams down, piercing the skin so that blood splashes on the snow – but the wound is merely a scratch.

Leaping to his feet, the ecstatic Gawain bids him cease, for he has received the return blow as promised. And then the truth is told: the first two feints, the Green Knight says, were for the returned kisses, and the cut for failing to tell him about the girdle! The Green Knight, it is revealed, is his merry host Sir Bertilak under enchantment (just as in the tale of Iron John, the wild man is an enchanted king, who resumes his true form at the tale's close). And the temptation was a test, wrought by the ugly old crone (who is actually 'Morgan the Goddess', Arthur's half-sister), to test the worthiness of Arthur's knights. Bertilak bids Gawain to wear the girdle with pride, as a noble knight who resisted the wiles of the lady; the failure to disclose the green-ribbon was seen as a slight failing that after all displayed a healthy lust for life. Arthur pronounces that all his knights should wear a girdle as a tribute to Gawain.

It is no wonder that many who have sought to fathom the mysterious deaths of the bog men looked to this medieval poem for clues, for this marvellous poem, as one of its translators J R R Tolkien states, has its roots deep in the pagan past – deeper than its author realised – in the 'ancient cults' of pre-Christian myth.[4] The provenance of such 'ancient cults' is not hard to fathom; from its very start the poem presents parallels to bog sacrifice: the magical beheading of a green-coloured victim clearly echoes the finds at Lindow Moss. What's more, the nick on the neck received by Gawain beside a body of water, and the mangy fox-fur given to him surely could be read as the literary equivalent of the slit jugular and fox-fur armband discovered on the Cheshire bog man. The parallels seem too good to be true; it is almost as if the poem had been written about him – with the green girdle being an echo of the thrice-knotted garrotte about his neck (a sinister love-lace from the hostess) and the three feints with the axe a memory of the three separate killing methods meted out to him.

The problem with using the Gawain story to illuminate the bog deaths is that Gawain, unlike Lindow man, survived his ordeal. Also troubling is the fact that both Gawain and Bertilak seem to possess qualities suggestive of the painted victims of prehistory, which obviously confuses the issue. Perhaps the Christian author had somehow swapped or duplicated the role of the victim, manipulating the pagan story to provide the audience with a moral heroic tale fit for Christian ears? I was soon to discover these inklings were correct: the tale was in fact crafted from older material, and in the earlier versions of the tale, the role of the protagonists was much clearer.

The first of the earlier tales from which the later poem had been forged is a story from the Irish Ulster Cycle named 'Bricriu's Feast', which tells of a competition between three Ulster champions – Conall Cernach, Leoghaire

Buadach and Cú Chulainn – to decide which one of them is fit to receive the *Curad Mir* ('champion's portion'), the prime cut (usually the thigh) of the boar, and the honour of sitting at the right of King Conchobar during the feast at which it is served. The boar, a magnificent seven year old, is offered at a feast given by the trickster Bricriu *Nemthenga* ('of the poison tongue'), and it is he who casts doubt on who is to be given the prime cut, telling each of the three heroes that it is his by right. When each stands to receive the portion, conflict immediately ensues.[5]

A general rout in Bricriu's hall solves nothing, so a number of tests of supernatural origin confront the three heroes: firstly, a giant appears out of a misty plain, described as 'not a handsome fellow … rough and rustic', black-browed, swarthy, with cropped black hair, carrying a huge club and walking with his rump sticking out from under his tunic. Only Cú Chulainn bests him, but the matter still is not settled because the other two warriors accuse him of using trickery. Secondly, from a *lake* appears another supernatural tester – Uath mac Immoman ('fear son of terror'). The challenge he presents to the three Irish warriors is the same as that given to the knights of Camelot in the Gawain poem by the bewitched Bertilak, except the return blow is to come the next night, not in a year and a day's time. Uath is beheaded: 'Uath rose, took his axe, put his head on his chest and returned to his lake.' But only Cú Chulainn returns to the scene the following night to accept the return blow. Three times the blade comes down; three times it magically twists upwards so that the blunt side hits his exposed neck. But again, Leoghaire and Conall do not accept the judgement.

For the third supernatural test the three warriors travel to the magical castle of Cú Roí mac Dáiri, which spins like a mill wheel so that it is impossible to find the entrance after sunset. Cú Roí is abroad, but his beautiful wife Blathnat greets them and they take turns in defending the fortress. Cú Chulainn is the only one of the three able to defeat an immense serpent that rises from the lake, and a giant who, with a tree in his hand (like the Holly branch held by the Green Knight) threatens the fort. Cú Chulainn offers to spare the giant's life if he will support his right to receive the champion's portion.

On their return to Ulster, Cú Chulainn's opponents continue to challenge his right to the *Curad Mir*, despite his victories. And so the strife continues, until, in a repetition of the earlier incident involving Uath, an ugly great figure comes into the feasting hall, a tree in one hand and an axe in the other, demanding that someone play the 'beheading game' with him. Once again Cú Chulainn proves triumphant, this time before the entire court so that no man can question his superiority. The supernatural foe, described as a rough 'churl', reveals himself as Cú Roí mac Dáiri, and admits that he was also the giant bested by Cú Chulainn in the earlier episode. He has now come to fulfil his promise to Cú Chulainn and support his claim to the champion's portion.

The similarities between the Gawain poem and its fourteenth-century source are obvious: most notably their 'Beheading Game' theme. The 'foe' of the original tale, Cú Roí mac Dáiri, disguised as the churl, is, of course, the equivalent of Bertilak, 'enchanted' into supernatural form for the express purpose of testing the heroism of the knight. But the connection between the figures is even more obvious than their shared plot line. The word used to describe the supernatural beings in the Irish is Bachlach ('churl'),[6] so it is not difficult to discern how the Gawain poet turned this name into Bertilak and Bachlach's test of warriorhood into Bertilak's test of morality. What's more, the Gawain poet gives away his source when in one line he describes the Green Knight, instead of bearing his axe, as 'clutching his club where he stands' (a club being Bachlach's usual weapon).

The Gawain poet, however, does not allow his hero to receive the return blow the following night, as in the Irish tale, but extends the challenge to a year and a day, thus allowing him to include within his poem a plotline gleaned from another Irish tale, 'The Death of Cú Roí mac Dáiri'.

In this tale a mysterious man aids the men of Ulster in a siege at Fir Falgae. After their victory they distribute the spoils but give none to their helper. In revenge he steals them all – an other-worldly woman named Blathnat ('flowers'), the three magical cows of Tuchna (which have three birds in their ears that cause them to produce the milk of 30 cows), and the enchanted cauldron into which the milk flows. Putting Blathnat under his arm, the birds in his belt and the cauldron on his back, he is challenged by Cú Chulainn. But the stranger buries him up to his neck, shaves off his much-admired hair, and anoints him with manure. Cú Chulainn seeks revenge – he follows a mysterious flock of black birds to a spinning fort where he realises that the grey stranger is Cú Roí mac Dáiri, the Bachlach of the other tale. Cú Chulainn cunningly enters the fort and colludes with the captured Blathnat, who has become his lover, in a ruse to defeat her husband Cú Roí. As Blathnat washes Cú Roí's hair in a stream that flows through the fort, she pours the milk from the cauldron into the flowing water as a sign to Cú Chulainn that her captor is off his guard. Blathnat binds Cú Roí to the bedpost with his hair, puts his head in her lap, and Cú Chulainn beheads him.[7] In a version quoted by poet Robert Graves, Cú Roí's soul is hidden in an apple within a magical salmon that appears in the spring once every seven years. Blathnat waits seven years and catches the salmon, then binds Cú Roí's long hair to the bedpost while he is bathing. She gives his sword – the only weapon that will harm him – to Cú Chulainn, who splits the apple in half, thus weakening the giant, and then beheads him.[8]

Had the Gawain poet remained faithful to this source it would have been Bertilak, not Gawain, who met his fate at the Chapel Green. But by meshing the two Irish plotlines into one tale, the Gawain poet decides to delay the hero's return blow until the latter part of the story, and so Sir Gawain receives the riverside blows originally meant for Bertilak. He survives them not through heroism, but because of his refusal to be tempted by his host's wife.

Many other Celtic tales repeat this ritual pattern of death and betrayal, not least the Welsh 'Math ap Mathonwy', the fourth branch of the *Mabinogion*, in which the murder of the victim beside a body of water is orchestrated, as in the tale of Cú Roí, by a woman whose name means 'flowers':

Lleu, the victim of the tale, is a magical figure; born of a virgin he is hidden in a chest and reared by his uncle Gwydion. Lleu cannot be killed when either on horseback or on foot, either indoors or out, and either in water or out of it. His deceitful wife, Blodeuwedd ('flower-face') takes a lover, Goronw 'Pebr' (the fiery), and plots her husband's death. Because he can be killed only in special circumstances she asks him to demonstrate how it can be done, lest in his ignorance she were to unwittingly bring it about. Foolishly Lleu shows her – he stands with one leg on the back of a goat, under a makeshift wooden shelter, on the bank of a river. At this point Goronw casts a magical spear, crafted while mass was being spoken, and kills Lleu, whose soul flies off in the form of an eagle. The magician Gwydion, Lleu's uncle, calls the soul of Lleu down from an oak tree and brings him back to life, and Lleu returns the compliment to Goronw, killing him with a spear. Blodeuwedd and her maidens flee the wrath of Gwydion and Lleu, but to no avail – her handmaidens are drowned in a lake, and Blodeuwedd herself is turned into an owl.

The similarity between this tale and the fate of the Green Knight/Cú Roí is obvious. Lleu is murdered on the side of an expanse of water, in a bizarre death involving a magical triple formula – betrayed by a wife whose name means 'flowers'. If Blodeuwedd is the Blathnat of this Welsh tale, then Lleu is its Cú Roí and Goronw Pebr its Cú Chulainn. A common theme of ancient ritual begins to emerge; a theme which tells again and again of a strange and unnatural death connected to the number three – either the number of blows dealt to the victim or the number of different ways in which he was killed.

The motif of the 'triple death' that appears most clearly in the myth of Lleu is quite common in Celtic and other Indo-European mythologies.[9] It appears in Greek myth in the murder of Agamemnon at the hands of his unfaithful wife Clytemnestra and her lover Aegisthus. Agamemnon is killed while stepping into the bath, half undressed.[10]

The triple motif also appears in the tale of Lailoken, a Scottish figure thought by some to be behind the character of Merlin, who lived as a wild-man in the woods, as did Iron John. Lailoken, it is prophesised, will die by drowning, and from stabbing and vicious blows. True to form he is chased into the forest and struck with sticks and stones. He then falls into the waters of the River Traved and is impaled on a stake placed there by fishermen.[11]

Lailoken's death recalls that of Lleu: both seem to defy normality, to be imbued with a sense of the impossible, and hence the magical. But what's more, they both seem to parallel the mysterious deaths of the bog men. Lindow Man, after all, was killed not by drowning, stabbing or strangulation, but in a bizarre combination of all three. Grauballe Man suffered blows to the head, a cut jugular and a broken leg, and was then drowned. Like Lleu, neither was killed on land or in water for they met their deaths in marshes and bogs – places that were neither one nor the other. And by wearing a fox-fur armband, Lindow Man – like Tollund Man, who wore a belt and a hat – was neither naked nor clothed.

Another reason for these triple deaths has become clear: they were not, as Lucan suggests, killed simply to appease three gods. They were killed in this magical fashion because that was the only way they could be killed; the bog men, like Lleu and Lailoken, were somehow special – magical – different from ordinary men.

My head was swimming with all these motifs and symbols, so I compiled a list of characteristics of the bog men and then of the mythic Bertilak/ Bachlach/Green Knight figure from the tales.

The bog men
1   Many had been beheaded.
2   Some were killed by a bizarre method involving multiple or triple deaths.
3   They were found in bodies of water – often liminal places, such as bogs and marshes.
4   Many were associated with wells and healing springs.
5   Some were painted green.

The mythic figures
1   They were associated with death and rebirth, through ritual beheading.
2   They were murdered with three magical blows – or suffered three impossible deaths.
3   They were associated with bodies of water or lakes.
4   Legends of the saints reveal their beheading to be associated with springs or wells.
5   Sir Gawain in the English poem is described as being green.

So far the lists matched point for point, but to the second list I could add two more:

6   They were betrayed by a woman.
7   They were murdered by her new lover.

If these tales really had preserved something of the rituals involved in the bog men's deaths, then they provided me with two important clues that I

Chapter 5

THE SACRED MARRIAGE

It was in Glob's *The Bog People* – where I had first stumbled upon the Grauballe and Tollund finds – that I was to discover further clues to the nature of the 'love triangle' that lay behind the sacred murders of the Iron Age. Glob, who from the start had believed the bog bodies to have been ritual sacrifices, connects their deaths to a passage found in *Germania*, by the Roman author Tacitus. This records a Germanic rite in which a goddess named Nerthus is borne around the country on a chariot, after which the priests and priestesses who accompany her are ritually drowned:

> On an island of the sea stands an inviolate grove, in which, veiled with a cloth, is a chariot that none but the priest may touch. The priest can feel the presence of the goddess in this holy of holies, and attends her with deepest reverence as her chariot is drawn along by cows. Then follow days of rejoicing and merrymaking in every place that she condescends to visit and sojourn in. No one goes to war, no one takes up arms; every iron object is locked away. Then, and only then, are peace and quiet known and welcomed, until the goddess, when she has had enough of the society of men, is restored to her sacred precinct by the priest. After that, the chariot, the vestments, and (believe it if you will) the goddess herself, are cleansed in a secluded lake. This service is performed by slaves who are immediately after drowned in the lake. Thus mystery begets terror and pious reluctance to ask what that sight can be which is seen only by men doomed to die.[1]

Tacitus is a reliable source, and his words are backed up by archaeological fact. On a silver cauldron found in a bog at Gundestrup, Denmark, such a goddess is depicted on a ritual cart or chariot (it also shows scenes of ritual drowning in a large vessel). Many of these carts had turned up in Danish and Celtic votive waters, including Llyn Cerrig Bach. Was Glob correct in his assumption that the bog victims were priests and priestesses drowned after such a rite? I thought of the drowned maidens of Blodeuwedd in the tale of Lleu, and wondered if they, like the two women found in the same bog as the Gundestrup Cauldron, had died because of what they had seen. But what was this secret 'seen only by men doomed to die'? It cannot have been the goddess herself, for the entire population of the countryside (among them the Angli tribe, the ancestors of the English) had seen her parade past on her chariot. Something else must have happened, some hidden rite – clues to which are provided by the Irish tales.

A suspiciously high number of Celtic kings and heroes, the tales reveal, die in incidents of a sexual nature. King Conchobar of Ulster, for instance, dies at a ford (neither land nor water) by a sling cast by Cet, son of Matu, when he is showing his 'nakedness' to a group of women. Cú Roí, of course, dies in bed with his wife, his head in her lap. Another tale told of Cumhaill, father of the hero Fionn – who could be killed only while sleeping with his wife, and, like Cú Roí, with his own sword. To protect him from death, on the night of his wedding to the daughter of King of Lochlann (Norway, but often used in the tales to mean the other world) seven marriage chambers are constructed around the bridal bed, but still his enemy, Arca the Black, the king's fisher, who has hidden in the inner room, is able to kill him. In a variant of this myth the couple sleep together on an island, but Arca hides in the grass and slays Cumhaill while in the act of love.[2] The island retreat seems connected to the sacred Island of Nerthus. Was the secret rite performed on the isle of Nerthus a sexual one? Might Lindow Man have slept with a 'goddess' before his death?[3]

There is a similar tale in which the theme of drowning the attendants is clearly present. It relates the killing of Fergus mac Roich on the command of King Ailill while he sports in the water with Ailill's wife, Queen Medb:

Now on a certain day the whole host went into the lake to bathe. 'Go down, Fergus,' said Ailill, 'and drown the men.' 'They are not good in water,' said Fergus. Nevertheless he went down. Medb's heart could not

bear that, so that she went into the lake ... Then Medb went till she
was on the breast of Fergus, with her legs entwined around him, and
then he swam around the lake. And jealousy seized Ailill ...

'It is delightful what the hart and doe are doing in the lake, O Lugaid,'
said Ailill. 'Why not kill them?' said Lugaid, who had never missed his
aim. 'Do thou have a cast at them!' said Ailill. 'Turn my face towards
them!' said Lugaid [he is blind], 'and bring a lance to me!' Fergus was
washing himself in the lake, and his breast was towards them ... and
Lugaid threw the lance, so that it passed out through his back behind.[4]

Certain elements of this tale parallel the myth of Balder, the son of the
Norse god Odin. Balder dreams of his impending death, and so the gods
make each creature and plant in creation swear that they will not harm
him, save for the mistletoe, which they think too young and innocent to
matter. Given his supposed immortality, the gods often shoot arrows at
Balder for amusement. Then one day the trickster Loki, disguised as an old
crone, persuades the blind god Hodr to throw a spear at him made from
this very plant. It kills Balder instantly and he descends into the underworld, from where he will emerge to rule the gods after the final battle
of Ragnarok.[5] Mistletoe had, of course, been found in the stomach of
Lindow II.

In the tale of Balder there are close similarities to the legend of the first
Christian martyr of these Islands, St Alban. Alban was condemned to
death by beheading for having sheltered a Christian from pagan persecu-
tion. On reaching the place of his execution he prayed, and a spring
bubbled up where he stood. But on cutting off his head, his executioner
suffered a bizarre fate – as the blow was struck his eyes fell from their
sockets and he was blinded.[6]

Archaeologists hoping to uncover traces of Alban's shrine during
excavations in 1999 unearthed no trace of a Christian shrine but found a
cult site or temple containing the skull of a teenage Romano-British boy,
which had been de-fleshed with a knife and mounted on a pole within a
shrine. The skull had four large holes in its crown – hard blows had been
driven down on it before the decapitation and his skull set up in the
temple.[7] The victim seems to have been killed in a rite similar to that which

accompanied the wounding and beheading of Worsley Man and Lindow I and III.

The motif of the blind killer appears to be of ancient provenance. Was Lugaid blind so that he would not see the mysterious and sacred conjunction of the holy lovers? And although Tacitus may have had no idea what Nerthus's fateful attendants had seen, the Celtic tales make it clear that the mystery they allude to is a sexual one – a sacred marriage, after which the husband joins this macabre Lady of the Lake, unseen by mortal eyes, in her own abode, for a last and bloody embrace.

Glob, too, had realised the sinister nature of this 'marriage', noting how on an Iron Age Danish carving of this ceremony, a twisted cord had been depicted around the embracing figures – a cord that he connected to the nooses found around the bog victims' throats. He states: 'The rope noose around the dead bog man's neck should also be seen as a neck-ring and also as the pass which carries him over the threshold of death and delivers him into the possession of the goddess, consecrating him to her for all time.'[8] This is the 'love-lace' of the bewitching Lady Bertilak, which offers her paramour eternal life, originally through sacrificial death.

Glob believes this twisted neck-ring to be a symbol of this goddess, an idea borne out in prehistoric Danish artefacts such as a Bronze Age statuette of this divinity wearing a double torc-like necklace. The Germanic Nerthus can be compared, both in name and role, to the Indian goddess Nirtti, a deity of dissolution, death, misfortune and witchcraft, who binds her victims with an unloosenable cord around their necks and drags them into the underworld.

In Germanic myth the goddess of fertility, Freyja, is famed for her magnificent necklace, known as the Brisingamen, which could also be translated as 'belt of fire',[9] a fact which links it to Lady Bertilak's girdle worn by Sir Gawain and the belt worn by Tollund Man. Perhaps the golden torcs worn in the Iron Age world are equivalent to the crucifixes worn by modern-day Christians – both are symbols of sacred sacrifices.

The image of the 'lovers' in deadly connubium in the lake is entirely in keeping with what I had learned of the Bachlach. Scholars have noted the connection between the figure of Cú Roí or Uath, the club-bearing churl, and the character named Fer Caille ('Man of the Wood'). He and his wife Cichuil appear in 'The Destruction of Da Derga's Hostel' as primitive and ugly lake-dwellers; in this tale Fer Caille is described as a black giant with one arm, one eye and one foot, carrying a huge club:

> *His hair was rough and bristling – if a sackful of wild apples were emptied over it, each apple would catch on his hair and none would fall to the ground … In his hand a forked iron pole. Behind him came a huge, black, gloomy, big-mouthed, ill-favoured woman; if her snout were thrown against a branch, the branch would support it, while her lower lip extended to her knee.*[10]

Similar lake-dwelling half-gods are to be found in English myth in the saga of Beowulf in the form of Grendel and his mother – primal troll-like creatures who attack the feasting hall of Heorot, much as the Green Knight arrives in Camelot, unannounced and uninvited. Their abode is reminiscent of the Chapel Green – a sub-aqueous cavern within a marshy pool beside a burial mound, into which Beowulf dives before decapitating them both.[11]

The identity of Fer Caille's mate is not in doubt. In Irish tradition she also appears 'As long as a weaver's beam, and as black, her two shins. Her beard reached her knees, and her mouth was on one side of her head.'[12] Standing on one leg, with one eye closed, she reveals her name is Badb ('battle crow'), another name for the Mórrígan, the demon-witch of Irish myth, who in the form of a raven gorges herself on the corpses of those slain in battle. In later legend she is Morgan le Fay, and she is no doubt also behind the figure of the loathsome damsel in the Grail myth, and obviously corresponds to the Indian Nirtti. She is also a goddess – her name translates as 'great queen'[13] – and so surely no mere slave, prisoner of war or simple country bumpkin could mate with her; her partner has to be divine, and the texts make clear that he is.

In an Ulster tale, the 'Intoxication of the Ulstermen', this divine personage is described as 'A man with a great eye, enormous thighs, wide shoulders, completely covered by a vast grey cloak, holding a thick iron cudgel in his hand.'[14] He wears a hood, like Tollund Man, and holds a great club. He is able to kill nine men with a blow from one end of this club and then revive them with the other. He is the Dagda.[15]

The Dagda ('good god', with good meaning 'all competent') appears in many tales in the Mythological Cycle. In the Book of Invasions, for instance, he is a king of the divine race of magical beings called the *Tuatha Dé Danann* ('the Tribes of the goddess Danu'), who fight with the demonic *Fomhoiré* over the sovereignty of the land in the Battles of Moytura. Known also as Ollathir ('All-Father') and Ruadh Rofhessa ('Red of Perfect Knowledge') – red being the colour of the dead in Celtic lore, but also hinting at the reddened hair of the bog men and Iron John – this 'god' strikes a bizarre and unlikely figure. Far from being 'godlike' in the modern sense of the word, he is shown as uncouth and pot bellied, with his genitals exposed below his woefully short tunic as he walks. He is forced to eat an obscene amount of porridge by the *Fomhoiré* in the prelude to one of the Battles of Moytura. But he is clearly a many faceted god – of war, fertility, the sky and, most importantly, magic. He is a druid god, possessing a magical harp which plays by itself and keeps the seasons in order.[16] To the Celts he was an underworld deity, thought to dwell in the Neolithic passage grave now known as Newgrange – a hollow hill or *sídhe* (fairy mound') to which he and his people retired after the coming of the Irish.[17] The track left by his club, which was so heavy eight men could not lift it, demarked tribal territories, a fact which revealed him as a tribal god. There are affinities here with his Germanic cousin, the red-haired Thunor (Lucan's Taranis), the hammer-wielding 'thunderer'. Both gods possess miraculous cauldrons that continually fill with good food – ancestors of the cauldron filled with the milk of three magical cows in the tale of Cú Roí's death.

As the archetype of maleness, and father of his tribe, the Dagda is also the fructifier of the Earth Goddess, possessing a voracious appetite for sex as well as food. In a scene highly reminiscent of the watery 'marriage' of the bog men he is depicted copulating with the Mórrígan while she straddles the river Unius, or in union with Boinn, his own sister, who personifies the river Boyne. In Gaul he seems to have existed under the local name Sucellos ('the Good Striker'), of whom over 200 figurines and inscriptions exist from the Romano-British period. He is accompanied by a goddess named Nantosuelta ('she of the winding brook'), who is associated, like the Mórrígan, with ravens.[18] Sucellos, in place of the Dagda's club, bears a hammer (as did Thunor) and is also often shown holding a small pot or vessel, the equivalent of the Dagda's cauldron. But he is also associated with the wheel (reminiscent of the turning castle of Cú Roí) and the Roman deity Silvanus (the god of the wood), and is thus linked directly to the primitive *Fer Caille*. Such gods, whatever their differing local names, represent the fundamental polarity of fecund goddess and her mate that lies at the foundation of primal Celtic religion.[19] It could be argued that later gods – such as the pan-Celtic Lugh, another 'all-competent' god of magic and the underworld – were not necessarily wholly separate deities but developments of the original god forms, which evolved as society itself evolved.

The Dagda can be seen as combining many elements within his person. As a club- or hammer-possessing sky god he is the thunderer, Taranis; as the 'good-at-everything god' he is Esus ('all-competent'); and as head and protector of his people he is Teutates ('God of the Tribe') – the three gods of Lucan's famous passage. Far from being dedicated *to* such a god, my researches into the Bachlach figure had revealed beyond doubt that the bog victims of prehistory had died *as* the god, with the three ways in which they died an expression of the fundamental triune-nature of this divinity.

Though the Dagda appears uncouth and comical to modern eyes (a fact that leads some to argue that he was a product of the medieval imagination), such a figure is almost universal in world myth. For example, in the Indian tradition there is an almost identical being, one who has not only been worshipped in Hindu countries from the earliest times (for at least 5,000 years in one form or another), but continues to have more worshippers than any other god on this planet today. He is Shiva, the destroyer – and a closer inspection of this god would help to illuminate the role played by the bog men.

Warriors of the Wasteland

Notes

1. Tacitus (trans. Mattingley, H and Handford, S A) (1986) pp.134–5.
2. Rees, A and B (1961) p. 337.
3. Glob, PV (1988) p. 166.
4. Meyer, K (trans.) (1993) pp. 33–4.
5. See Crossley Holland, K (1980) pp. 147–61.
6. Bede (1955) pp. 53–4.
7. *British Archaeology*, no 11, February 1996: 'The skull contains four large holes caused by blows at the time of death, suggesting the boy was battered to death before being decapitated and defleshed – though whether he was killed and defleshed by the same people is unknown.'
8. Glob, P V (1988) p. 166.
9. Ellis Davidson, H R (1988) p. 116.
10. Gantz, J (trans.) (1986) p. 71.
11. Connections between Beowulf and bog bodies are given in Stead, Bourke, Brothwell (1986) p. 174.
12. Gantz, J (trans.) (1986) p. 76.
13. Mor ('great'), Rigan ('queen'), from the proto-Celtic *Rigantona (Proto-Indo-European words are prefixed by an asterisk to show they are reconstructed); also the origin of the horse-goddess Rhiannon in the first branch of the *Mabinogi*.
14. Markale, J (1995) p.135.
15. Gantz, J (trans.) (1986) p. 207.
16. For a good introduction to the Dagda see Markale, J (1999) pp. 89–102.
17. And as lord of the underworld, he is linked to a passage found in Caesar's *Gallic War*, chapter 18: 'All the Gauls assert that they are descended from the god Dis [Dis Pater, a god of the dead], and say that this tradition has been handed down by the Druids.' Dis Pater, according to Tertullian, is depicted with a hammer.
18. See Green, M (1986) pp. 95–7, 140.
19. Cunliffe, B (1997) p. 186.

Chapter 6

THE WILD HERDSMAN

Shiva, meaning the 'auspicious one',[1] is the supreme god of the Hindu religion. As lord of the cosmos – 'Lord of the cosmic Dance' – he is shown holding the fire of immortality in one hand, and the drum of the beat of time in another; in his hair lies the crescent moon, containing the divine elixir of life, *soma*, a sacred narcotic; and on his head flows the River Ganges.[2] As the 'Lord of Yoga' who withdrew from the world into the woods, he is reminiscent of the druids who undertook their 20-year training within forest groves. Serpents are twisted about his neck and phallus, and he is often depicted in the form of the generative organ, known as the 'lingam'. In one Indian tale he is described as:

> *A hideous person – one with enormous pointed teeth, his hair standing on end, his hands busy with fire brands, his eyes red and tawny, his penis and testicles adorned with red chalk.*[3]

But it is not only this Bachlach-like description and his overtly sexual characteristics that link him to the Dagda. He is also known as *vina-dhara* (the lyre player), and is depicted wielding a trident, an axe or a club. One of his partners is the destructive Kali – she of the dreadful teeth, lolling tongue, four arms and an insatiable taste for blood. As her lover he is known as Shava ('the corpse'), and they are often shown resting on an island in the ocean of the cosmos, with Kali dancing on top of him wearing a necklace of severed human heads and carrying a noose to lasso and strangle her victim.[4]

'Shiva' is a Sanskrit word, but there are signs that the god is much older than this Indo-European language. Even in early myth he was treated as something quite ancient and primitive, a lord of forests who hunted with a bow and arrow. This proto-Shiva was also called Rudra, a name that links him to the Dagda in his aspect as Ruadh Rofhessa ('Red of Perfect Knowledge'), for Rudra means, among other things, 'the Red One'. Rudra was associated with the bull; he was a 'Herdsman, owner of cattle, lord of the animals';[5] he was also known as 'wielder of the bolt'.[6] Both functions were passed on to his later form, Shiva. He was a god of thunder and lightning, riding on a boar on stormy nights.

As Pasupati ('Lord of the Beasts') Shiva appears on cylinder seals of the Vedic period from the Indus Valley dating to around 2000 BC. He is depicted seated in a yogic posture, with great horns upon his head, and serpents and forest creatures in attendance.[7] This early form of Shiva sheds light on a Celtic god, for a figure similar to Rudra/Pasupati is depicted on the Gundestrup Cauldron. On one of its silver panels, surrounded by animals, including a stag and a wolf, is an antlered figure holding a serpent in his right hand. He is squatting in a yogic manner identical to the Indian god, although his 'horns' are obviously the antlers of a forest dweller of northern Europe. Some have associated him with a Gallic inscription to a god named Cernunnos ('the horned one').

What is of interest is the fact that about a mile/2 kilometres from the spot where the Gundestrup Cauldron was found, in Borre Fen, the bodies of a man and two attendant women were found – all three of Iron Age date. The man had suffered a triple death: he had been strangled with a triple-stranded hemp cord, his skull had been smashed in at the back, and his right leg had been broken above the knee. In the stomach of this red-haired man lay the same vegetable gruel found in other victims – and, importantly, like the yogic Pasupati and the Gundestrup horned god, he was sitting in a cross-legged position within the peat bog.[8]

The antlered man on the cauldron brought to my mind that figure of English folklore, Herne the hunter, leader of the Wild Hunt, who would lead the souls of the dead through the air on stormy nights. Herne was derived ultimately from Herian, an epithet of the Germanic Wotan, who, as a god of wizardry and the dead, shared many characteristics with the Dagda.[9] I had scratched the surface of the Green Knight and found a primitive god of the hunt!

The one image that fuses together these two aspects, seemingly poles apart, is to be found in the story of Owein in the Welsh *Mabinogion*:

The Wild Herdsman

On that mound you will see a great black man, no smaller than two men of this world. He has one foot, and one eye in the middle of his forehead, and he carries an iron spear ... Though ugly he is not an unpleasant man. He is keeper of the forest, and you will see a thousand wild animals grazing about him.[10]

This 'Wild Herdsman' as Owein is also called, was able to summon all the creatures of the forest to him by striking a stag, which subsequently roars, with his club. He was Bachlach and horned herdsman in one. But I was about to chance upon some information that would reveal something else about the bog men: the fact that they were probably shamans.

In Siberian lore such a one-eyed and one-legged figure is known as *Burgestez-Udagan* – an *Udagan* was a medicine man, or a witch doctor, usually translated into another Siberian word that has attained common (mis-)usage: shaman.[11] Briefly, a shaman is an individual who through some initiatory illness (often psychological in nature) leaves the community for the wilderness, where he lives like a beast before undergoing a psychologically transforming experience (usually hedged in death/dismemberment/rebirth symbolism). He thereby attains the ability to enter ecstatic trances at will and to heal others whilst in these states of altered consciousness. The shaman believes that whilst in this state of trance, induced by drumming, dancing or ingesting narcotics, his soul journeys to another world (the upper- or underworld), usually via the 'world tree' that connects the three worlds in shamanic cosmology. There it meets with animal helpers and with the spirits of the ancestors, who impart knowledge to him. The shaman is thus surrounded and aided by a host of spirit-animals or familiars who help him heal and perform magic. He sometimes takes on the characteristics of these familiars by wearing feathers or fur and acting as if possessed by them, either swooping with arms outstretched like an eagle's wings, or on all fours like a bear, wolf or horse. Shamanism is seen by many as the earliest form of tribal religion, used in hunting magic since Palaeolithic times. Perhaps, then, the squatting men of Vedic India and prehistoric Britain were primitive wizards – shamans – a possibility that would become more important as my quest continued.

Nowhere is this shamanic background more apparent than in the figure of Merlin, whom Jean Markale called the 'last of the druids' and

49

Count Nikolai Tolstoy called a 'late British shaman-figure'. A passage in the *Vita Merlini*, written in 1132 by Welshman Geoffrey of Monmouth, describes what happened to Myrddin after the battle of Arderydd, in which his lord, Gwenddolau, is slain:

> ... *fury seized him and departed secretly, and fled to the woods ... He became a sylvan man. For a whole summer after this, hidden like a wild animal ... found by no one and forgetful of himself and of his kindred.*[12]

Myrddin/Merlin is charmed back to civilisation by his sister Gwendydd, wife of his enemy Rhydderch, but again flees into the wilds, whereon Rhydderch has him brought back to court, Iron John-like, in chains. He escapes once again, only to return riding a stag. He kills his wife's new lover with an antler (which he takes off his own head – he has been wearing them, like the figure on the Gundestrup Cauldron). Merlin then spends the summer in the company of a grey wolf, and clothes himself in a wolf skin.[13] The wolf is no doubt his familiar. In the French text *Merlin*, he is described as clothed in wolf-skin and bearing a cudgel, which he strikes against the oak trees, seemingly summoning a train of deer and 'russet' animals.[14]

According to Geoffrey, Merlin's teacher is Blaise, a name hinting at further wolfish origins, for in Welsh *Bleidd* (*Bleiz* in Breton) means wolf. Another Blaise, the Catholic St Blaise, is obviously nothing but a wolf-shaman in Christian clothing: He retired to a mountain in Turkey and was found outside a cave, surrounded by a horde of wild animals, and was able to talk to wolves, like St Francis of Assisi.[15] His martyrdom is suspect: thrown into water to drown, he is then beheaded and his flesh ripped off with wool combs. Surely a triple death? Blaise is not the only wolfish Celtic saint. St Ronan – whose abode was Neved, a word derived from the Celtic *Nemeton* ('sacred grove') – could not only converse with wolves, but could also become one.

These saints left humanity behind to become forest hermits. Celtic myth is thronged with such men who thus went mad and became identified with 'the wild man of the woods'. Owein, for instance, sprouts long hair all over his body and lives with the animals. His hairiness, like that of Iron John, is suggestive of the lycanthropy (transformation into a wolf) of Ronan. Are such tales dim remembrances of shamanic transformations? Lycanthropic creatures are not rare in the shamanic world: shamans across the globe, especially among the Eskimo, the Chukchee and the Lapps, boast the ability to shape-shift into animal form, often the wolf. The Lapps often become bears and fish, too.[16]

There are many signs that in the Celto-Germanic world – the world in which the bog men lived and died – special attention was given to such a wolf or canine shaman. A wolf, after all, appears next to the horned 'god' on a scene from the Gundestrup Cauldron – and on the panel that shows men being ritually drowned. And an Iron Age carving from Kells, Co. Meath, shows what could be a horned figure between two wolves, its face more canine than human.[17] What's more, in the poem *Beowulf*, Grendel and his mother are described as *werga, heorowearh, brimwylf* – all of which contain Old English words meaning 'wolf'. Two of these names – *werga* and *heorowearh* – are derived from the word *waergh* (or *warg*), itself a derivative of the Indo-European **werghez*, which means to *strangle*.[18] (Proto-Indo-European words are prefixed by an asterisk to show that they are reconstructed.)

The gallows in Germanic tradition are known as the Warg-Tree, and a hanged man as a 'Vargr'.[19] Had this connection between the wolf-man and the hanged-man come from a time when those condemned to death by strangulation were the wolf-shamans of prehistory, drowned in connubium with the noose-carrying goddess?

And then it hit me! Perhaps the fox-fur armband worn by Lindow II was a totemic badge. If being strangled by the garrotte marked him out as a 'Vargr', then maybe his rust-red armband was a shamanic symbol that hinted at some sort of magical transformation, that turned him into a hairy wild man – a werewolf or werefox.

There is much folklore to connect the wearers of animal-skin armbands with werewolves, and none more intriguing than the case of Peter Stubb, executed for lycanthropy in 1589 in the village of Bedburg, near Cologne. This bizarre story, countersigned by four witnesses, was recorded on two pamphlets dating from 1590 (now both in London, in the British Museum and Lambeth Library). They describe Stubb as 'a most wicked sorcerer, who in the likeness of a wolf committed many murders, continuing this devilish practice for 25 years, killing and devouring Men, Women and Children'.[20] But despite its purported historical reality, the tale of Herr Stubb hints more at a pagan rite than an actual occurrence, for he was killed in a complex triple method: after being tied to a wheel, he was beheaded, burned and dismembered. The wheel is associated with the Gallic Sucellos, and with Cú Roí and his castle that spun 'like a mill-wheel'. Could the account of Peter Stubb's execution have been the memory of the victim of a ritual death, especially given the date, 31 October – the Celtic festival known as Samhain that marked the start of winter and from which modern-day Halloween is derived? But more important to my theme was Peter's confession, in which he declares that he became a wolf by wearing a girdle given to him by the devil.[21]

The magical girdle crops up many times in werewolf lore, and I was intrigued to discover that such a belt could also transform a person into a *fox*.[22] And, interestingly, in light of the strangulation of the bog men, according to German tradition the 'wolf-belt' is crafted from either wolf's fur or the skin of a *hanged man*.[23]

Admittedly these folktales and semi-historical records are aeons away from the era of the bog victims – yet the wilds of Germania had resisted Christianisation for longer than much of Europe, and if pagan motifs from the Indo-European world had survived in folklore, Germany was where this was most likely to have occurred. It is possible that by wearing his fox-fur armband Lindow Man somehow took on the properties of the fox and became identified with this rust-red hairy animal – not by a personal name or tribal affiliation, as other authors have suggested,[24] but through some kind of shamanic transformation, as if by wearing the armband he became 'enchanted' into a red-haired wild man, the horned one and wild herds-man, whose companions were the snake and the wolf. And why not a fox? Red hair in Celtic tradition marks out an animal as other-worldly; and the fox dwells below the earth, as medieval Welsh poet Dafydd ap Gwilym hints when he wrote:

> *No easy thing for me to follow him*
> *Since his dwelling is far down in Annwfn*[25]

Annw(f)n – meaning literally 'not world' – is the Welsh other world. Lindow Man, I surmised, had played the role of the fox of Annwn, to be killed while mating with the goddess of the chariot – a fact remembered in the Gawain poem where a fox pelt is given to Gawain (originally the host) on the eve of his death, on the same day that the hostess gives him a 'magical' girdle. But there is something more that conclusively links the bog men to the lycanthropic forest shamans: the 'Tooth of the Wolf'.

A certain poisonous fungus which grew on barley, especially in the damp and misty conditions of north-western Europe, had caused many deaths throughout history. The effects of eating these rotten grains were horrific: intense burning pains caused by vasoconstriction that could lead to loss of limbs, or in certain cases, if the dose was high enough – death.[26] Even ingesting only a minute amount of this fungus caused a loss of motor control, writhing, intense shaking, fits, rolling eyes, extreme thirst, ravenous hunger, and a sense of suffocation caused by an intense wry-neck. It also caused vivid hallucinations, and the sense of being transformed into a beast. In German it was known as 'Wolf' or 'Tooth of the Wolf'.[27]

I had read how the name of this fungus, and the symptoms it caused, suggested that the accidental eating of affected barley grains might lie behind the phenomenon of lycanthropy. The werewolf of German folklore is sometimes known as the Roggenwolf (the 'Rye Wolf'), who was said to ambush and strangle unwary peasants in the fields – indeed, a metaphor for this fungus.[28]

Beowulf means 'Barley Wolf' – hinting that behind the tale of his battle with the wolfish Grendel and his mother lay a cult of the 'Tooth of the Wolf'. Had this fungus been taken in small doses by prehistoric warriors seeking to become like beasts in battle? The Berserkers (literally, 'bear shirts'), Germanic warriors who were said to become bears in battle, are comparatively well known, but few are familiar with the twin tradition of the Ulfhednar' (the 'Wolf-Heads').[29] Was it possible that Beowulf had been an Ulfhednar? And in Iranian lore there exists a similar band of warriors known as the Haomavargaz (the 'Haoma' or 'soma' wolves)[30] – soma being the unidentified drug that Shiva possessed in the cup of the moon – who become wolves after taking this sacred substance. All the evidence points to the existence of a lycanthropic-warrior drug cult in the ancient Indo-European world – including the Celtic lands.

The nearest figure to a Berserker in Celtic myth is the Irish warrior Cú Chulainn, whose famous 'battle fury' (the *fearg* – 'fury', 'rage') transforms him into a monster:

Thereupon he became distorted. His hair stood on end so that it seemed as if each separate hair on his head had been hammered into it ... He closed one eye so that it was no wider than the eye of a needle; he opened the other until it was as large as the mouth of a mead-goblet ...The champion's light rose above his head.[31]

It was obvious that in his fury Cú Chulainn took on the appearance of the Bachlach or Wild Herdsman – one-eyed, with rigid spiked hair. Were there any clues of a wolfish connection? In the *Iliad*, such battle-fury, demonstrated by Achilles, is called 'Lyssa' – meaning 'wolfish rage', stemming from the word *lycos* ('wolf').[31] And on closer inspection the Irish *fearg* yields similar etymology, being quite evidently the same word as *waergh* or *vargr*, but spelled with an 'f' (there is no 'v' in the Irish Gaelic alphabet).

The lycanthropic connection did help to explain the names of Cú Chulainn and Cú Roí – 'hound of Culann' and 'Hound King'. The canine-totemic connection had been in their names from the start. The evidence of prehistoric lycanthropy in warrior-bands then led me to assume that the shamans of the north also used such narcotics. The 'Tooth of the Wolf' had no doubt been taken to induce ecstatic trances and visions of other worlds, for this barley fungus was none other than ergot, whose active ingredient, lysergic acid, is used in the production of LSD.

The connection between ergot and lycanthrope was one of the Eureka moments in my quest. Ergot (the word itself derived from *wearg*) had been found *in large quantities in the stomachs of both Tollund and Grauballe Man*, mixed in with other seeds in their last meal! And as Glob points out, these were no prisoners of war or labourers, but probably priests of Nerthus. They were shamans. What's more, ergot, causing as it did a feeling of strangulation, was known in seventeenth-century England as the *'suffocation of the mother'* (a name that probably originated in much earlier times).[33] It was the necklace of Nerthus in chemical form.

Alby Stone has stated that the intense burning suffered by the taker of the drug might lie behind the image of the burning of the cosmos at the end of time found in Norse myth, when a giant conflagration destroys the cosmos after the battle of Ragnarok, caused by the loosing of the *wolf* Fenris from his chains. From my work on Shiva I knew that in Indian myth the universe is said to end in a similar conflagration associated with Rudra (the 'red one'), whose name, I was not surprised to read, also means 'the howler'.[34] Such clues led to a growing realisation that the deaths of the bog men might have had a more cosmological significance than a simple tale of love and betrayal.

I also began to recognise that my quest for the meaning behind these deaths was entering new territory. Where there was once just a man in a museum, now there was a wounded shaman god – a howling red one, bizarrely murdered in connubium with a dark goddess, who possessed a cauldron of plenty, a soma-filled moon-vessel that offered glimpses of other worlds to those who sought it. Could this amazing character be any other than the Wounded King of the Grail legends?

Could an ancient wizard-god whose fate was aped in all its gory fullness by the bog men really lie behind such a figure? One legend that certainly points to this being the case concerns Shiva. It tells how the great phallic god enters the forest, dishevelled and hairy, his member coloured with red chalk, and asks for sex with the daughters of the sages who lived there. Understandably, the sages are not enamoured with the idea and castrate the god, unaware of who he is, thinking him a simple madman. But the wound to his 'thigh' has dreadful consequences.[35] 'Nothing shone forth; the sun gave no heat ... and the constellations and planets were all topsy-turvy.' It is only after worshipping Shiva in the form of a lingam for a year that spring returns.

Here was a connection between the Wasteland motif of the Grail and the wound to the genitals. But did such a wound exist in the early Celtic sources? I had uncovered plenty of beheadings (of the Green Knight/ Bachlach) that might provide a background to the Peredur story, and plenty of wonder-working cauldrons to link to the Fisher King's Grail. As for crippling wounds to the thighs, I knew one source in Celtic myth that included such a motif in stunning perfection – the tale of Bran ('raven'), also known as Morddwyd Tyllion ('the wounded thigh'), who not only possessed a cauldron of plenty, but was beheaded, to boot. In examining his myth I would gradually begin to fathom the exact identity of his killer. My quest for the 'why' behind the killing of the bog men had become intrinsically linked with the quest for the Grail.

Notes

1. Campbell, J (1962) pp. 206–7.
2. See Campbell, J (1974) pp. 356–9 and Zimmer, H (1974) pp. 151–7.
3. Doniger O'Flaherty, W (trans.) (1975) p. 142.
4. Campbell, J (1962) pp. 90, 334 and Zimmer, H (1974) pp. 206–7.
5. Zimmer, H (1974) p. 171.
6. Campbell, J (1962) pp. 208–9.
7. Campbell, J (1962) pp. 168–9.
8. See Ross, A and Robbins, D (1989) pp. 164–8.
9. See Matthews, J (1993) p. 51.
10. Gantz, J (trans.) (1985) p. 196.
11. Matthews, John (1991) p. 36.
12. Quoted in Stewart, R J (1986) p. 25.
13. For a summary of the career of Merlin see Markale, J (1995) pp. 1–34.
14. Markale, J (1995) p. 134.
15. Markale, J (1995) pp.164–5.
16. See Eliade, M (1989) pp. 93, 241 and 467.
17. Ross, A (1996) p. 187.
18. Stone, A (1994). This essay is available online at http://www.indigogroup.co.uk/edge/
19. Stone, A (1994).
20. The information on Peter Stubbe is found in Summers, Montague (1934) pp. 253–9, quoted from http://www.pitt.edu/~dash/werewolf.html
21. As note 20.
22. 'In the village of Dodow near Wittenburg there lived an old woman who possessed a fox-strap. With its help she could transform herself into a fox, and thus her table never lacked for geese, ducks, and all kinds of poultry.' (Karl Bartsch, *Sagen, Marchen und Gebrauche aus Meklenberg* (Wilhelm Raumuller, Vienna 1879, v.1, no. 181, p.146), again quoted on http://www.pitt.edu/~dash/werewolf.html
23. A A Wuttke: 'Der Deutsche Volks und Aberglaube der Gegenwart', 1925, quoted online at http://www.pitt.edu/~dash/werewolf.html
24. Anne Ross, who has had the dubious honour of actually coming face to face with an ancient Celtic lycanthrope!
25. Bromwich (trans.) (1985) p. 88.
26. In AD 994, 40,000 people died of ergot poisoning.
27. Stone, A (1994).
28. The source for this folklore is Frazer, J G (1987) pp. 448–9
29. Lincoln, B (1991) p. 134.
30. Lincoln, B (1991) p. 134.
31. Kinsella, T (1990).
32. Lincoln, B (1991) pp. 131–7.
33. Stone, A (1994).
34. Zimmer, H (1974) p. 181.
35. Doniger O'Flaherty, W (trans) (1975) p. 145.

Chapter 7

THE WOUNDED THIGH

The story of Bran is found in 'Branwen daughter of Llyr', the second branch of the *Mabinogion*. The tale begins with Bendigeidfran ('Bran the Blessed'), king of all Britain, in negotiations with the Irish king, Matholwch, who, wishing to cement an alliance between the two countries, proposes to marry Bran's sister Branwen ('white raven'), the eponymous heroine of this tale. Bran's half-brother Efnissien arrives to find the marriage has taken place without his being consulted, and in his fury he mutilates the horses of King Matholwch. In reparation Bran offers Matholwch a gift – a magical cauldron that can bring the dead back to life, whole *save for the power of speech*. Bran tells how the cauldron was a gift from a strange couple to whom he had once shown hospitality. Matholwch reveals that he, too, knows of them: a monstrous red-haired couple who emerge from the lake known as the 'Lake of the Cauldron'. Matholwch had attempted to kill the couple by roasting them to death in an 'Iron House'. They, however, had escaped and fled to Britain.

Within three years, although she had borne Matholwch a son, Branwen is put away in disgrace. She suffers abuse from a butcher in the kitchens where she is forced to work, but she manages to send a message to Bran, beneath the wing of a trained starling, detailing her predicament. Leaving seven men in charge of his kingdom (under his son Caradwg), Bran, who is depicted as a giant, immediately sets off for Ireland with his army, wading across the sea. He is soon spotted from Ireland, though at first his immense form is mistaken for a mountain. Branwen explains that it is her brother come to rescue her. The Irish army retires beyond the Shannon, destroying its bridges, hoping to prevent the invasion, but to no avail, for Bran allows his men to cross the river over his immense body, saying:

'He who is chief, let him be a bridge.'[1]

Matholwch surrenders and offers to abdicate in favour of Branwen's son Gwern. A great feasting hall is built for the occasion (Bran being too large to be contained in any normal house), in which the kings and their warriors assemble. The king-to-be, Gwern, is passed from man to man, but when he reaches the hands of his uncle Efnissien, the latter throws him into the fire. There is uproar and Bran shouts 'Dogs of Gwern, beware 'Morddwyd Tyllion' ('the wounded thigh')!'[2]

A rout ensues in which there is great slaughter. The Irish, however, fire up Bran's wedding gift, the great Cauldron of Rebirth, and begin to re-suscitate their dead. Efnissien, in an act of remorse and redemption worthy of any Hollywood villain-turned-hero, places himself amongst the Irish dead, and on being thrown into the cauldron, stretches out so that it is destroyed – dying in the process.

The Irish are eventually wiped out, but the cost to the Britons is immense, only seven men return home: 'Pryderi, Manawyddan, Glifieu son of Taran, Taliesin and Ynawg, Gruddieu son of Muriel, and Heilyn son of Gwyn the Old.'[3] Bran, grievously wounded has a bizarre request: he asks to be decapitated, and for his severed head to be buried in the White Mount in London, facing France.

With Bran's severed head for company the seven men set out for home, but the journey is to be magically long – 87 mystical years of feasting, in which time none grew older, and all the while they were entertained by the head of Bran. Eventually curiosity leads Heilyn to break the prohibition set on the seven by opening a door facing Cornwall, and the feast ends. They return to Britain to find it desolate. Caswallawn, son of Beli, has killed and replaced Bran's son, Caradwg, and only one man, Pendaran Dyfed, has escaped alive. Bran's men are true to their word and bury his head in the White Mount, where it acts as a talisman, protecting the land from invasion. After many years it is uncovered by King Arthur, who wishes to defend the land as sole protector.[4]

It is easy to see how many took this Bran who had been wounded in the thigh as the precursor of the Wounded King of the Grail legends. For a start his name echoes that of Bron (De Boron's Fisher King) and also his magical cauldron of rebirth easily matches in enchantment the Holy Grail. Its resurrecting qualities shed light on the famous image on the Gundestrup

Cauldron of a man being submerged in a cauldron, for on closer inspection the image depicts an army of men led by a wolf, carrying spears on the points of which rests a giant sprouting tree. They walk towards the cauldron, and come away from it on horseback (reborn presumably), led by a snake (which through the shedding of its skin symbolises the concept of rebirth). In the tale of Peredur there is an episode in which the hero, while in the hall of the 'King of Suffering', witnesses corpses being taken off their horses, placed in a tub of warm water and brought back to life.

Bran's head entertaining his men at the other-worldly feast also seems to offer an origin for the head on the salver seen by Peredur, for it is indeed the head of the Wounded King, pierced in the thigh. The mysterious castle of the Grail, that timeless realm which appears magically out of the mist, is also no doubt akin to the other-worldly feasting hall of the so-called 'company of the noble head' in 'Branwen'.

It came as a shock to discover that some thought the tale of Bran purely the invention of the medieval storyteller who first put these stories down on paper. It is true that many of the motifs found within the tales do match – and are indeed inspired linguistically by other, especially Irish, myths, but it is possible that the basic plot of the tale, so close to the theme I had unravelled from a host of other sources, preserves a very ancient story indeed. According to Breton scholar Jean Markale, Bran's myth lies behind the so-called 'historical' raids of the two Gallic warriors named Brennus on Rome in 390 BC and Delphi in 279 BC. It has been argued that Brennus means 'king', but Markale has put forward good evidence that it is in fact a corruption of Brannios, i.e. Bran,[5] whose myth has somehow accreted itself onto the historical Gallic incursions into the Classical world.

The parallels between Roman 'history' and Welsh myth are astounding:

1   In Livy's *Ab Urbe Condita*,[6] Brennus is recorded as attacking Rome to avenge one Aruns, whose adopted son and wife are betrayed by the Romans,[7] an explanation that parallels Bran's journey to Ireland to rescue his sister and her son from the wicked Matholwch.

2   Much as Branwen, Blodeuwedd and Blathnat betray their husbands, Rome is betrayed by a maiden named Tarpeia who is in love with a Gallic warrior.

3 The Romans and Gauls meet at the river Allia, where the Romans flee in terror from some supernatural force. The Gauls wait outside the city until the solstice arrives, then launch their attack. Rome, here, is clearly a magical place, like the spinning castle of Cú Roí in that it is difficult to enter, or like the castle of Bertilak that opens its doors to Gawain on Christmas Eve.

4 In the Delphic myth, Brennus crosses the River Sperchios *by wading across* (because its bridges have been destroyed), just as Bran crosses the Shannon.[8]

5 Brennus returns to Heraclea, *thrice wounded*, and takes poison, or, as Justinus (whose work is based on *World History* by Trogus Pompeius, who was of Celtic stock) says: 'He put an end to his days with a blow from a dagger', much as Bran commands his men to end his life by decapitation. And in both raids, the Gauls, like Bran's Britons, are wiped out almost to a man.

Jean Markale concludes that these references to the historical incursions of Brennus originated in Celtic myth, and have been woven into the histories of Rome by authors unaware of their ritual content.[9] If he is correct, versions of the Bran myth, which some claim to be a medieval invention, existed many centuries before the birth of Christ.

Another variant of the story of Bran appears in a near contemporary source to the *Mabinogion* – Geoffrey of Monmouth's *History of the Kings of Britain*, written between 1129 and 1151. This work by the author of the *Vita Merlini*[10] contains elements of Celtic tradition not found in other surviving sources. It tells the story of a prehistoric prince named *Brennius*, whose father, Dunvallo, dies, leaving Brennius and his brother Belinus to fight for the throne. On Dunvallo's death, the kingdom is divided between the two, with Brennius, the younger, getting the smaller portion – Northumbria from as far north as the Humber to Caithness. But Brennius is unwisely counselled to marry the king of Norway's daughter (Norway, as noted earlier, had connotations with the other world) and invade the rest of Britain. But while Brennius is at sea preparing to attack Belinus, his wife is abducted and ends up in Belinus's hands. Belinus seizes the entire kingdom and the two eventually meet in a pitched battle in the forest of Calaterium.

Geoffrey records that in the end it is Belinus and the Britons who are victorious, and Belinus keeps hold of the kingdom. Brennius and Belinus then decide to unite and conquer Europe – heading ultimately for Rome. After much combat, Brennius takes the city – but of his fate Geoffrey makes no mention, saying only that 'the histories of Rome explain these matters'.[11]

Geoffrey's Brennius and Belinus are clearly the Welsh Bran and a figure that appears in the *Mabinogion* as his uncle, called Beli son of Mynogan (or Beli the Great, King of Britain, as he is referred to in the tale of Lludd and Llefelys). The taking of Britain from Brennius by Belinus clearly parallels the ousting of Caradwg son of Bran by Caswallawn son of Beli at the end of the second branch of the *Mabinogion*. What is of interest is that when Geoffrey states that 'the history of Rome' explains the subsequent history of Brennius, he is clearly linking his Brennius to the Gallic chieftain Brennus.

But what is important in Geoffrey's work is his demonstration that Brennius's adversary, to whom he loses the kingdom, is none other than his *brother*.

An alternate version of this Bran/Beli conflict appears in a strange Welsh poem named 'Cad Goddeu' (The 'Battle of the Trees), in which the opposing armies of Bran and the sons of Beli are turned into trees and shrubs to fight;[12] the whole conflict is a ritual battle in which Bran and Arawn, gods of Annwn (the underworld), are vanquished. A gloss on the poem states:

And there was a man in that battle, who unless his name were known could not be overcome. And Gwydion ap Don guessed the name of the man, and sang the two englyns following:

Sure-hoofed is my steed impelled by the spur;
The high sprigs of alder are on thy shield;
Bran art thou called, of the glittering branches.

Sure-hoofed is my steed in the day of battle:
The high sprigs of alder are in thy hand:
Bran thou art, by the branch thou bearest –
Amathaon the Good has prevailed.[13]

A similar plot involving the enchanter Gwydion seems to lie behind the defeat of the hero Pryderi son of Pwyll, lord of Annwn, slain at the hands of this son of Beli, at a place called the Yellow Ford (Y Felen Rhyd). In this tale, found in the fourth branch of the *Mabinogion*, the war is over the magical self-reconstituting swine of Annwn, just as in the poem 'Cad Goddeu' it was over a 'whelp and a roebuck' from Annwn. Was the 'Cad Goddeu' also being hinted at in Geoffrey's forest battle of Calaterium, where Brennius meets and is defeated by Belinus? What the tales seem to reiterate over and over is the defeat of Bran, or an equivalent underworld deity, within a sacred grove or ford, at the hands of Beli ('bright/light') or his sons.

The name of Bran's adversary brought to mind yet again the Grail legend, for according to Malory, the Fisher King, Pellean, is wounded by the 'dolorous stroke' of one of a pair of warring brothers named Balin (or Balainn) and Balan, identified by many scholars as Beli and Bran. Balin attacks the Grail King Pellean with a spear that he finds floating in the air, point-down above a cauldron. As soon as he drives the spear through the king's thighs the castle walls collapse, the crops fail and the trees lose their leaves.[14] In the *Mabinogion* Bran's assailant is unnamed; he is merely recorded as being wounded in the thigh or foot with a poisoned spear, but in the Grail legends, in the legend of Brennius in Geoffrey's *History*, and in 'Cad Goddeu', enough evidence is presented to make it clear that it is his brother Beli who does the deed.

Having discovered the 'brother-battle' motif deep within this sacrificial tale, I was then able to link it to other stories that contain this theme – and not all from Celtic lands.

In the Fionn mac Cumhaill cycle of Ireland, for instance, Diarmuid O Duibne is slain by a magical boar that is also his brother under enchantment. And bearing the boar in mind I recalled that in Egyptian myth the god Osiris is killed while hunting for boar one night on the marshes of the Nile delta by his brother Seth. In some versions Osiris, who is depicted as being *green*, is drowned in these marshes and is later decapitated and dismembered by Seth (who in some forms of the legend is himself depicted as a boar).[15] Osiris is later reconstituted, save for his penis which is eaten by a fish, neatly linking this green man to the emasculated Shiva. I was also aware that Osiris's son Horus was conceived when his wife Isis was in the Nile marshes while he was *dead* – an image of the sacred connubium of god and goddess in a watery place, with the god, like the Indian Shava (or Shiva), a corpse – wounded and emas-culated by his brother and then drowned. I had not expected to find such clear parallels in Egyptian myth. To add to this mystery, in the third branch of the *Mabinogion* Pryderi is depicted chasing a boar into an other-worldly castle, where he becomes stuck to a golden bowl and the land falls under an evil enchantment. The appearance of the boar and its connection to the brother in these myths is most interesting.

I remember finding a brilliantly simple form of this myth in a Grimm's fairy tale, 'The Singing Bone', in which two brothers hunt a magical boar in order to win the hand of the king's daughter. The youngest kills the boar, but his jealous brother kills him and claims the boar, and the princess, for his own. He buries his brother's body beside a river, where one day a shepherd chances upon a bone, and from it creates a pipe. On blowing it he hears these words:

> Ah friend, thou blowest upon my bone!
> Long have I lain beside the water;
> My brother slew me for the boar,
> And took for his wife the King's young daughter.[16]

Of course, he goes to the castle, where the truth comes out and the evil brother is banished. But the story neatly summarises what I had found so far – I could almost imagine Lindow Man, who himself had long lain beside the water, singing these verses. And if the tale sounds familiar, it is because it was used by Shakespeare in *Hamlet*, where the slain king's ghost appears to his son to tell of his 'murder most foul' at the hands of his own brother, now married to the dead king's wife. It is up to the son, Hamlet, the less than willing Grail Knight of this epic, to 'revenge his foul and most un-natural murder' and expose the wickedness that has corrupted the land: 'There is something rotten in the state of Denmark.'

The first question posed by the bog men had now been answered. They were playing the role of the defeated god of Celtic myth – the primal god or herdsman, the old tribal triune god of magic – the shaman, possessor of the cauldron of immortality, defeated and emasculated in connubium with the dreadful goddess by his brother, an act that blasted the fertility of the land. I had discovered the original plot of the drama enacted by the sacrificial victims, but for all my research I was no closer to the 'why' of these murders. The myth clearly meant something; it was not just a story. What did this brother battle mean? What were its origins? Having exhausted the main leads in Celtic myth and legend I had, it seemed, come to a standstill.

But then a thought occurred. I had already accepted that Rudra, the Indian reflex of the Bachlach figure, was a pre-Indo-European deity, appearing as the horned Pasupati on seals from the Indus Valley dating back to at least 2000 BC. Could it be that the origins of the Celtic myth dated to this time? Might it be that I would discover what I wanted to know about this strange tale of brother-battles and wonder-working cauldrons in a more distant age?

And the boar was to be the first clue, for its connection with Pryderi, the Irish Diarmuid, the 'Singing Bone' and Osiris hinted that all these tales share a common origin: the motif of the god slain by the boar, the son and lover of the Great Goddess, dying and being reborn with the seasons, who under various names and forms (Osiris, Attis, Adonis) was worshipped throughout Old Europe and the Near East from the time of the first farmers – the vegetation god of Frazer's *Golden Bough*.[17]

Was it possible that the appearance in Celtic myths of the god slain by the boar was of ancient provenance? The modern view that the Celtic language had developed indigenously in the Atlantic coastal zone since Neolithic times raises the possibility that these ancient traditions might have been passed down to an Iron Age population from their Neolithic ancestors.

If these traditions really did date back to the Neolithic, it would be necessary to journey back to those times and attempt to discover exactly what was the meaning behind them. And so with great anticipation I turned my gaze on the ancient timeworn stones of megalithic Britain in search of a Wounded King.

The Wounded Thigh

Notes

1. Doniger O'Flaherty, W (trans.) (1975) p. 34.
2. Doniger O'Flaherty, W (trans.) (1975) p. 37. Also see Matthews, C (1987) p. 45.
3. Doniger O'Flaherty, W (trans.) (1975) p. 37.
4. This event is known as one of the 'Three Unfortunate Disclosures of Britain' in the Welsh triads (trans. Bromwich, University of Wales Press).
5. Doniger O'Flaherty, W (trans.) (1975) p. 72.
6. Livy is an interesting character who, like Geoffrey of Monmouth, was of Celtic stock, being born into a Cisalpine Gallic family. And in a similar fashion to Geoffrey he used much of his Celtic literary heritage to forge elements of his half-fact, half-fiction history of Rome. See Markale, J (1993) p. 51.
7. To begin with, this reason for the Gallic invasion is suspect for it is derived from a completely unconnected event, the murder of Aruns by King Tarquinius Superbus, which is originally found in an account by Dionysius of Halicarnassus (IV, 15). The original date of this event is 508 BC, over 100 years before the Gallic incursion. But this confusion is revealing.
8. Markale, J (1993) p. 67.
9. Markale, J (1993) p. 78.
10. See introduction to the Penguin translation by Lewis Thorpe. Geoffrey's work was probably completed by 1136.
11. Markdale, J (1993) p. 99.
12. Composed some time between 1080 and 1350 by a poet calling himself Taliesin, this poem had been crafted in the age of the Gogynfeirdd ('fairly early poets'), professional bards in the courts of the Welsh princes who plundered the remnants of the old myths and legends to create works which they saw as being 'inspired' by the old poets and even prophetic. See Hutton, R (1991) pp. 322–4.
13. Source: Graves, R (1961) p. 49.
14. See Loomis, R S (1992) pp. 77, 110–12 and Lacy, N (ed.) (1988) p. 40.
15. Rundle Clark, R T (1959) pp. 97–123.
16. Grimm, W and J (1993) p. 150.
17. Campbell, J (1968) p. 124.

Part Two

THE GRAIL

Chapter 8

THE HOUSES
OF THE DEAD

I vividly recall the moment in 1994 when I crossed a small wooden bridge spanning the River Kennet, in Wiltshire, and continued up a gentle slope to where, on the crest of the hill, a low-lying mound was just visible. It was higher at the eastern end than at the west, and was toothed with great stones, stark against the sky. This 10-foot/3-metre-tall man-made earthen hillock – measuring some 330 feet/100 metres by 80 feet/25 metres – was West Kennet longbarrow, once a repository for the bones of the ancient Neolithic dead. It was well over 5,000 years old, and in it I would find a clue to the origins of the Celtic cult behind the Grail.

Behind me lay the colossal dome of Silbury Hill, the largest man-made mound in prehistoric Europe and one of the most enigmatic features of this magical landscape. Even from my present vantage point this vast pudding-bowl-shaped hill seemed immense, a marker that drew me in to the mysteries of the surrounding landscape, including the stone circle of Avebury, whose hallowed turf I had trodden earlier in the day.

The circle at Avebury was so vast that a modern village now nestles within its bounds. Inside its huge exterior ditch (originally 55 feet/17 metres high) and bank (once 30 feet/9 metres deep and built around 2600 BC) were 28 acres/11 hectares of land and *three* stone circles: a huge ring of 98 mighty stones near the inner edge the ditch and two smaller circles, aligned roughly north and south, each bigger than the later Stonehenge. The northern circle contained a box-like 'cove' of three stones, the southern an obelisk 21 feet/6 metres high – perhaps a 'female' and a 'male' circle.

The circles at Avebury were but the latest of the ritual structures to appear in the area: West Kennet longbarrow and Windmill Hill causewayed camp had given an air of sanctity to the landscape a thousand years before ever a stone was placed at Avebury. The circular wooden 'sanctuary' on Overton Hill and the mound at Silbury, too, predated the circles, but in time would be linked to them by the West Kennet Avenue. This consisted of 100 pairs of stones: on one side column-shaped and on the other triangular or diamond-shaped – again, expressive of male-female polarity.

But it was the early tomb at West Kennet to which my attention was drawn that day; for here, 4,000 years previously, the body of a man with an arrowhead embedded in his throat had been buried. The tomb, which until then had been open, was then shut for eternity behind him.

In time I would discover that this murder was not just a personal tragedy; it was the physical evidence of a change in the mindset of pre-historic man – a change that offered a possible clue to the origins of some of the more mysterious symbols found within the Grail legend. For here, in prehistory, a religious war had been fought between the tomb builders and the sun-worshipping warriors of a new tradition – a war in which this man was no doubt a casualty. And in tracing the origins and outcome of this conflict I would unearth a major clue to the meaning of the Wasteland.

The West Kennet tomb is just one among many thousands of Neolithic monuments that cover the British Isles. The differing geographies of Britain saw the flowering of many different tomb styles: in the lowlands of the south and east where stone was rare, earth and wooden burial structures were the norm,[1] whereas in the highlands of the north and west there were magnificent constructions in stone. Among these impressive structures were local creations such as the 'portal dolmens' of Wales and the South West, which consisted of a massive stone slab, like a tabletop, resting on four or more 'legs' that from the front resembled a huge doorway, with a single huge stone blocking the entrance. Other tombs had great façades with small rectangular 'mortuary areas' behind them; some, like the 'Cotswold-Severn' tombs, consisted of round stone graves with a central cist, which soon developed into multi-chambers reached by a short passage. West Kennet is a good example of this design. In the so-called 'passage graves' this passage was long, leading to a central chamber or chambers; such monuments were common in north and west Scotland, Wales and Ireland.[2] Passage graves were the princes among tombs; one example – Bryn Celli Ddu ('The Mound in the Dark Grove') on Anglesey – had often been my destination on moonlit walks whilst I was studying at Bangor.

The crowned king of tombs was Newgrange in Ireland, part of an important ritual centre built in the Boyne Valley around 3300–3200 BC. Newgrange was 340 feet/105 metres in diameter and 40 feet/12 metres high; its internal passage was lined with 60 stones, many of them intricately patterned in an undeciphered frieze of labyrinthine spirals, lozenges and serpentine curves. In Irish it was called Brugh na Boinne ('The Palace on the Boyne') – and of obvious importance in my quest for the Wounded King was the fact that it was said to be the home of the cauldron-owning, club-wielding Dagda. This royal palace for the dead was so cunningly crafted that on the morning of the winter solstice a beam of light from the rising sun penetrated the passageway through a 'light box' – a gap above the doorway – and crept up the passage until it alighted on a triple-spiral pattern carved into a stone.

It is apparent that such places were more than simple reliquaries; as Ronald Hutton says: 'To call such monuments tombs at all is stretching the meaning of the word.'[3]

In general, the space in these monuments dedicated to burial was just 5 per cent of their entire area (West Kennet was no exception – the major part of the site consists of a great comet-like expanse behind the main stone chambers). These were not just tombs: they were the cathedrals of pre-history – places of worship, no doubt, but also tribal or territorial markers. These sites were also, we might assume, centres of initiation and other forgotten ceremonies. Many of them were in continual use for 1,000 years, and individuals were inhumed within them over many hundreds of years, during which time the houses of the dead were open – as is West Kennet today, since archaeologists moved the hefty blocking stone placed there after the old man had been interred.

The tradition of tomb building arrived in Britain with the introduction of farming, around 4000 BC. With this revolutionary lifestyle, which had arrived in Europe from the Near East and Anatolia some 3,000 years earlier, came cereal crops (emmer wheat, einkorn wheat and barley – which were more hardy than any native grasses that might have been casually harvested by the native hunter gatherers), new breeds of livestock such as pigs and cattle (smaller and more domesticated than the native varieties), and goats and sheep.[4]

The first British farmers did not live in villages as did their Continental cousins. There is evidence to suggest that the natives were essentially nomadic, having hardly changed their lifestyle since their hunter-gatherer days[5] when they had inhabited relatively unchanging 'tribal territories', but travelled across them seasonally, following the migratory herds. It appears that the Neolithic farmers did the same, only they drove tame herds of cattle to the summer pastures, treading paths long used. Their lives were essentially a seasonal pilgrimage from one sacred spot to another; their homes small farmsteads or even mobile shelters of hide.

West Kennet would not have been like a cemetery for a local village; it was more like a cathedral, visited perhaps by pilgrims on their way to convene at the vast 'causewayed camp' at Windmill Hill – a Neolithic meeting place bounded by multiple ditches in concentric rings that dominated the landscape before the great stone circle and giant artificial mound were built here. What its use was – perhaps a cattle kraal or place where the bodies of the dead were held prior to being put in the tombs – no one knows for sure.

In this stone womb 46 individuals had been deposited – probably over a considerable period of time. But that is not to say that 46 complete skeletons were uncovered; each individual was represented by a mere handful of various bones, except for the old man in the north-east chamber whose remains were complete.

At West Kennet, the bones of the dead had been deposited with some semblance of order: in the main west chamber were the remains of adult men; to the south-west and north-west, a mix of male and female adults; nearest to the door, to the south-east, children; and to the north-east, old people.[6] But these distinctions, found relatively rarely in Neolithic tombs, hinted at family rather than tribal structure.

Generally, once within the tomb, very few individuals remained intact; their disjointed bones were placed in random heaps or sorted into piles, based not on age or sex but on bone type. At Tinkinswood in Glamorgan, for instance, the entire contents of the tomb consisted of 3 thighbones, 7 skulls and 22 jawbones. In many tombs only skulls remained, in others most bones except the skulls. In some cases individuals had been placed in the tombs whole – their bones still joined together with ligaments – and were then pushed back into the general mêlée once their flesh had rotted; in others the remains had clearly been left to rot elsewhere – perhaps on wooden platforms (as was the practice of certain Native American tribes) or in shallow graves – before being taken to the tomb.[7] The number of individuals represented in the tombs was a mere fraction of the entire community. What gave certain individuals the right to be 'buried' in these Neolithic cathedrals is not known.

But what happened to the body parts that were not found in the tombs? It is agreed that the most probable explanation is that they were taken from the tombs to be used in rituals. I had been intrigued to discover that some of the missing skeletal parts of the 46 individuals buried in West Kennet were later found at nearby Windmill Hill. I imagined a grand gathering of tribes and the exchange of ancestral relics – or immense feasts, with the skulls of the dead looking on. Such images brought to mind the old traditions of Christmas and Halloween, when food was left on the hearth for the spirits of the dead, to ask for their blessing and protection in the coming year. Had something similar been going on in Neolithic times? Were the dead invited to dine with the living? The whole uncanny scene made me think of the severed head of Bran at the feast at Harlech in the second branch of the *Mabinogi* – and of the head borne on the dish before Peredur.[8]

The idea that these people went to their deaths anonymously is at once suggestive of a group mentality in early planting cultures – where the individual was seen as but an ephemeral manifestation of some greater force, a leaf on a mighty tree; where the fate of the individual was subsumed within the eternal play of death and rebirth suggested by the vegetable world. The planting societies' concept of life mirrored the vegetal world: they knew that hacking back a plant would cause it to grow new shoots – thus death was seen not as a finality, but as the prelude to rebirth. From the way in which the Neolithic ancestors of the Celts buried their dead, it is apparent that they held such a view of themselves; and this would also have been reflected in their everyday life. It has been argued that in Neolithic society there was no marked hierarchy or caste system – that perhaps they lived in a kind of prehistoric communistic collective.

Whatever the manner of their daily lives it is certain that their concept of death was radically different to that held by most people today. The doors to the houses of the dead were always open, reflecting, perhaps, the belief that the boundary between life and death was not unbridgeable, that one realm infringed upon the other. The dead were not hidden away or feared, but revered; and the living knew that one day they would merge into the general collective of the ancestors.

But what had granted them this vision of the interface between the dead and the living? What exactly did they believe? It was time to investigate the religion of these first farmers.

Notes

1. The megalithic structures of the Medway being the exception.
2. Imposed upon this schema were other trends, such as that of building 'long mounds' – some up to 330 feet/100 metres long – which stretched, comet-like, behind the main chambers; some built over older tombs. These long barrows were common in the east of Britain – and are thought to reflect houses of the living, with their entrances facing south-east, and flanking ditches on each side, and a timber façade in front. For a good introduction to the tomb types see Lynch, F (1997).
3. Hutton, R (1993) p. 29.
4. Darvill , T (1997) p. 44.
5. Before the introduction of farming the inhabitants of Britain had dwelt within the great oak, elm and lime forests that had grown up after the retreat of the glaciers around 10,000 BC.
6. Malone, C (1989) pp. 75–6.
7. Evidence of which exists at Windmill Hill.
8. If this was the case, it might be pertinent to ask whether those remains that were left within the tomb might be seen not as the special few who were 'chosen' to abide there *but the sad few that had not been chosen to join the feast, the relatives not invited to tea*? That both ideas can be entertained reveals how little is known of life in the Neolithic.

Chapter 9

THE MOON BULL

Joseph Campbell is one of those who argue that the religion or religions of these islands has derived from, or at least been influenced by, those of the Fertile Crescent, where the god gored by the boar held sway.[1] Given the appearance of the destructive boar in many Celtic myths I see no reason why the British farming cultures could not have adopted and passed down this religion, just as they had adopted the agricultural technologies that accompanied it. As I was to discover, the myth of the dying god and the boar was intricately bound up with the practice of farming itself. From the evidence for the worship of this god it is clear that parallels can be drawn between this practice and the forgotten cults of the megalithic tomb-builders.

The god gored by the boar went by many names in the regions where his cult, always associated with planting societies, has been practised. In Egypt he was Osiris, in the Middle East he was Adonis, and from there he entered Greek mythology under the same name. In this tradition Adonis (from the Canaanite *Adon*, meaning 'lord')[2] is a fertility god, the lover of Aphrodite, and of Persephone, queen of the underworld.[3] Gored in the thigh by a boar while hunting, Adonis is sent below to live with Persephone, but the land above is blighted by his absence; his death, like that of Balder, is accompanied by such an outpouring of grief that the gods decree he can be reborn in the spring and spend a portion of the year back on earth before returning below at winter.

Clearly, as Frazer suggests, the lifecycle of these wounded gods mirrors the seasonal round and the death and rebirth of the vegetable world. However, this god is not, as Frazer implies, simply an anthropomorphic symbol for wheat, like 'John Barleycorn' who is cut down, threshed, buried and reborn. The death and rebirth of the vegetable world is *a metaphor for the god*, not the other way round; indeed, *all* great cycles – those of birth and death amongst man and animals and the death and rebirth (waxing and waning) of the moon in the heavens – are used to express the eternal rebirth of this deity, of which man himself is a part. Primitive though the worship of a god steeped in vegetal metaphors might seem, it is in essence no different from the Christian imagery of Christ as the 'Bread of Life', or the 'One True Vine'.[4]

The whole vegetal complex appeared in its earliest written form in the Near Eastern myths of the death, descent and rebirth of the god/goddess.[5] John Gray summarises this myth well:

> *Inanna, or Ishtar, is associated with Tammuz, the dying and rising god of vegetation, whom she seeks in the underworld in his season of recession, according to the motif of the search of the fertility-goddess for the dying and rising god of vegetation. This motif recurs in Canaan in the search of the goddess Anat for the dead Baal, in Egypt in Isis's search for Osiris, in Greece in Demeter's search for Kore ('the maiden') and Aphrodite's for Adonis.*[6]

It is a seasonal drama: when the god is in the underworld the land lies barren, for it is winter and the divine grain lies 'dead' in the ground, waiting to be reborn in the spring. The goddess, who journeys in search of the god's underworld abode, brings about his/her rebirth, and therefore the rebirth of the land, through his 'rescue'. But the underworld is a realm she knows well – for as the goddess of both life and death (like Kali) she is also its ruler.

Tammuz (and his cronies – Osiris, Dionysos and Adonis, amongst others) is both the lover and the child of the mother goddess, reborn from her after his sacrificial death. The god, often born in a cave, returns into it at death – into the womb of the earth – and from there emerges reborn as a child. The moon and the serpent were his earliest symbols[7] – a direct link to Shiva, who holds the moon in his hair, and has a serpent twisted about his neck and phallus. The Celtic Cernunnos is also depicted holding a serpent, or, as on one Gallic image, with serpent-like legs. The crescent moon is also thought to be behind another symbol for this god, one that reflects the pastoralism of the first farmers – the crescent-horned bull, which became as powerful a metaphor for the god as the grain.[8]

The best example of this vegetal bull deity is the Greek god Dionysos, a god of vegetation, ecstasy and wine whose cult arrived from Asia Minor via Crete. This bull-horned god, like Rudra, is known as 'The roaring one' and, like Osiris, is killed, torn into seven pieces, and reborn (from a cauldron, no less).[9] The symbols of this god are legion.

The first clue that such a god might once have been worshipped in Britain is the fact that the entrances to the vast majority of megalithic tombs tend to face the rising and setting of the moon. Clearly these monuments were places of the night and the rituals that took place there began with sundown and ended with sunrise. Such heavenly alignments seem to support Joseph Campbell's belief that the religion of the megalithic builders of Britain is akin to the Dionysian 'lunar bull' religions of the pre-Homeric Aegean and ancient Near East. But more evidence for the existence of such a Neolithic British bull cult is to be found in the tombs themselves.[10]

To begin with, at Sherrington near Stonehenge, an ox skull and deer antlers were discovered buried in cists beneath a Neolithic barrow – suggestive of a meeting of the traditions of the pastoral bull god and the old antlered-shaman god of the hunt. At Manton an ox skull had been laid at the entrance of the tomb, as if guarding the contents, as had been the case at the impressive passage grave at Bryn Celli Ddu on Anglesey. And at Fussel's lodge (Berkshire), the hide of an ox had been stretched over the wooden mortuary house (which would eventually have been covered by the earthen mound) so that its legs hung down the sides and its head looked to the front, so that at death the deceased would enter the body of the divine ox. Perhaps the most impressive manifestation of this bovine cult was at Beckhampton, near the great Avebury ring. A longbarrow had been raised here that was devoid of any human deposits, but three ox skulls had been carefully positioned along the axis of the mound.[11] Whatever cults were practised in prehistoric Britain, whether akin to that of the lunar bull of the Near East or not, the moon and the bull certainly played a part in them.

In some religions the moon was seen as lopsided or lame – like the lame king of the Grail.[12] But unlike the later Celtic manifestation of this deity, the vegetal god of the Near East is not killed or emasculated by his brother. In Near Eastern myth the figure of Attis, the son/lover of the mother goddess Cybele *castrates himself* before his rebirth. Similarly, in some tales Shiva castrates himself, without the aid of the Brahmins; his castration blasts the cosmos – hence his epithet 'the destroyer' – but also ushers a new one into being.[13]

But why castration? On the surface, the seasonal waxing and waning of vegetal life may have suggested that the fertilising principle in nature periodically became 'infertile' or 'impotent', unable to fecundate the earth. But on another level, threshing grain or planting a crop could be seen as an act of castration, for it involves removing the seed, the generative organ, from the plant and placing it in the earth, where it remains inert, apparently dead, until it emerges, reborn, in the spring.

The planting cycle thus informed the rise and fall of Adonis and his kind and led to the formation of two basic images – that of *self-emasculation* (perhaps the earlier image, based on the self-seeding of the natural world) and *murder* (a reflex of the process of farming, where another was responsible for cutting down the corn, killing the crops so they might grow anew). It was, presumably, in the second of these images that the motif of the killing of the god by the boar originated; the young god wounded in the thigh by the boar's deadly curved tusks was the corn cut down by the crescent-shaped sickle. It was a murder, but a fortuitous one, for it created the world, and through the god's death food was brought to mankind.

The severance of the generative organ played a major part in the Mystery cults of the Classical world: in the Mysteries of Dionysos the phallus of the god was preserved after his death and placed in a cauldron or winnowing basket – a *liknos*, used in farming practice to separate the grain from the chaff – from where in the spring he would be reborn as a child known as Liknites ('he of the winnowing basket'). The phallus of Dionysos – no doubt taken from him with a sickle, as was that of Uranus – was the grain cut from the stalk, the divine shard or 'seed'.

According to Robert Graves, the murderous boar was in fact a *sow*; it was the goddess in animal form taking her chosen victim to her lands below, a reflex of the betrayal of Blathnat, it would seem. Such an origin is not surprising, for there is an Irish folk tale in which the daughter of the king of the other world, who lures heroes into her timeless kingdom, has a pig's head. Also, in Classical myth, Persephone, to whose kingdom Adonis travels after the wound to his groin, is clearly linked to this animal, for suckling pigs were sacrificed to her at the yearly Thesmophoria rite at Eleusis, being thrown into a chasm in the ground in memory of the rape of Persephone (Kore) and her abduction into Hades.[14] The boar, then, stands in the same position as the 'Black One' (Kali), who dances on her victim and takes his life. Kali, like the Greek Medusa, is an oxymoron: a great goddess who is both creator and destroyer, like ugly Morgan and beauteous Lady Bertilak. Is it, then, a coincidence that Adonis's lover, Aphrodite – a name perhaps linked to the Latin *aper* ('boar')[15] – is also known as Melaenis ('the Black One'), Scotia ('the Dark One') and Androphonos ('Man Slayer'), hinting that she and Persephone were originally a single yet two-faced goddess of life and death?[16]

Whatever the origin of the motif of the god gored by the boar, this lamed/castrated lunar god – whose wounding in the groin blasts the fertility of the land, and who needs 'rescuing' from the underworld – was a prefiguration of the Fisher King of the Grail legends and thus the very god whose role was played by the bog men. Also, the dual goddess seems to be connected to the figure of the grail maiden and her shadow, the loathsome damsel who rebukes the Grail knight for failing to ask the Grail question.

But the legend of the slain god as it appeared in medieval Celtic literature had obviously undergone many transformations of content and meaning over time. To say that the Celtic cult was merely a 'continuation' of a fertility myth of the Near Eastern sort (aside from being far too simplistic an explanation) does not explain the intricacies of the tale. The Grail legends were penned in the thirteenth century – 5,000 years after this myth was first told – and over time the god's castration had become an act performed not by himself or his lover, but by his victorious brother who had usurped his kingship. What's more, the seasonal blighting of the land when the god lay in the underworld had become a tragic blasting that could be undone only by the asking of a question; it had lost its calendrical significance and taken on another that for the moment remained hidden. Clearly a number of transformations had occurred to this myth over time, so I could not guarantee that its meaning had remained static. I could not return to the British museum and simply label Lindow Man a British Adonis, Dionysos or green-coloured Osiris. His role had become a lot more complex and suffused with new meanings – of which the 'brother-battle' was just one. And to unearth those meanings I would have to continue my examination of Neolithic Britain.

Already in my study of the rites of the tomb-builders I had unearthed evidence of a ritual regard for both the moon and the bull or ox. This suggested that Campbell had been right in arguing that a reflex of the ever-living, ever-dying Near Eastern god of the grain had existed in prehistoric Britain. Other clues support this, such as the chalk phalli and testicles uncovered from many Neolithic sites that hint at a connection to the castration of the deity. But perhaps the greatest clue of all is the evidence for a death and rebirth cult found within the graves themselves.

The form of the Neolithic burial mounds – a domed rise of earth, entered and exited through a passage, often flanked by a curved façade – is of course reminiscent of the female form. Entering the tomb is like stepping into the womb of the earth mother for rebirth. The late gallery graves of Brittany show a female form carved into the uprights of the chamber, so it is possible that the mounds were the dark realms of the female where the dead came to be reborn – a representation in stone and soil of the dark maternal underworld, the realm of Persephone, into whose embrace the dead journeyed, their bodies, like that of Dionysos, dismembered. Even today the act of entering into these dark, damp, claustrophobic resting places for the dead and then exiting through the passage into the light and the land of the living evokes a sense of rebirth. With a potent mythology and religion supporting such a symbolic act, these places would have been efficient ritual centres for transforming experiences.

I myself experienced a much watered-down sense of death and rebirth when I first visited Newgrange, on a cold but brilliantly sunny day in the February of 1998. Archaeologists had reconstructed the Dagda's palace earlier last century, rendering what was a dilapidated ruin into a national treasure that many people can safely visit. Some were against this kind of work, and for good reason, but on seeing the brilliant white curve of the walls against the azure grass and blue winter sky the effect was breathtaking – so much better than seeing an artist's impression in a book.

Newgrange and its sister tombs Knowth and Dowth – built around 3300–3200 BC in a curve of the River Boyne[14] – are to my mind as spectacular as the three pyramids of Giza, only they were built over 500 years before their Egyptian counterparts. For the modern visitor, Newgrange is the most impressive of the three, with its ring of hulking stones like a crowd of en thralled onlookers gazing at the vast white walls of its drum-shaped form. Above the perimeter wall, pocked with great lumps of quartz, rises the immense grass-covered dome. But the eye is soon drawn to the small curved forecourt of rectangular blocks with its low square entrance, the view of which is clocked by a huge altar-like stone, carved with seven spirals within a frame of lozenges and whorls.

Fighting claustrophobia I entered the long passage, bending my head as I did so, and to my relief found the stone-lined interior relatively spacious. I was soon within the cruciform chamber that lay at the end of the passage, with the splendid corbelled roof extending above my head. Listening with interest to the tour guide, I let my eyes wander from stone to stone, catching a glimpse here and there of strange symbols pecked into their rough surfaces. At this point the lights went out; the interior of the tomb was suddenly so dark I literally could not see my hand before my face. From feeling a little constricted, I suddenly felt as if I was alone and floating within an immeasurable void. I couldn't tell if my racing pulse was caused by panic or elation. And then my sense of space returned as a burning red glow appeared in my peripheral vision, creeping towards me up what I could now discern was the chamber, snaking its way along the passage and crawling up the stone carved with three spirals on the back wall.[18] When they reconstructed the mound, archaeologists fitted lights in the chamber to emulate the effect of the midwinter sunrise – and it was this that I was seeing. How might this sight – accompanied by the blowing of horns, or the entrancing beat of a drum – have affected Neolithic man? It was with a measure of reluctance but also relief that I emerged into the light of day again. I felt elated, privileged, as if I had witnessed something miraculous. I felt *changed*.

On a purely intellectual level it seems obvious to me that astronomi-cally aligned tombs such as Newgrange, in which the sun was allowed entry only on a certain special day, lie behind the spinning castles of myth. Cú Roí's castle, for instance, turns on its axis like a mill-wheel, and its entrance cannot be found after *sunset*. These mysterious castles can be equated to Rome in the tale of Brennus; his men had to wait outside the city until the solstice arrived, at which point they are able to invade. It is clear that the solstice somehow acted as a doorway between the worlds, opening the underworld to those who wished to enter therein.

Similarly, at the Celtic feast of Samhain (31 October), seen by many as the Celtic equivalent to the New Year, the doors to the other world were believed to open, and the *sídhe*, or 'fairy folk', could enter the real world and, conversely, a mortal could enter fairyland.[19] Might a similar impulse have lain behind the idea of the light-box at Newgrange, which signalled to those dwelling within the mound that the time had come for the souls of the dead to travel between worlds? It identified the most auspicious of dates, when the old year died and the new year was born, a date that was neither the old year nor the new, on which the phallic ray of the sun penetrated the womb of the mound.[20]

Newgrange in legend is the home of the cauldron-owning Dagda, and I was intrigued to discover that this mythical image seems to be based in reality, for Newgrange had contained cauldrons. Within the east and west chambers archaeologists found two shallow stone basins, thought by some to have once contained cremated bones, though empty when found.[21] Beneath the rise of this female mound I could imagine a dismembered skeleton curled up within each chiselled-granite *gradale* (a vessel of rebirth), like the seven body parts of Dionysos that were placed in his magical cauldron to be reborn. Perhaps these stone basins were the physical counterparts of the mythic cauldron of the Dagda, which, like that of Bran and his Germanic cousin Thunor, could bring the dead back to life. Newgrange was clearly a place where the dead came to life again.

But, as I was to discover, such rites were not restricted to the dead.

Notes

1. Campbell, J (1968) p. 203.
2. Cotterell, A (1986) p. 16.
3. Like Lleu in Welsh myth, he is put in a chest after his birth.
4. See Campbell, J (1959), especially chapter 5.
5. In its earliest form the myth tells of the raping of the Sumerian goddess Ninlil 'in the stream Nunbirdu' by a deity named Enlil, who is then banished to the underworld (i.e. he is killed). In a variant, the goddess Inanna descends to the underworld – *kur nu gia* ('the land of no return') – through its seven gates and is forced to remove a garment (in the dance of the seven veils). She is hanged on a stake, but is brought back to life thanks to a plea from Enlil. However, she has to give a life in return – that of Dumuzi (her faithful son). Source: Hooke, S H (1963) pp. 24–5, 39–40.
6. Gray, J (1988) p. 24.
7. see Campbell, J (1964) pp. 9–10.
8. Campbell says the early form of this myth (c. 4000 BC) was of 'the earth goddess fertilised by the moon bull who dies and is resurrected'. Campbell, Joseph (1962) p. 37.
9. 'The bull is father to the snake and the snake to the bull.' Links Dionysos with the serpent.
10. Astronomer John North points out that at the time of the construction of the longbarrow (around 3600 BC) the tip of the constellation of Taurus's right horn, beta tuari, would have shone through the crack in the door, where it could be viewed rising from the horizon from the back chamber wall. Not only this; to the east, from the 'sanctuary' at Overton Hill – part of the Avebury ritual complex – at certain times of the year the red eye of the bull, Aldebaran, would seem to sink into the West Kennet barrow from the sky. See North, J (1996) pp.72-85. The plan of West Kennet, with its great curving forecourt and v-shaped chambers, and its stone façade as it would have appeared before the tomb was blocked by the followers of a new religion, are suggestive of a bull's head and the five visible stars that make up the v-shape of the sky bull Taurus.
11. Burl, A (1979) pp. 98–9.
12. The ultimate origin for Christ's three days in the tomb 'on the third day he rose again, in accordance with the scriptures'.
13. Doniger O'Flaherty, W (trans.) (1975) p. 139.
14. This connection is explicit – see Kerenyi, K and Jung, C G (1985) pp. 118–19, 132.
15. Markale, J (1986) p. 98.
16. In an ingenious conclusion, Graves theorises that the whole complex of the goddess slaying her lover in connubium stems from the image of the 'queen-bee' who kills her partner, the drone, 'by tearing out his sexual organs' after mating. The goddess as a bee – a queen of her hive – appears from early times, especially in Crete. See Graves, R (1960) vol. 1 p. 71
17. Hutton, R (1993) p. 60.
18. Brennan, M (1994) p. 36 Apparently the first man (in historical times) to have witnessed this marvel was Michael J O'Kelly, the tomb's excavator, who decided to keep watch here in the winter of 1969 – seeking to substantiate local legends and hearsay that told of 'beams of light' and an astronomical component to the mound's structure.
19. A memory of this window effect might be preserved in a description, found in Geoffrey of Monmouth's *Vita Merlini* (The Life of Merlin), concerning the building of Merlin's

observatory. It has: 'seventy doors and as many windows, through which I may see fire-breathing Phoebus with Venus, and watch by night the stars wheeling in the firmament; and they will teach me about the future of the nation.' See Tolstoy N (1997) p. 141.

20. The four main pagan festivals still remembered in Christian times, to give them their most common Gaelic names, begin with *Samhain* (1 November); *Imbolc* (1 February); *Beltane*, 'Bel's fire' (1 May); and *Lughnasadh* (1 August).

21. O'Kelly, M J (1994) pp. 24–5, 103–7.

Chapter 10

TIR NA N'OG

As I stood in the centre of Newgrange watching the fiery beam of light burning into the triple spiral on the back wall of the chamber, I knew that these carvings must have been of central importance to the tomb-builders.[1] The spirals, whorls, lozenges, zigzags, concentric circles and serpentine undulations found on decorated stones in Britain and Ireland appeared to be symbolic – but of what? Some see them as a sophisticated astronomical code or calendar, others as maps of the land of the dead, but the most promising and illuminating theory proposed is that they are representations of neurally induced geometric patterns of light known as phosphenes, or 'ectoptic phenomena' that are often experienced during altered states of consciousness, or in conditions such as epilepsy and migraine.[2]

Some of these ectoptic patterns – the lozenge and zigzag, for the most part – also appear in the designs scraped into the sides of a Neolithic type of pottery known, after its patterned exterior, as 'grooved ware', which archaeologists have traced to the remote northern isles of Orkney, a major centre of innovation in Neolithic times.

The grooved-ware pots were first uncovered within the Neolithic village of Skara Brae, a hive of small cell-like domiciles crafted from the local sandstone, whose hearths were specifically orientated to either the sunrise or sunset at midsummer or midwinter.[3] The builders of these houses were obviously interested in the motions of the heavens, and not without good reason: only from Orkney do these important solar events occur perpendicular to each other; in all of the British Isles this place was astronomically unique.[4]

The windswept and treeless Orkneys had been uninhabited until the arrival of the Neolithic tomb-builders. Had they gone there to live under that holy sky? Was it a coincidence that the heaven-gazing henge-building tradition, that would reach its apex in the marvel that was Stonehenge, would be conceived there?

Whatever the reason for their arrival, these ancient Orcadians were forced by limitations of space and building materials to live a more settled life than their mainland counterparts. Their stone hives were the first 'villages' in Britain, and this in itself might explain why new traditions emerged there. The inhabitants would have had to adapt to becoming 'villagers', because life in a stable community needed different laws, perhaps different hierarchies, from those in a nomadic one. On a more mundane level, solutions to practical problems posed by settlement would have resulted in innovation: Neolithic pots had always been round-bottomed, but on the flat stone floors of the Skara Brae such pots would have rolled over and spilt their contents, and so the flat-bottomed 'grooved-ware' came into being. With a stable base such vessels could now be made larger than any previously crafted, allowing foodstuffs to be stored away. And now that the people were sedentary, they could begin using these pots to experiment with the art of fermentation.

From the early fourth millennium BC the people of Orkney, like their mainland counterparts, had built houses for their dead – but in the centuries leading to the end of this millennium a transformation in tomb building took place. The new tombs contained masses of human remains, representing hundreds of individuals, in the main probably taken from the old tombs.[5] Perhaps the most magnificent of these monuments (and rivalling Newgrange for the title of 'most impressive prehistoric tomb') is Maes Howe passage grave. Set within a roughly circular man-made mound some 100–130 feet/30–40 metres in diameter, was a central chamber of polished stone, 15 feet/4.5 metres square in area and 16 feet/5 metres high, under a magnificent corbelled roof. At midwinter the rays of the setting sun would penetrate the smooth stone passage and enter the chamber. The entire barrow was placed within an innovative and monumental concept: a circular ditch with an outer bank (in this case carved from solid rock) – a form that would later be called a 'henge.'[6] The very nature of the monument meant that the rites performed within its bounds were open to the expanse of the sky.

With its circular ditch within an exterior bank, in opposition to that of a defended site, the henge's boundaries were symbolic – a 'magic circle' to define the space within it as sacred and to distinguish it from the mundane world outside – and such 'sacred spaces' could range from 13 feet/4 metres to 1,700 feet/520 metres in diameter.[7] Henges normally had two entrances on opposing sides, leading some archaeologists to believe that they were built on trade routes or sacred ways, with the henges punctuating these sacred paths at regular intervals like service stations on a motorway or churches along a route of pilgrimage. Though henges appeared with or without stones, later in some areas the stones seemed to replace the need for a ditch and bank, acting as the scared boundary themselves.

The henge was a wholly British phenomenon that would in time dominate the landscape after the tombs were no longer used. Stretching from 3500 to 1200 BC, the henge tradition eventually reached its climax in the construction of Stonehenge and the massive Avebury circles. The tradition then began to disintegrate, up until its sudden abandonment in the Late Bronze Age.[8] But what interested me was the relation of these early circles to the passage graves. While some scholars argue that the two monuments developed at different times, there is good evidence to suggest that the earliest circles were contemporaneous with the tombs.[9]

It was not just in Orkney that the two stood side by side; they did so also in Ireland, at Newgrange, strengthening the idea that these two regions were in close maritime contact. I was therefore intrigued by the fact that the race to whom the Dagda was said to have belonged – the divine *Tuatha Dé Danann* – was credited in Irish myth as having come from '*isles in the north*' (or, alternatively, 'from the sky'), bringing with them the art of magic and druidism that they had learned whilst dwelling in the four mystical cities of *Tir Na N'Og* ('The Land of Youth'), namely Gorias, Murias, Finias and Falias. Although the Land of Youth was clearly other-worldly, perhaps it is possible that behind the *Tuatha Dé Danann*, seen in legend as the divine predecessors of the Celts (and later their gods), lay a dim memory of a Neolithic Orcadian priesthood who had brought their inspired rites with them to the Boyne valley at the end of the fourth millennium BC.

Whether they had ever journeyed to Ireland to spread their new sky-based religion or not, the inhabitants of the northern isles of Britain were certainly caught up in a fantastic game of orientating their monuments to provide visually stunning effects involving the heavenly bodies. Perhaps the most spectacular of these was conceived on the Hebridean isle of Lewis at the site of Callanish, one of the earliest stone circles. Here, every 19 years (18.6 to be precise), when viewed from the avenue that juts from the north of the circle, the moon, at its most southerly extreme, is seen to rise from out of the hillside (shaped like a pregnant woman and known as Sleeping Beauty) and skim its way over the horizon – like a ball rolling along the tops of the distant hills. The moon then vanishes behind a mound named Cnoc Na Tursa before reappearing, for a brief, blazing moment (reminiscent of when the sun hits the door at Avebury and Maes Howe) at the centre of the circle. Such alignments were not undertaken merely for entertainment – they were obviously symbolic and of religious import. The meaning of such a celestial display no doubt involved the birth of the moon god from mother earth, his death and disappearance into the underworld, and his blazing rebirth.[10] The entire spectacle was a symphony in stone dedicated to the moon bull.

As Julian Cope points out it was probably the phenomenon seen at Callanish that Roman author Diodorus Siculus was referring to when he wrote:

> *Beyond the land of the Celts there lies in the ocean an island ... situated in the north ... inhabited by the Hyperboreans ... and there is ... both a magnificent sacred precinct ... and a notable temple ... spherical in shape ... The moon as viewed from this island appears to be but a little distance from the earth ... and the god visits the island every nineteen years and ... dances continually through the night until the rising of the Pleiades.*[11]

Given that astronomical knowledge was one of the qualities Classical writers attributed to the druids, I couldn't help seeing the 20 years it took for a druid to qualify as somehow reflecting the 18.6 years of the lunar cycle. Caesar mentioned that druidism originated in Britain; conceivably it had arisen in these northern isles.

But what was important about Orkney to my quest was the evidence found there of the ritual use of grain connected with the grooved-ware pots that explicitly linked the cults of the Neolithic British with the Classical mysteries.

The first clue that the Neolithic inhabitants of the British Isles had been using grain for non-secular purposes lay in a study of the chemical make-up of their bones which suggested that their diet consisted largely of meat – and only a very small amount of plants or cereals.[12] This came as a surprise, for it had been assumed that after the introduction of agriculture their diet would have been high in these foodstuffs. What were they doing with these grains if they weren't baking bread?[13] The answer was surprising. Archaeologists argued that its importance might not have been dietary to begin with, for many of the sites where evidence of grain existed were ritual in nature. It was possible that grain was grown (or imported) solely for *religious* use.[14]

If this were true it would explain the absence of grain in their diet. A modern comparison might be the Christian mass wafer; even a dedicated churchgoer might consume only a few thousand of these paper-thin discs in a lifetime – hardly enough to fill a bucket – yet on a symbolic note they were the most important foodstuff he could eat. It was possible that the cereal grains of the Neolithic had been consumed as part of a ritual, and I was soon to discover how this prehistoric communion was taken – as a drink.

Evidence for a ritual grain-based drink was first found in excavations at Skara Brae. A kiln for malting grain was discovered, associated with the flat-bottomed grooved-ware pots that could hold 6 gallons/27 litres of liquid – an ideal size for fermentation.[15]

The residue from the bottom of these grooved-ware vessels was most interesting. As well as an excess of meadowsweet, a common ingredient found in beer in the ancient world that acted as both a preservative and a flavouring agent, there were traces of two toxic plants: deadly nightshade and henbane. Both contain tropane alkaloids – hyoscamine, atropine and scopolamine. The effects of these psychoactive substances include distorted vision, hallucinations, ecstatic states, a sense of the dissolution of the body, and sensations of flight.[16] The Old English name for deadly nightshade, 'Dwale', means 'trance' – and it was used in ancient Greece as an additive to wine in the orgiastic celebrations of the god Dionysos. Traces of henbane were found in other grooved-ware vessels in a rectangular wooden enclosure at Balfarg/Balbirnie in Fife.[17] So this was not a simple beer; it was a ritual hallucinogen that would have formed the sacrament of the mysteries of a British vegetal god and his cycle of death and rebirth.

It was the ingestion of such a brew that was likely to have been the origin of the phosphene patterns etched onto the walls of Neolithic tombs. This is an important point, for the use of ritual hallucinogens links the British rites with those of the Classical world; it indicates that the rites practised in tombs or in henges were not simple fertility rites undertaken to ensure the growth of crops, nor primitive attempts to awaken the dead, but ceremonies based on a religion of self-transformation that offered to its initiates a sense of immortality.

Notes

1. Especially in light of the serpentine spiral path newly discovered on Silbury Hill.
2. See Dronfield, J (1995) and (1996).
3. Parker Pearson, M (1993) p. 59.
4. Parker Pearson, M (1993) p. 59.
5. And each tomb suggestive of a certain tribe or clan. At Isbister, Ronaldsay, 312 individuals were found – as well as the bones of sea eagles – perhaps a local totem. At Quaterness, 400 were found burned and smashed. And of great interest are elements of a later tradition: at Cureen Hill, as well as 5 human skulls there were 23 dog skulls, all mixed together, and at Burray, 23 people and 7 dogs. See Hutton, R (1993) pp. 62–4.
6. The name 'henge' is derived from 'Stonehenge', which really means 'hanging stones'. Ironically, Stonehenge, with a ditch outside the bank, should not be classed as a 'henge'.
7. Burl, A (1999) p. 7.
8. Burl, A (1999) p. 8.
9. See Bradley, R – 'Stone Circles and Passage Graves', in Gibson and Simpson (1998).
10. Cope, J (1998) pp. 66–9.
11. Cope, J (1998) p. 69.
12. Bones of 23 Neolithic people from ten sites in central and southern England, ranging in date from 4100 BC to c. 2000 BC. See Richards, M (1996).
13. Farming, however, did not come as a complete culture shock to these people. As hunter-gatherers they knew all about land management: they harvested hazel nuts in the forest, thinning out the other trees so that the hazels could spread and grow; and they created artificial glades in the oak woods to encourage wild pigs to gather for the mast, where they could be more easily picked off by hunters (for example, at Oakhangar in the Weald of Kent).
14. Sherratt, A (1996).
15. *British Archaeology*, no 27, September 1997.
16. 'Hallucinogenic effects and ecstatic states which often involve frenzied activity and erotic fantasies.' Rudgley, R (1999) p. 32.
17. Excavated in the 1980s by Gordon Barclay and Christopher Russell-White.

Chapter 11

THE STONED AGE

In many depictions the lunar god of the Near East is shown holding a sacred vessel and offering it to his celebrants; on an Akkadian seal (2350–2150 BC),[1] the bull-lord is shown on a throne, behind which are two entwined serpents. Before him stands a fire altar, and above his miraculous cup is the crescent moon. In Indian tradition this same lunar cup is possessed by Shiva, and contains 'soma' – the Eastern equivalent of the ambrosia drunk by the Greek gods. Soma, or *amrita* as it was also known, was an intoxicant that granted its drinker a sense of immortality, a quality reflected in its very name, for *amrita* means 'not-mortal'.[2] In Tantric Buddhism *amrita* is seen as the divine female essence; this is important for it provides a link to the dying and resurrecting goddesses Demeter and Persephone, in whose rites such a ritual drink figured prominently.

The mysteries of the goddess Demeter and her daughter Persephone, and the god man Iakchos, an alter ego of Dionysos, were celebrated at the site of Eleusis, 14 miles/22 kilometres west of Athens, each September for at least 2,000 years, until the destruction of the sanctuary by Alaric the Goth in AD 396. The story behind these rites tells of the rape of Persephone (Kore – 'maiden'), her abduction into the underworld by Hades, and her return to her sorrowing mother Demeter after a long search, during which time the land is barren. It is clearly a reflex of the ancient planting myth that in time would come to be associated with the moon bull, of which there was evidence in Britain.

The word 'mystery' (from the Greek *mysterion*) stems from the root-word *muein*, meaning 'to close the eyes or mouth'. Indeed, whatever the initiates of this popular cult saw in the sanctuary they certainly kept their mouths shut, for the 'miracle' of Eleusis was kept a secret for over 2,000 years.[3] Whatever the content of the revelation, its effect was clear, as the ancient writers noted:

Happy is he, who having seen these rites, goes below the hollow earth; for he knows the end of life and he knows its god-sent beginning.[4]

The result of the initiation into the secret of this divine mother and daughter offered nothing less than a sense of immortality. For here the agrarian metaphors were revealed as not mere analogies of the growing year, but ultimate symbols of the death and rebirth of the initiate.

Details of the lead-up to the ceremony itself are not lacking, and can be reconstructed from the layout of the temple ruins. Following a lengthy preparation period (including a nine-day fast) the neophytes would cross a bridge into the main sanctuary, led by a priest bearing a statue of Iakchos/ Dionysos. Here a sacred object was taken from a basket – probably a phallus, hinting at the castration myth – and the celebrants entered the main temple, the Telestrion. Inside this magnificent columned hall was a small sanctuary in which a hierophant was enthroned before a large fire. The role of this priest was to declare to the neophyte, in the form of a riddle, that the goddess had given birth to her son in the fire – an allusion to an episode in the tale of Demeter's search for her daughter when she becomes a nurse and places a baby named Demophoön into a fire to give him immortality. The hierophant then beat a huge gong and the celebrant would begin to see visions … most notably of the lost daughter Persephone/Kore rising from the underworld.[5]

But what were these visions? Very clever men such as the Athenian playwrights Aeschylus and Sophocles saw and accepted them, so what-ever they experienced it must have been *real*. Modern writers who have researched the mysteries agree that the ritual offered the neophyte a psychologically transforming experience – an experience of the supra-individual, so that the initiate detached his or her focus of identity from the mortal 'I' to some deeper and less transient part of their being that seemed to exist beyond the limits of time and space.[6,7]

The experience, in whatever form it took, was connected to the revelation that the two goddesses – Demeter and Persephone – were in essence one being (in the same way that Aphrodite and Persephone in the

Adonis myth, and the Lady of Life and the Lady of Death, were but two sides of the same coin). To initiates this experience granted them the knowledge that they, too, consisted of both a mortal and mundane Demeter side (known in the mysteries as the *eidolon*) and a hidden, but gloriously revealed, 'immortal' Persephone side (the *daemon*), that would live on after physical death.[8] The notion of the twin-aspect of the personality is neatly symbolised in the Dioskouri, the divine twins Castor and Polydeuces, of whom only the latter was immortal. The revelation granted by the mysteries is that we all possess an immortal twin – or, as Carl Jung describes it: beneath the ephemeral 'flower' of physical life there exists an enduring root or 'rhizome' which remains even after the blossom has fallen.[9]

The Mysteries of Eleusis offered an experience in which it was revealed to the celebrant that such a *daemon* rhizome existed, and that it would continue to exist after the demise of the *eidolon* flower. Further, it revealed that the *daemon* was itself a shard of the original god, the universal Daemon, which had been dismembered by evil forces at the creation and had entered matter. The initiate who realised his unity with this original godhead thus himself became a 'god'. *This* was the true meaning of the vegetal myth – that just as the corn was threshed and its grains scattered over the soil, so each of us contains the divine seed, unknowingly, until we experience the moment of revelation, at which point we die to our old selves.

But how was such a revelation achieved? A clue is in the ritual 'password' used by those who had seen the vision:

> *I fasted; I drank the* kykeon; *I took out of the chest; having done my task, I put again into the basket, and from the basket again into the chest.*[10]

Despite what early commentators on the myth supposed, the disclosure of what was in the basket would not by itself have offered some miraculous revelation to the neophyte; it is thought that the basket or chest, like those of the Dionysian mysteries, contained a phallus fashioned from fig-wood – hardly a catalyst for immortality, but perhaps a loaded symbol that might evoke a response from a mind somehow primed for revelation. And this was the function of the *kykeon* that broke the neophyte's nine-day fast – to prime the mind for revelation. The ingredients of the *kykeon* are preserved in the Homeric hymn to Demeter (seventh century BC): 'Meal and water with soft mint and give her to drink.'[11] 'Meal', in this instance, means barley grains. For the majority of the rites this barley drink was held in large sheet-metal vessels with holes around the rim from which barley sprouted. They were borne along by the priestesses in the ceremonial procession towards the Telestrion.

The *kykeon* was subsequently drunk from small goblets that offered a controlled dose of the divine potion. But what was so sacred about this barley brew? How can we be sure that it lay at the heart of the Eleusis vision? The answers to these questions were provided by an Athenian named Alcibiades, who scandalously stole this sacrament in 415 BC and used it at a dinner party, proving conclusively that it was *kykeon* that triggered the experience.[12]

So what was in this miraculous drink? Some believe that it was derived from a psychoactive mushroom,[13] perhaps the magic mushroom *Psilocybe cubensis*.[14] But although mushrooms may have been used widely throughout the ancient world, another explanation seems more obvious: ergot.[15] If this was the case, it would explain some of the more puzzling motifs found in the Eleusinian myth, such as that of Demophoön being burned in the fire by Demeter to 'give him immortality'. The motif was not restricted to the Eleusis myth: Isis enacts the same deed, burning a child of the King of Byblos, in whose court she acts as a nurse when in search of her maimed husband Osiris. In all probability it also lay behind the strange incident in the tale of Bran (who journeys Demeter-like to Ireland to rescue his sister Branwen), in which Efnissien burns Branwen's son Gwern ('Alder') on a fire – a motif strongly suggestive of the burning sensation caused by ergot. Such a motif, symbolic of burning away the *eidolon* to reveal the *daemon*, may have been included in the myth to warn of the uncomfortable visceral sensations that might accompany the initiate's ergot-inspired visions. Was this also the reason why the *kykeon* was administered in such a regulated dose – providing enough lysergic acid to promote the vision, but not enough to cause permanent physical damage or death? The bad side-effects could be limited by macerating the ergotised grain in water, separating the water-soluble psychotropic chemicals from the harmful fat-soluble ones. Thus, by drinking the water rather than eating the whole mash, the change could be effected without harm.[16]

It is clearly important that the ingredient used in the Classical mysteries was discovered in the last meals of the Danish bog men. It seems entirely possible that the later sacrificial cults of the Celts, which I had already linked to the myth of Adonis, had followed an even closer course to the Classical mysteries than I had first thought, even down to the use of a similar narcotic drink. And as if to further highlight these connections, the motif found in the tale of Bran – of the dead being 'reborn' from the cauldron deprived of the power of speech – seems to state directly that these figures were in fact initiates of a mystery cult, their silence reflecting a ritual state of *muein* that kept what they had seen a secret from the uninitiated. It was no accident, then, that the figure plunging the warriors, led by a wolf, into the vessel on the Gundestrup Cauldron was a goddess. She was, of course, the goddess of life and death; and the vessel, always interpreted as a female symbol, was her womb, into which the dead, like the bodies of the Neolithic Britons in the pregnant belly of the earth, journeyed in order to be reborn. The vessel might often have been depicted as the property of the god, but it was always a symbol of the mother. To the initiates of Eleusis, their minds opened by the *kykeon*, the fig-wood phallus in the basket, or *cista mystica*, symbolised their own rebirth from the mother's womb.

Modern research into the ergot derivative LSD has revealed that the drug can evoke experiences similar to those associated with these mysteries. Psychologist Stanislav Grof, who has personally observed some 4,000 'trips' and had access to 2,000 more, conducted by colleagues in the USA and Czechoslovakia, argues that such experiences of non-ordinary states of consciousness seem to give access to supra-personal knowledge and a sense of rebirth,[17] a sentiment that mirrors Greek mythographer Karl Kerenyi's belief that: 'The Eleusinians experienced a more than individual fate, the fate of organic life in general.' They became aware of their Persephone nature, the *daemon* at the root of their *eidolon*, their mortal personality, after which their previous everyday concerns seemed trivial.[18]

It is precisely the fostering of such a sense of immortality and a disregard for ego-centred individuality – invoked through drinking the contents of the grooved-ware pots – that seems to lie behind the communal non-personal burial tradition found in British Neolithic tombs.

The evidence, then, was mounting for the existence of a mystery cult in ancient Britain involving a native dying and resurrecting god – a dim memory of which had been preserved in the myth of the Dagda and his resurrecting cauldron at Newgrange. Such a mystery rite, although coded in metaphors of murder and sacrifice, was wholly psychological, not literal – as practised at Eleusis. The death and dismemberment of the universal *daemon* and the sacrifice of the *eidolon* were not enacted in physical reality. However, this had not always been the case, for there is evidence that in the ancient world – including Neolithic Britain – the death of the god had once been enacted literally.

Notes

1. Campbell, J (1964) fig. 3 p. 11.
2. Campbell, J (1968) p. 80.
3. Gilbert, R A (1991) pp. 4–5.
4. Pindar, Fragmenta 137a, quoted in Kerenyi, K and Jung, C G (1985) p. 145.
5. See Kerenyi, K (1967) pp. 67–102.
6. Kerenyi, K and Jung, C G (1985) pp. 153–4.
7. Campbell, J (1964) p. 15.
8. Freke, T and Gandy, P (2000) p. 124.
9. Jung, C G (1990) p. 18.
10. Clement of Alexandria *Protreptikos*, quoted in Kerenyi, K (1967) p. 66.
11. Kerenyi, K (1967) p. 65.
12. Wasson, G, Hofmann, A and Ruck, C (1978), discussed in McKenna, T (1992) p. 135.
13. Graves, R (1964) pp. 106–7.
14. McKenna, T (1992) p. 115. Might it also be possible that the one-eyed, one-legged wisdom-giving gods of Celtic myth are symbols of this monopedal mushroom? A similar thought is voiced by Wasson, in Wasson, S K; Ott, J; Ruck, C and Doniger O'Flaherty, W (1986).
15. Wasson, G; Hofmann, A and Ruck, C (1978), quoted in McKenna, T (1992) p. 135.
16. McKenna, T (1992) p. 136.
17. Grof, S (1998) p. 15.
18. Drug ingestion was only one amongst a plethora of 'technologies of the sacred' that could have been used to experience this state; others include drumming, rattling, dancing and breath control – methods documented as being used by practitioners of 'shamanism' throughout the world. Grof himself would later fasten on to the use of hyperventilation, in place of LSD, to achieve the non-ordinary state, thus following an age-old tradition of breath control to promote changes in consciousness, a technique which appears to have been used by the ancient shamans and the initiates of Eleusis.

Chapter 12

THE DANCE OF DEATH

Whereas the older tombs, and some of the early circles such as Callanish, seem to have directed their focus on the moon, in time more and more sites (for example, Newgrange and Maes Howe) would begin to show a fascination with the sun. One such site was the so-called Woodhenge, a structure 2 miles/3 kilometres north-west of the later Stonehenge and dating to 2300 BC. It consisted of a 'henge' of six concentric oval rings of huge oak posts, with lintels across the top of them in a manner suggestive of the Stonehenge trilithons. The monument was aligned solsticially, with a special alignment of posts towards the midwinter sunset.[1] Woodhenge is just one of a number of ritual complexes known as 'super-henges' that appeared in prehistoric Wessex, accompanied by grooved-ware pots. Some reconstructions depict them as forests of carved totem-pole-like posts, others as a huge thatched hall; but one thing is certain: after the arrival of grooved ware and the cult associated with it, the local population embarked on a frenzy of ritual activity – which included sacrifice.

On the central axis of Woodhenge, pointing to the midwinter sunrise, was the grave of a child with its head cut in two. The skull was completely split in half, initially leading archaeologists to assume that it was the remains of two individuals. This child was undoubtedly the victim of a ceremonial death. But was there any other to point to a sacrificial use of the henges or earlier tombs? I was to learn that sacrifice might possibly have played a part in the religion of the first farmers brought from the Near East, and that it could have been associated with a sudden entrancement with the sky, like the cults developed on Orkney.

According to Joseph Campbell there is evidence to suggest that ceremonial human sacrifice developed precisely at the same time as fascination with the heavens began, and that societies observing the skies chanced upon the idea that the laws that governed the heavens were linked to, and therefore should be aped by, man below.[2]

This idea was expressed in the concept of 'cosmic harmony' – a divine order within the cosmos known in different cultures under a variety of names. In Egypt it was *Maat*, and was symbolised as a goddess; in ancient Sumeria it was *Me*; and in the East it was *Tao* or *Dharma*. This cyclic cosmic process was in reality a continuation and adaptation of the cycle of the vegetal world, but also taking into account the cyclic motion of the heavens.

It was through this revision that the 'lunar king' of Near Eastern society increasingly became symbolised as the sun, and his wife as Venus. For just as Inanna/Ishtar followed her dead lover to the underworld, so Venus, the evening star, followed the sun at sunset; and just as Innana led the god out of the depths to live again at dawn, so Venus, the morning star, led the sun out of the horizon. It seems as if heavenly motifs were grafted onto the vegetal symbolism of the death and rebirth of the god, adding a new dimension to his myth and providing a new cosmic timetable to his life – which would end when the skies dictated.[3]

In the Near East there is evidence to suggest that the king and a priestess, representing the goddess, actually performed this ritual drama of death and resurrection, either each year or after a specific reign. The timing of the king's death probably differed from region to region. In some lands it may have been yearly, in others perhaps it was timed to coincide with an eclipse. This sacred union was enacted in the temple,[4] and is depicted on a cylinder seal from Tell Asmar (mid second millennium BC).[5] It clearly shows a priestess sitting on top of the king in the act of love (in other words, in the same position as Isis on the dead Osiris, or Kali/Shakti on the dead Shiva – the so-called 'yab-yum' position of Tantric sex) and a man to the side of the couple holding a sword ready to strike. Another seal (from Lagash, c. 2300 BC) shows the priestess squatting on top of her mate, while to her right stands a figure with a raised knife.[6] In this magical cult, it seems, once the king's powers waned, or a strange or uncanny sign was seen in the heavens, he was killed and replaced – to be 'reborn' in his successor, just as the god was reborn in the new spring growth, or the murdered ox in his calves. Clearly it is this ritual death that is celebrated in the work of Frazer – but Frazer is wrong in assuming that in every case the king was killed by his successor; this is clearly not so.

But it was not just the king who would periodically die. On his death, or ritual murder, the wife and court of such kings would follow him – alive – into the grave.[7] Because Venus followed the sun below the horizon – so the queen, priestess or entire royal court would submit to an untimely death to follow her sacrificed lord into the underworld. By joining him, the original unity that existed before the first murder was recreated, and from their connubium the new cosmos would be born: the queen, by following her husband below, as Inanna followed Tammuz/Adonis, effected his resurrection. Evidence of such rites of 'suttee' as they are termed (from the Sanskrit *sati*, meaning a dutiful wife)[8] exists at burial sites in Ur, Abydos and Nubia. A grave at Ur of a man named A-bar-gi contained no fewer than 65 attendant sacrifices – in all probability the entire royal court – as well as six oxen; his wife or priestess, Shub-ad, lay in an adjacent pit in the company of 25 servants.[9] An investigation of such graves revealed that the attendant sacrifices had gone into the graves alive. But a golden cup in the hands of the 'queen' hints that before the earth was closed over their heads, a sacred drink had been administered; either a deadly potion to usher them into the nether world, or a *kykeon* to reveal to them the new life to which they were to go. These individuals died not as personalities but as parables of the cosmic process – aware of their *daemonic* immortality that allowed them to willingly slough off the *eidolon* of mortal existence.

One interesting point is the fact that on the regalia buried in the tombs the figure of the lunar bull was prominent. In Shub-ad's chamber lay the head of a cow rendered in silver, and in her divine consort's boudoir were two magnificent harps with golden bulls' heads. And in a suttee grave from ancient Nubia, the legs of the bed on which the dead king lay were fashioned into the legs of a bull. The presence of the bull is important; it reminded me of the barrow at Fussel's lodge with its wooden mortuary house set within the hide of an ox. Similar practices, it seems, were going on within the henges or megalithic tombs of Britain.

As far as I am aware, no one has suggested that the remains found in the megalithic tombs of Britain and Ireland might be those of the victims of suttee rituals. Indeed, the whole Neolithic is (wrongly) seen as an age of peace, with little evidence of war.[10] But clearly some of the dead met with violent, perhaps sacrificial, ends. At Giant's Grave in the Vale of Pewsey there is evidence of a skull 'forcibly cleft before burial'; at Rodmarton (20 miles/32 kilometres north-west of Avebury) 'four skulls with fatal gashes to the head'; at West Kennet, again, two skulls with traces of fractures, injuries inflicted, it is supposed, before death; at Belas Knapp, more of the same; and another skull beaten to pieces at Oxendean Down. The most stunning evidence is a skeleton from Boles Barrow, where the neck vertebrae had been sliced when the individual was beheaded. Although these cases represent only a small fraction of the many hundreds of bones buried, many victims might have been strangled, or given a potion similar to that taken by the attendants of A-bar-gi and Shub-ad – and these modes of death would not be evident from the skeleton.

Although I knew it was a controversial theory, I thought it prudent to at least consider the possibility that the tombs of Neolithic Britain had contained the bones of victims of sacrificial rites that were celebrated in much the same fashion as those in Mesopotamia and Egypt. Maybe this was why there were so few bodies in the tombs. Perhaps the rest of the population were cremated or buried elsewhere, while the mansions of eternity were reserved for the kings, queens and courtiers of British prehistory, who went to their deaths when the heavens sent a sign, their bodies rent apart and disarticulated like the Greek bull god Dionysos, whose body was placed within the cauldron in seven pieces and later restored to life.

Perhaps on a given day, when the doors between the worlds were open, members of the court of the dead were brought out of their tombs to feast again with the tribe, their bones painted with red ochre.[11] I thought of Dagda and Rudra – the 'red ones' – and again of Bran, his severed head entertaining his men at the 87-year-long feast, entertained by the singing of the three magical birds of Rhiannon, whose name derived from the proto-Celtic *Rigantona* meaning 'Great Queen'. And what was the Grail castle if not a tomb or henge – a place of magic where the worlds of the living and the dead met; the spinning fort of the labyrinth, whose entrance and exit was hard to find, where the Wounded King lay in his torpor, a wound in his side, the cup of rebirth processed before him?

But the appearance of the sun on the horizon had marked the beginning of a change. The nameless Sons of the Mother were giving way to rulers who bathed in the light of the sun, and who were becoming less willing to go 'gentle into that good night'. And in time they would kill off the god of the old religion so that they would not have to give up their lives to the unrelenting cycle of the heavens.

Notes

1. North, J (1996) pp. 347–58.
2. Campbell, J (1959) pp. 146–7.
3. Frobenius, L, quoted in Campbell, J (1959) p. 166.
4. For instance, at Isin in the third millennium BC (see Gray, J (1988) p. 20).
5. Gray, J (1988) p. 20.
6. Shown in Campbell, J (1962) p. 42.
7. Campbell, J (1962) p. 69.
8. Campbell, J (1962) p. 66.
9. Campbell, J (1962) p. 44.
10. Though some see the Neolithic as an age of peace, there is evidence of war. Two male Skeletons from Wor barrow and Crichel Down near Stonehenge had arrows in their vertebrae and ribs respectively. At Ashton under Wychwood two of the occupants of the tomb had been killed by arrows. And in the north-east chamber of West Kennet longbarrow, the old man had a wound in his left arm and an arrow in his throat. Examples could be repeated ad infinitum. Source: Burl, A (1979) pp. 81–2.
11. As was done to the bones in the tomb at Nympsfield. Two lumps of ochre were also found in the sanctuary at Avebury. Burl, A (1979) p. 123.

Chapter 13

THE LABYRINTH

By examining the Neolithic past I had discovered the ultimate ground of the Wounded King in the dying and resurrecting lunar deity who was wounded in the thigh and whose cup of immortality (ultimately a symbol of the goddess herself) was once filled, at least ritually, not with the blood of Christ but with a narcotic brew that offered the individual a sense of immortality. As long as that individual remained in the underworld, winter reigned – but spring was never far away.

However, things were about to change.

Until this time the immolation of the god gored by the boar, the divine dismembered *daemon*, was seasonal and natural, aped by the sacred king (and his court) in a mummery of the motion of the heavens and the reaping and sowing of the fields. But from around 3000 BC evidence emerges of a change in burial traditions that would be of great importance to my quest: the appearance of individual burials.

Perhaps the finest example of this development was found under a 30-foot/9-metre-tall pudding-bowl-shaped barrow known as Duggleby Howe in North Yorkshire. Here archaeologists uncovered the graves of a number of old men – buried, so it seems, with an entourage specifically sacrificed to accompany them into the afterlife.[1] Beneath the tranquil rise of this man-made hill were two shafts containing principally the remains of four old men – one buried with a pot of red body paint, accompanied by maces of antler, and *boars' tusks*. Apart from one 70 year old with a semi-transparent flint held up to his face as if skrying, the others were in their fifties and sixties, each accompanied by a youth and child – some of whom had sinister holes in their heads. The entire barrow was clearly a suttee burial.

These were not kings slain in their prime; they were old kings, not killed as part of the cosmic dance but allowed a natural span of years, even though it would seem that those who accompanied them below had not been so fortunate. In the previous age the god king had died when the cosmic cycle decreed, and he had been slain and placed within the cosmic mountain (the pyramid, the barrow).[2] The mountain (representative of the goddess herself) had remained, in the form of the great white chalk mound of the Howe. This was copied at Silbury, that ultimate of mother hills which, like the Near Eastern temples of the 'love-death' ritual, the ziggurats, and the abode of the gods of Indian myth, Mount Meru, consisted of multiple tiers. But the fate of the king who entered the mountain, however, had changed dramatically.

The appointed slaying of the king had become a custom to be avoided. In ancient Babylon the death of the king at the New Year had been replaced by a mummery of the former rite – he was stripped naked and struck, while another 'substitute' king was hanged in the marketplace.[3]

Similarly, at Duggleby the kings were no longer killed off. The reason for this can be easily postulated: maybe with the growth of a more settled way of life, twinned with an increase in population, the role of the tribal god-king (or whoever was the figurehead of these primal societies) had become more political and he was more of a statesman, a war leader, and thus his death no longer as expedient. And if his appointed time came in the middle of a tribal conflict, when for the stability of the tribe his wisdom and experience were needed, a substitute sacrifice may have been made.

In Mesopotamia the substitute for the king was another human being, but elsewhere it could have been an animal, most probably the sacred animal of the god: for Dionysos, the kid or the bull; for Persephone, the pig.

It is possible that the killing of a 'divine' animal in place of the king exists in Celtic myth, in the tale of Conn the 'hundred fighter', King of Ireland. Conn, so the tale begins, marries an other-worldly woman named Becuma, who is secretly in love with his son, Art. By her wiles the boy is banished from Tara for a year – an act that blasts the land. In order to rectify this enchantment, Conn's druids ask that the son of a sinless couple should be sacrificed at Tara so his blood will heal the land. Conn travels for a year in search of such a lad. Eventually he is made the welcome guest of a boy named Segda, who, it turns out, possesses the desired qualities. And to Tara they travel, to attend the council that will decide his fate.

The council decides that the boy must die, but before the sentence is enacted they hear the lowing of a cow, and see a woman behind the beast driving it into the assembly. The woman is Segda's mother, who rebukes the druids for offering her son, adding that the cow has come to save the innocent youth. It is to be slaughtered and its blood mixed with the soil of Ireland, so that the boy will be unharmed.

Is it not indicative of such a substitution that as the great communal tombs of the Neolithic slowly begin to fade out of use after the appearance of the first individual graves, some of those that continued to be built contain not human but ox bones? Recalling the Beckhampton tomb (empty save for three ox skulls along its axis) and Thickthorn Down[4] (with no humans but one ox skull and cattle bones within its chambers), I would have expected to see precisely such remains if indeed the sacrifice of sacred cattle *had* gradually taken the place of the sacrifice of the king. Such evidence also adds credence to the idea that the tombs had been the charnel houses of the victims of some kind of ritual death and dismemberment.

A similar substitution took place in ancient Egypt. By the time of the historical pharaohs, the king had been excused from undergoing a ritual death and in his place a sacred bull was offered.[5] Known as the Apis bull, an animal identified by sacred markings, it was ritually slain every 25 years in place of the pharaoh, and would be mummified and buried, with all royal due, in the temple of the Serapeum at Memphis. Perhaps the same was true of the kings of ancient Crete, whose periodic death (as a bull-headed god – the origin of the Minotaur) was transferred to the drama of the sacred bull-court. In Egypt, the pharaoh, instead of being stripped and struck, as in Babylon, underwent a mock-death in the so-called Heb Sed, or Sed, ritual, of great interest to my theme for it preserved elements of the original ritual death of the king.

The Sed ritual, which took place beside the stepped pyramid of Djoser at Saqqara was probably held every 30 years.[6] The rite began with the king dressed as a bull, wearing a belt depicting the four faces of the cow goddess Hathor, and a bull's tail. He entered the ritual enclosure, dwarfed to the north by the pyramid, preceded by the priestess dressed as this cow-headed goddess. The second day of the rite saw the pharaoh circumnavigating the Sed enclosure – symbolic of the bounds of his land. On day three, entering the 'Court of the Great Ones' within the Sed enclosure, the pharaoh was preceded by six priests in wolf-skins, bearing the shrine of the wolf god Wepwawet ('The Opener of the Way'). On a platform in the court the pharaoh saluted the four directions, wearing the double crown of Upper and Lower Egypt – and, again, the bull's tail.[7]

The next day was special – the populace did not witness this part of the rite, which took place after a ritual feast taken by the Royal Family in the 'Hall of Eating'. Seth, the fiery one, lord of the scorching desert and Osiris's rival, approached the pharaoh with a knife. The king was *stabbed and beheaded* – his face painted *green*, his body wrapped in white cloths and laid on a bier. Then a secret rite involving the severed head of the dead pharaoh took place. No one knows what this entailed. His body lay in his tomb, while his soul descended to the nether world.

The following day, as the sun rose, the pharaoh emerged from the tomb, having vanquished death. He re-established the boundaries of Egypt, laid waste at his death, by firing arrows to the corners of the court (the cosmos) with a mighty bow. He then joined the Apis bull in circumnavigating the complex, again with a bull's tail attached to the back of his kilt. He was then led forward by the wolf god Wepwawet, accompanied by the goddess Mert, symbolic of the sovereignty of the land, and handed a scroll, known as the *imyt per*, the 'Secret of the Two Partners'. Recorded on this was his right to rule Egypt, and his victory over Seth, given to him by his father, the god Osiris. He proclaimed that he had passed through the land, touching its four sides, holding the *imyt per*.[8]

This was the Heb Sed as it appeared in historical times. What, though, had it entailed before the kings became men instead of gods?

Originally the point of the Heb Sed was akin to the initiations of Eleusis – to give the pharaoh, through a rebirth experience, awareness of both the upper- and underworld aspects of his nature (the Demeter and Persephone or *eidolon* and *daemon*). At some point in the past, however, enamoured by the cycle of the heavens, the rite had been enacted in bloody reality and the old king would have literally lost his head (a fact borne out by Sir Flinders Petrie's discovery of decapitated pharaohs at the early site of Nakada II)[9] and become identified with the universal *daemon* within, the god Osiris in the underworld. His successor would then have been granted the kingship following the secret ritual involving the head.

By the time the Heb Sed is recorded, the literal death of the king had been replaced by the death of the bull, and so the rite returned to its original psychological meaning, in which the king became aware of the two sides of his nature. Accordingly, he was to wear the crowns of Upper and Lower Egypt – not as a memento of a historical uniting of the two lands, as is normally suggested, but as a symbol for the unification of the upper and lower worlds.

In Britain, the move away from the literal death of the king, as evidenced at Duggleby Howe, paved the way for a complete reversal in the make-up of prehistoric society. By 2000 BC all the great tombs had been abandoned (except in parts of Ireland), replaced by round barrows containing individual inhumation. But this reversal was not limited to Britain.

In the tombs of the pharaohs the bulls' legs on the beds were replaced by lions' feet, and a new solar religion, the cult of Re, was established. In Crete, the bull-horned man god became a monster, the man-eating Minotaur (Asterion, 'star'), into whose labyrinth at Knossos the hero Theseus travels not to rescue the god but to kill him. The motif is familiar, for Theseus is helped by 'thrice holy' Ariadne, the Minotaur's sister, who betrays him (Blathnat-like) by giving Theseus a ball of string (in Greek, *clew*, the origin of the English 'clue') that enabled him to find his way out of the labyrinth (the spinning castle of Cú Roí) after stabbing the bull-headed beast. What's more, the labyrinth is the Minoan palace of Knossos (meaning the house of the *labrys* – the 'double axe', the ritual weapon used to kill the king). And it was in Knossos that the rites of Eleusis had their origin; it was here that the *kykeon* was drunk in ceremonies to the bull.[10] Perhaps Theseus, like Cú Chulainn, stole off with a cauldron of this *kykeon*, too.

In February 2002 English Heritage released the results of a detailed three-dimensional seismic survey of Silbury Hill, revealing that it had contained not stepped layers, as previously thought, but a spiral pathway winding anti-clockwise to the summit. The spiral form of course suggests the spinning fortress of Celtic myth, as well as the spinning of the stars around the pole (as the countryside would seem to spin around an individual climbing the hill). What is perhaps more intriguing is the fact that the pathway is not curved, but made up of short straight sections forming the sides of a nine-sided polygon, so that from above it would have looked exactly like a spider's web. The link between this and the labyrinth became clear when I imagined Theseus and the ball of string threading through the maze as an image of a spider spinning its web. Silbury Hill, it could be postulated, is the dancing ground of the British Minotaur – the moon bull, slain in connubium, just as the male spider is killed by the female after mating – and perhaps the original of the 'white hill' where Bran's head was buried in Welsh myth.

But soon the death of the bull god in his spinning fort would be at the instigation of a male rival. In Britain, victory over Asterion (the starry bull) was on the horizon. Just as the ritual sites reached their apogee in the super-henge tradition of Wessex – when the rulers behind their construction achieved absolute power – a new cult suddenly swept Britain. Identified by its tradition of burying individuals singly under round mounds, clutching delicate pottery vessels known as 'beakers', this cult was to change the make-up of power, and the nature of religion. And the deathblow issued to the bull god of the Neolithic was echoed in the dolorous blow of the Grail. For the new god would seal him in the underworld not just for a season, but for ever. A Gallic coin[11] depicts this take-over, with the sun steed leaping over the old earth bull in victory, and it was shown in the heavens, too.

In his book *Stonehenge: Neolithic Man and the Cosmos*, John North points out a strange yet fascinating property of the famous chalk hill-figure known as the White Horse of Uffington. This 360-foot/110-metre-long piece of ancient artwork, a stylised evocation of a leaping equine elegantly carved into the Berkshire hillside, has been attributed to every people who had inhabited the land from Roman times up until King Alfred the Great. Recent archaeological work on the site, however, confirms what many have argued all along, that the horse could in fact date back to as early as 1400 BC.[12]

When North examined the site from an astronomical perspective, he came up with another interesting clue. He made the obvious point that the horse is very difficult to see, and would be much more visible if it had been crafted lower on the hillside.[13] He therefore suggested that the white horse had been placed where it was for a specific purpose – as a *star marker*. From a position on the modern-day road at the foot of the hill, which affords a moderately good view of the beast, one of the clearest night-time constellations rises above the horizon, seeming to emerge from the body of the horse itself: the constellation of Taurus.

To the north of the horse, at the foot of the slope, lies Dragon Hill, a natural cone-shaped rise with an artificially fashioned top. Local tradition states that it was here that St George slew his adversary. According to North's analysis, as early as 3230 BC (within a century or so of the completion of the nearby chambered tomb known as Wayland's Smithy), at the moment when the star *Zeta Tauri* (which forms the tip of the bull's horns) emerged from the top of Dragon Hill, two of the three stars which form the bull's face would have been seen to emerge from specific points along the hillside. These points were later defined as important parts of the body of the horse – from its eye rose *Gamma Tauri*; and from its testicles (suggested by a mound) rose Aldebaran, the fiery red eye of the bull. At the level of the horse's heart sat, below the horizon, the third star.[14] The alignments, if correct, imply that this was an old site of the bull god, changed and reclaimed by the new religion to suggest their own cult animal, the horse – a native victory over the sky bull.

It was at this period that the body of the old man was placed in West Kennet longbarrow with an arrow in his throat – just before the doors of the tomb were sealed for ever. The rule of the immortal moon-bull would soon come to a violent end, giving way to the sons of the sun horse. The dolorous stroke was about to be dealt.

Notes

1. Hutton, R (1993) p. 82.
2. As quoted in Cambell, J (1959) p. 166.
3. As quoted in Cambell, J (1959) p. 168.
4. Hutton, R (1993) p. 67.
5. Campbell, J (1962) p. 89.
6. The festival was a five-day affair – perhaps symbolic of the 'five days out of time', the days in which the cosmos was created. These five days were the first five of Peret – the 'Season of coming forth', the winter period, a time of rebirth after the flooding of the Nile. Preceding the festival proper were five days known as the 'lighting of the flame', which, Campbell argues, in the earlier form of the rite would have been quenched 'on the dark night of the moon when the king was ritually slain'. Campbell, J (1962) p. 75.
7. A good description of this rite is given in Rohl, D (1998) pp. 360–72.
8. Campbell, J (1962) p. 76.
9. Rohl, D (1998) p. 370.
10. Kerenyi, K (1967) p. 24.
11. Campbell, J (1968) p. 208.
12. Castleden, R (2000) p. 48.
13. North, J (1996) p. 191.
14. North, J (1996) p. 193.

Part Three

THE
DOLOROUS STROKE

Chapter 14

THE ARYA

No subject in archaeology typifies the twists and turns in academic fashion more than that of the Beaker Folk. Thirty years ago it was an accepted fact that around 2700 BC a new population of round-headed warriors arrived in Britain who buried their dead singly under round barrows, clutching red-clay drinking vessels called 'beakers'. Ten years ago, saying you still believed in the invasion of the Beaker Folk was like professing a belief in ghosts or fairies.[1] But this change in opinion had little to do with the archaeological evidence, which has remained constant throughout.

The evidence for some kind of 'Beaker event' is overwhelming: 1,240 single inhumations and 40 cremations have been excavated so far, dating from their thousand-year *floruit*. All contained the superior-quality, narrow-waisted, red-clay drinking vessels, with their wide open mouths and intricate linear patterns.

One beaker found at Ashgrove, Fife, contained the remnants of linden pollen, undoubtedly from honey,[2] hinting that these vessels were most likely used for the drinking of mead.[3] Unlike the grooved ware that existed before, the beakers were compact enough to be used by a single individual, suggesting that the communal rebirth cult of the henge builders had been superseded by a 'limited-access cult', restricted to the elite – and a mainly male elite at that. Beakers appeared in the graves of men, women and children, but the finest were found with the warrior males – archers armed with daggers and man-killing arrowheads, and wearing wrist-guards (bracers) to protect their arms from the whiplash of the bowstring.[4]

It is believed that the 'Beaker event', like the megalithic building tradition, began on continental Europe. The first glimmerings of it appeared around 3000 BC in an area spreading from eastern Germany to the Ukraine. A new type of warrior society had developed there, called the *corded-ware* (after their distinctive pots decorated with impressed cords) or *battle-axe* (after their favoured weapon) tradition. Its members were buried singly, usually in a crouched or foetal position in round barrows. It was at the western edge of this cultural province that the corded pots began their transformation into beakers. Over the next 200 years these quickly spread as far as the Netherlands, Brittany and Iberia. It was only a matter of time before they arrived in Britain.[5]

If the 'Beaker event' had signified merely a change in pottery, then little ink would have been expended on it; however, it seems that monumental changes occurred in the religious make-up of these islands after the arrival of beaker pottery. The beakers were the physical remains of a cultural revolution that saw a complete change in the prehistoric mindset. The old sites were abandoned; woodland sprang up on previously cleared land. There was an increase in defended settlements, and evidence of a substantial growth in warmongering.[6] As a result, farming was affected and went into a decline. But the most important outcome of these changes was the ending of the communal burial tradition in favour of the individual burial. While it is true that individual burials had taken place in Britain before the arrival of the Beakers (at Duggleby Howe, for instance; though I believe these were the tombs of men-gods), after their appearance the corner was fully turned. What had been an undercurrent became mainstream, and those buried were war chiefs or kings rather than gods.

Nothing revealed the extent of this revolution so much as the blocking of the doorways of the great communal tombs, such as those at Tinkinswood in Glamorgan, and Nympsfield in Gloucestershire.[7] This is most dramatically demonstrated in the closure of West Kennet longbarrow. After a millennium of use, the great doorway to this house of the dead was sealed – and not just with great sarsen blocks at the entrance. The very chambers were filled with some 2,500 cubic feet/700 cubic metres of infill, including shattered beaker pottery – a clue to the perpetrators of this deed. The last person buried within this tomb was the old man slain by an arrow in the throat.[8] Possibly he was a beaker user, but more likely he was the priest or god-king of the old religion, gloriously defeated and imprisoned for eternity.

Although the tombs went out of favour with the construction of the henges, and increasingly fewer new burials were placed within them, their doors remained open[9] – the divine ancestors could still look out on the living, and their bones were no doubt still used in rites within the henges. |But then all this suddenly changed. What impulse lay behind the closing of the tombs? Was it a respectful laying to rest of the old souls, or was it an attempt to sever the old contacts – to lock them away within their mounds and throw away the key? And why was the womb of the earth mother blocked? The importance of this act cannot be understated. The world-view that had seen the land of the dead and the land of the living as neighbours, perhaps even one, had changed. The communal dead were silenced. Clearly something fundamental had happened to society to so alter a millennium of tradition.

It is tempting to conclude that the Beaker event was the result of the increasing importance of the chief, who came to be seen as a political indiv-idual rather than a religious puppet fated to die when the heavens sent a sign – a continuation of the individual leaders from Duggleby, and therefore an indigenous change. But the clues seem to hint at an outside influence – either an incursion of newcomers or just new ideas. For it is clear that the henge builders themselves did not adopt the cult – they were overtaken by it.[10]

What this meant was that the whole 'Beaker package' – the new goods, the new religion – had somehow slipped in through the back door without the help of an invading population (a similar 'cultural package', the 'peyote cult', spread from Mexico to Canada in 1850 without any population movement).[11] But why was it that the beakers, which required great skill to produce, unlike most innovations from the Continent, were taken up not by the current elite but by members of the population *away* from the great henge sites? Who were these others? What connections did they have which gave them the ability to partake in this new cult when the great henge builders did not? Rather than attempt to identify this rogue element in society it is simpler to argue that these beaker-using people *were* newcomers, albeit a minority – missionaries of this new religion of the individual that had already taken root on the Continent, a religion that somehow sought to undermine that of the god kings of the henges.

In the past archaeologists had argued that a change in skull shape between the occupants of the Beaker graves (broad or round-headed, bracycephalic) and the earlier Neolithic skeletons of the communal graves (long-headed, dolichocephalic) was clear evidence for a new population.[12]

Later this evidence was challenged; it was possible, some argued, for native head shapes to have changed in the 500 years that had elapsed between these two burial traditions, and, in any case, the actual difference in skull morphology was not that pronounced. The most recent study has been unable to prove or disprove this theory.[13,14]

Perhaps newcomers *had* arrived, even if they were just cousins from over the water or trading partners, who had arrived with the new pioneering spirit of individual enterprise that the new cult seemed to preach. Perhaps they came to tap into the lucrative metal trade which was beginning at this time, ushering Britain into the Bronze Age.[15] But whatever their origin, whether foreign or local, these outsiders and the rites they brought with them were to overtake the native belief system and turn it on its head.

There is evidence, especially in the Wessex area, of a conflict of interests and ideologies at the henges. At Mount Pleasant, around 2200 BC, the ring of stones was destroyed, the entrance to the ring narrowed and a huge palisade built, enclosing an 11-acre/4.5-hectare area, which was subsequently burned to the ground – evidence perhaps of hostility or a take-over.[16] At Woodhenge the sarsen stones were also destroyed by fire; other henges were levelled. And at Avebury and Stonehenge, which were nearing their completion, there seems to have been a shift in use, with Beaker burials now appearing in these once grave-free enclosures. They had possibly been foundation sacrifices to dedicate these sites to the Beaker deities, or to build the foundations on a new blood line.[17] These burials could be seen as evidence for some kind of military or religious take-over, a conflict between beaker and grooved-ware users that archaeologists agree did take place.[18,19] Whatever form the war took, whether it was one of weapons or words, the beaker cult triumphed and the old sacred enclosures became graveyards – not for great ancestors or nameless gods, but for known individuals.

In spite of all this upheaval, henges continued to be built, evidence perhaps that the revolution brought about not the adoption of a wholly new religion, but the redefinition of the old one – a shifting of emphasis, a reinterpretation of its symbols to suit the individual rather than the group. Many of the old cults remained: the veneration of the sacred ox, and the use in some burials of boar tusks, or, as at Chaldon Herring, of antlers. The major change was that these symbols of power now celebrated the individual, not the egoless god king.

The best example of this reinterpretation of the old system is evident at Stonehenge. When this unique site, originally an unremarkable circular enclosure, was completed the old super-henges had long since been abandoned. It was like nothing built in Britain before, or after, and can, perhaps, be seen as the central site in the beaker cult. Thirty huge sarsen stones formed the outer ring, capped with hefty horizontal sarsens to form the famous 'trilithon' goalpost-shaped 'doorways'; and within this ring was a horseshoe of five magnificent trilithons. Though dwarfed by the sarsens, there was a smaller horseshoe of so-called 'bluestones' within the sarsen horseshoe, and a ring of them between this horseshoe and the outer sarsen ring.

The bluestones are intriguing because they are not native to Wessex. It is thought they were brought over land and sea from the Preseli mountains of South Wales, where they may have originally been set up in an existing circle – perhaps even as a circle of trilithons. It is possible that the beaker users brought the famous bluestone circle to Salisbury Plain from Wales, perhaps, as some believe, as a symbol for the subjugation of the old national religion and one of its shrines. The new temple, however, was to have a wholly new purpose; unlike the Neolithic henges, Stonehenge 'becomes a huge symbolic burial mound, the final resting place of a single entity, a man elevated from leader to god'.[20]

Archaeologist Colonel William Hawley had found this 'god' in 1924 along the midsummer solstice axis of the site, with a 'damaged' skull (though the bones were subsequently lost, so the date of the burial cannot be checked). Another body found at Stonehenge, this time buried in the ditch, showed signs of a violent death – it was riddled with six arrows.[21] These men, I suspect, like the old man in West Kennet, were not beaker users but leaders or priests of the old religion – an assumption supported by what I was to discover about the Beaker religion and its Indo-European origins.

If the Beaker Folk were a bone of contention, then the Indo-Europeans were an entire graveyard. The Indo-Europeans are normally seen as a single linguistic group speaking a number of tongues (Celtic, Germanic, Italic, Greek, Balto-Slavic, Anatolian, Armenian, Indo-Iranian and Tocharian) thought to have derived from a parent language (known as Proto-Indo-European) somewhere around 6–8,000 years ago.[22]

The Indo-Europeans – or *Arya* (not *Aryans*, as is commonly thought), a name they sometimes used in reference to themselves [23] – are believed to have had a common cultural make-up, which was carried with them to the various lands where their languages are now spoken. Part of this make-up was a threefold division of society into priests, warriors and herders/cultivators: in India the Brahmas, Ksatriyas and Vaisyas; in Rome the Flamines, Milites and Quirites; and in Celtic Gaul, according to Caesar, the Druides, Equites and Plebes. [24] Scholars have sought, using these cultural and linguistic connections, to discover exactly where the parent language first appeared, with by far the most commonly held opinion being that it originated in a region that stretched across the Pontic Caspian region and into north or central Europe. [25,26,27]

One notable exception to this theory is that put forward by Colin Renfrew in his *Archaeology and Language*. He suggests that Anatolia is the homeland and that the spread of the Indo-European language accompanied the spread of agriculture – and thus arrived in Britain around 4000 BC. [28] However, other scholars point out that Indo-European myth exemplified and glamorised the warrior individual, and that because it was a mythology that sought to justify invasion, subjugation and raiding, it is more likely that its spread occurred not through farming but as the result of the violent expansion of a warrior race – the so-called Kurgan people (a Russian word for a tumulus), horse-riding warrior nomads from the Steppes who exploded out of their homeland, down through the Balkans and perhaps as far west as the Danube, some time after 4000 BC. [29] It was there, in the heartlands of western Europe, c. 3200–2300 BC, that the 'battle-axe' and 'corded-ware' traditions arose – the origins of the Beaker Folk. And from there, over the next few centuries, these traditions, if not the people themselves, spread to Britain.

What is impossible to say is whether an Indo-European language accompanied this spread – or whether the language had arrived in Britain before the cult of the individual and was the medium through which the cult took hold.

The idea of the arrival of an Indo-European language in Beaker times clashes with the idea of an Atlantic Celtic language developing over many millennia. But might not a solution fall midway? Could a form of Indo-European have spread early on with farming, as Renfrew has suggested, only to be eclipsed by a secondary wave that brought with it a refashioned mythology and lexicon, so that the old (Anatolian) and new (Kurgan) seamlessly merged into one? The Beaker event in Britain could then be seen as an updated religious package in which the sacred sites of the ancestors are converted to those of warrior kings.[30]

What is sure is that with the rise of the individual came a change in mythology and religion, and it is this, more than any population or language change, which was of massive importance to my theme. For the Beaker Folk closed the tombs and turned henges into graves; they sealed up the old gods within the earth and turned to the sun. The new religion that these Indo-European peoples promulgated told of a victory over the old gods; where the old lunar deity had died and been reborn periodically in accord with the cosmic cycle, the new religion lauded his defeat and banishment to the underworld at the hands of a new breed of warrior deity. In place of the god of the cauldron's annual self-immolation there was now cruel murder and banishment, more violent and negative than anything that had gone before – and it was this change in mythic (and psychological) emphasis that lay behind the dolorous stroke of the Grail legends.

Notes

1. Pitts, M (2000) pp. 293–4.
2. Parker Pearson, M (1993) p. 85.
3. Analysis of pollen from Beaker times shows an increase in barley – possibly for brewing. Also, the fact that many of the herringbone and rectilinear patterns incised on their sides were impressed with a twisted cord of hemp, hints that perhaps this plant may have been used in the drink itself.
4. Other early Beaker graves contained boars' tusks, antlers and axes. See Darvill, T (1987) p. 90.
5. Cunliffe, B (2001) pp. 217–21.
6. Such as Crickley Hill – sacked and burned – and covered in leaf-shaped arrowheads. See Darvill, T (1987) p. 76.
7. Darvill, T (1987) p. 76.
8. Malone, C (1989) p. 79.
9. Apart from sites such as Newgrange, where archaeologists claim there is evidence that it was sealed immedieately after use – hence the need for a lightbox above the door. But might there have been a temporary wooden door – as in the houses of the living?
10. Parker Pearson, M (1993) p. 87.

11. In Clarke, D V; Cowie, T G; Foxon, R (1985) p. 82. Thanks to Jonathan Holden for pointing out this connection to me.

12. Parker Pearson, M (1993) p. 85.

13. Brodie (1994).

14. Archaeologist Mike Pitts has been braver than most in suggesting that this Pandora's box ought to be reopened. He says: 'It has to be said that the immigration hypothesis was rejected in the 1970s as much as any reason because of academic fashion. The possibility that at this time in Europe certain people were on the move, in search of land and other resources, needs to be revisited.' Pitts, M (2000) p. 294.

15. With evidence appearing of gold, copper and tin mines in Ireland, and tin mines in Cornwall.

16. Pitts, M (2000) p. 292.

17. Beaker burials appear beneath the great sarsen avenue leading to the main circles. A Beaker youth is buried in the sanctuary – and more burials appear in the circle itself. Burl, A (1979).

18. Parker Pearson, M (1993) p. 88.

19. In Darvill, T (1987) p. 92.

20. Pitts, M (2000) p. 294.

21. For a discussion of these finds, see Pitts, M (2000).

22. Perhaps the best introduction currently available on the Indo-Europeans is Mallory, J P (1991).

23. Lincoln, B (1991) p. 148. The term 'Arya' is also useful to distinguish this prehistoric people from the self-styled 'Aryans' of Nazi ideology.

24. Mallory, J P (1991) p. 131.

25. Based on studies of the linguistic development of Amerindian tribes, scholars have suggested that a homeland of between 96,500 and 386,000 miles (250,000 and 1,000,000 square kilometres) would have been necessary (see Mallory, J P (1991) p. 146) for a language group to develop.

26. Reconstructing the Proto-Indo-European language has been one of the more interesting sides to their study. It is accepted, for instance, that the Proto-Indo-Europeans knew of sheep, given the widespread use of the word *owis for sheep. Similarly, they were familiar with horses, cows, mountains, lakes, rivers and plains. Unfortunately, the reconstructed lexicon is not a great help in the identification of their homeland.

27. Mallory, J P (1991) p. 177.

28. Renfrew, C (1998).

29. Mallory, J P (1991) p. 184.

30. For simplicity I have not so far gone into the fact that there are actually two branches of the Celtic tongue – Q Celtic (or Gaelic) and P Celtic (or Brythonic). Q Celtic is found in Ireland and is taken to be the earlier of the two forms. Is it perhaps important that Beaker traditions never caught on in Ireland? Or that no beakers are found in the south or west of the island, and that those found elsewhere are not associated with grave goods at all? Evidence of some incursion exists at Newgrange, where they erected a shelter or shrine(?) against the side wall of the mound. Later myths tell of overcoming old population here – but Q Celtic stayed put. Did the Beaker event see the introduction of P Celtic from the Continent (where it existed in Brittany)? It is a possibility.

Chapter 15

THE DRAGON SLAYER

In the old religion of the Neolithic farmers, which continued into the later Neolithic, the king or chieftain, fuelled by a drug cult that offered him a sense of unity and identification with the universal *daemon*, played out in a great ritual game the cosmic order of the heavens as an embodiment of the lunar serpent bull – living then dying, dying then living.

The serpent, which as a symbol of the wisdom of life beyond death, slithers on Hermes' staff in Greek myth, holds a different notion in our modern world. To a Christianised Westerner the serpent is the symbol of evil, of the devil, which tempted man to eat of the fruit of the tree of knowledge, and hence initiated his expulsion from Eden. Genesis tells of the angel with a fiery sword who prevents man's return to paradise, but I had seen for myself that in Britain at least the doorways to the paradisal land of the dead were closed with stones and debris by the followers of the Beaker cult. They had exiled themselves from Eden – they had left the half-light for the harsh light of day. And at this point the glorious sun achieved supremacy and the serpent was cast down.

The principal holy symbols used by the Arya/Indo-Europeans were the horse and the sun. The horse was the Indo-European animal *par excellence* and took the place of the ox as a symbol of divinity in their religion. The horse was what made them swift and deadly in battle; it pulled their chariots and provided them with victory and new land – for they claimed as their own the very soil over which their horses travelled (indeed, *gabar*, the Irish word for horse, forms the basis of the word for 'invasion').[1] On rock carvings from Denmark the so-called 'Celtic cross' – a cross within a circle, which appears as a solar sign – often accompanies the horse and the chariot, and it is also seen on Beaker goods (gold buttons, for example).[2] The artistic apogee of both these traditions is the Trundholm Chariot, a wheeled horse drawing a bronze and gold disk 10 inches/25 centimetres in diameter, found in a bog in Denmark.[3]

In this new solar cult the once life-sustaining lunar serpent of the Neolithic was characterised as an abomination – a negative symbol of the older ego-negating culture – destroyed by the victorious solar hero. The myths of the Indo-Europeans are rife with such imagery.

In Indian myth Indra, king of the gods, destroys the serpentine demon Vritra; he drinks three great draughts of soma and then blasts Vritra with a thunderbolt, scattering his foe into many pieces and thus releasing the flood waters that the 'dragon' had jealously guarded and kept from humanity, leaving the land dry and barren.[4] In later Hindu myth this water-serpent Vritra can be slain only at dusk by the foam of the ocean – by something neither dry nor wet, neither by day nor at night, nor with a weapon.[5] The link to the triple death of the bog men is obvious.

In Babylonian myth the water-dragon Tiamat is slain by Marduk – an early version of the slaying of the Leviathan by Yahweh in the Old Testament.[6] The list is endless – from Apollo slaying Pythia the python at Delphi, to St George slaying the dragon.

The beheading of the serpent-maned gorgon Medusa by Perseus also fits into this pattern, as does the defeat of the serpent Apophis each morning by the sun god Re in Egyptian belief. Perhaps its most potent form is in the theme of 'war in heaven'. This tells of the expulsion of Lucifer ('bearer of light') from Heaven by Yahweh, reiterated in the Book of Revelation where St Michael casts down Satan in the form of a seven-headed dragon, back into hell. It is also of great importance that Tiamat, Pythia and Medusa are all female: the defeat of the dragon was also a victory over the dark maternal underworld and its denizens. Clearly the Arya were seeking to curtail the power of the goddess who demanded that her lovers die anonymously according to the cosmic order. No more would they dance to her tune.

The enigmatic 'Battle of the Trees', the conflict between Gwydion son of Beli and Bran, is also visibly such a battle between the new gods and the old. The war was over the other-worldly treasures of the underworld – in this case a 'whelp' and a 'roebuck', but obviously in the same vein as the three cattle and the cauldron seized from Cú Roí by Cú Chulainn.

But this battle seems to have been one of magic rather than of swords: a war of intelligence in which the victor had only to name his opponent, Bran, to win. But the clues to the dragon slaying are to be found within certain lines of the 'Battle of the Trees' poem where there is mention of a hundred-headed beast, a 'spotted serpent ridged with a crest' and with gaping jaws, on whose tongue and head a battle was fought.[7] (Here, surely, is the Celtic counterpart to the great water monster Tiamat, slain by Marduk with a blow to the mouth.) After the fight with the serpent the battle begins, the warriors become trees, Bran is defeated and his treasures taken.

The widespread occurrence of this motif points to its obvious importance in the ancient world. Whereas before this time the body of the god was willingly given up to form the cosmos – shown in the self-castration of Shiva and Attis, or by consent to deathly connubium with the Dark One – such a deed was now practised by a young upstart, a demiurge, who slew the old deity but offered no part of himself in the act (the body of Tiamat formed the waters of heaven and earth, but the slayer remained whole). In other versions of this myth, the slayer of Tiamat is *Bel* or Bel-Marduk. The similarity between his name and that of Beli, the brother of Bran, who kills the giant and blights the land, is perhaps no coincidence. This common myth, summarised here by Bruce Lincoln, was clearly of great importance to my theme:

> In this [myth] it was told how the first warrior, whose name was 'Third' (*trito) conducted the first cattle raid. Here it is related that cattle originally belonging to the Indo-Europeans were stolen by a monstrous three-headed serpent (his very name was 'Serpent', *Ng(w)hi-), who was a non-Indo-European, an aborigine living in the land entered by I-E invaders. Following this theft it fell to 'Third' to recover the stolen cattle, and he began his quest by seeking the aid of a warrior deity to whom he offered libations of intoxicating drinks. Having won the god's assistance, and himself fortified by the same intoxicant, 'Third' set forth, found the 'Serpent', slew him, and released the cattle which had been imprisoned by the monster.[8]

It was a myth that would justify to the Indo-Europeans their conquests over non-Indo-European neighbours.[9] The Indian *Rig Veda* – a collection of 1,080 hymns written between 1200 and 900 BC and celebrating the victories of the Vedic Arya – contains this tale:

> *Trita, knowing the ancestral weapons*
> *and impelled by Indra, did battle*
> *Having killed the three-headed, seven-bridled one,*
> *Trita drove off his cattle …*
> *Driving forth the cattle of Visvarupa,*
> *he tore off those three Heads.*[10]

I soon realised that fragments of this myth appear in Celtic legends. The *Táin Bo Froech* (the 'Cattle Raid of Froech'), part of the Ulster Cycle, is a good example. It tells of Froech's recovery of his own stolen cattle (and his wife) from beyond the Alps where they are guarded within a fort by a monstrous serpent, which is caught by the Ulster hero Conall Cernach in his belt. The cows, along with Froech's wife, are then rescued.[11]

There are similar motifs in an Irish tale called 'Balor of Tory Island'.[12] Balor, who lives on Tory Island, covets the magical cow of the smith Gavidim, which could fill any vessel with milk. Gavidim's appointed guard, Fin, loses the cow and Balor captures it. Aided by a magician named Gial Dubh, Fin sleeps with Balor's daughter and rescues the cow. Balor, enraged, kills Fin, but not before his daughter gives birth to a son – Lui – who is hidden away.

Balor travels to Gavidim's forge where Lui is waiting for him with a red-hot spear, which he casts into Balor's single eye. The dying Balor instructs Lui to behead him and to place the decapitated head above his own, so that he might have all the knowledge that is in the world. The boy refuses and throws the head down, blasting a hole of immense depth in the earth. This tale parallels the god Lugh's defeat with his magical spear of the one-eyed Balor in the Irish second battle of the Moytura, told in the Book of Invasions.

But what is more important is that Lincoln's reconstruction is directly applicable to the legend of Cú Roí (who stole Blathnat, the cauldron and the *three cows* of Tuchna from the Ulster men, who in turn sent sent Cú Chulainn – the Irish Theseus – into his labyrinthine spiral castle to get it back, which resulted in the death and beheading of Cú Roí in a variant of the beheading game). Cú Roí's role is clearly that of 'Serpent' – the god of the old religion who had stolen treasure once belonging to the Arya.

However, the treasure – the sacred cows and the wonder-working cauldron (full of *kykeon*?) – had presumably belonged originally to Cú Roí. His wife Blathnat, too, was in origin no spoil of war but the goddess herself, who, with her other half, the old deity, would undergo the cosmos-renewing love-death. As the lunar god of the Neolithic, the old deity had owned the cauldron of transformation for over a thousand years before the mead-drinking Arya brought their beakers across the Channel. He had been the mate of the deadly goddess since that time, too, as the tusk-shaped wound to his groin showed – and were not his three magical cows buried in Fussel's lodge long before the tombs were blocked up by the solar horsemen?

From what I had discovered about the cults of the Neolithic it was quite clear that this Arya myth was a late invention. The Ulstermen had been lying; the spoils weren't theirs after all. But the followers of the new religion had invented this myth to justify their pillaging and plundering; or, rather, they had manipulated an old myth – that of the rescue of the god from the underworld – and applied it to the cauldron, the cattle and the sovereignty of the land. The once-mighty goddess became a spoil of war – stolen and raped (although, as they would tell it, she had willingly betrayed her old spouse) to legitimise their taking of the land. The theme of the rescue of the moon god was thus adapted so that it was the drink of that god that was quested for – and obtained by wile.

The theft of the cauldron is a theme that appears again and again in Indian myth; for the cauldron contains soma, the same drink that resides in Shiva's hair in the moon cup, and that Indra quaffs before killing Vritra.

What is soma? Many suggestions have been made, ranging from opium, ephedra, Syrian rue and harmel to the *Amanita muscaria* mushroom.[13] Whatever its origin it seems likely that soma was originally the drug of the moon-worshipping farmers[14] and was possibly something that the Indo-Europeans obtained from them.

The most famous account of the soma theft is found in the *Mahabharata*. It tells first of how the gods (*devas*) and the demons (*asuras*) create soma together by churning the Cosmic Ocean, using Mount Mandara as a pivot and the serpent King Vasuki as a rope (an analogy gleaned from the preparation of butter). With both gods and demons pulling the snake in a great game of tug-of-war, the central mountain churns the sea, creating milk, butter and, finally, soma.[15] Eventually the god Dhanvantari appears, bearing the pail of ambrosia.[16]

The gods, however, trick the demons and drink the ambrosia themselves. But as they are supping, the demon Rahu disguises himself as a god and steals some of the precious drink. The moon and sun spot him and inform Vishnu, who decapitates the demon with a discus. The head of Rahu, which falls to the earth as a mountain, periodically swallows the sun and moon in revenge – thus causing eclipses.[17] The battle is ended when Nara takes his celestial bow and fires at the demons so they flee into the earth and the oceans. Nara, it seems, casts the demons into the underworld, just as Zeus casts the Titans into Erebus in Greek myth.

Clearly there are parallels in motive between the beheading of Rahu and the beheading of Cú Roí: the former to allow the gods to win back the soma that Rahu had stolen from them, the latter to seize the cauldron with the three magical cows' milk which had been seized from the Ulstermen. Not only this, surely the 'milky ocean' of the *Mahabharata* is paralleled in the Irish tale by the pouring of the mystical milk into the river by the lovely Blathnat, as a sign to Cú Chulainn to enter the 'spinning fortress' (Mount Mandara in the Indian myth). According to Santillana and Von Dechend's *Hamlet's Mill*, the spiralling of Mandara represents the pole star spinning on its own axis, and the milky ocean the Milky Way. Whatever the origins of these motifs, they clearly sprang from the same soil.

However, the soma theft as found in the *Mahabharata* is a relatively late version of the tale. Earlier Hindu tales presented the theft as occurring not during some cosmic tug of war, but during an all-out battle between gods and demons – a symbol for the battle between Arya and non-Arya. There is an incredible similarity between these tales and the Celtic myths. In one version the demons own a magical lake that revives the dead and heals any wounded warriors placed within it.[18] (The comparison to Bran's cauldron in 'Branwen Ferch Llyr' – which brought dead warriors back to life, whole save for the power of speech – is overt.)

The Indian gods are wily thieves, sending an envoy to capture the heart of the demon king's daughter, who betrays the secret of this lake out of love.[19] Is this not similar to the story of the betrayal of her countrymen by the maiden Tarpeia in the account of Brennus' sacking of Rome? And is it the same role that Branwen plays in the Welsh tale, where she betrays her husband, Matholwch, and summons Bran to Ireland to help her escape? She is Lady Bertilak, Blodeuwedd and Blathnat.

In another Indian version of this myth Indra, king of the gods, sends a spy, Sarama, to steal the ambrosia from the demons. Sarama crosses the magical River Rasa that divides the world of the living and the dead and enters the land of the demons. Here she requests the secret of soma, which is represented, in an exact parallel to the Cú Roí myth, as the *milk of three magical cows*. Sarama asks for a draught of the magical milk, which is granted, but once she has crossed back over the river, under the influence of the demonic liquor she lies to Indra and denies that she has drunk any – but he kicks her in the stomach and she throws up the milk.[20]

In the Irish text of the 'Battle of Moytura', in which the god Lugh with his magical spear defeats then beheads the demonic 'Balor of the Baleful Eye' (like the Indian Rahu), there is also a resuscitating aid – this time, like the lake of the Indian demons, a well of immortality. It is held by the Irish gods, *Tuatha Dé Danann*, but is discovered by Ruadhan the Fomhoiré who disguises himself and enters their camp to find out why the Dé Dananns cannot be killed. On finding their revivifying well he fills it with stones so it cannot be used, but is found doing so and is destroyed.[21] This event, though, seems to be a corruption of an original version in which it is the *Tuatha Dé Danann* who steal this resuscitation aid from the demonic Fomhoiré, through the cunning of the *Tuatha* deity the Dagda (literally, 'The Good God'), disguised as Ruadh Rofhessa.[22]

The Dagda steals into the camp of the Fomhoiré on the eve of the battle, and is subjected to a humiliating meal. His enemies pour a huge quantity of *porridge*, consisting of 'fourscore gallons of *new milk*, with meal and bacon in proportion … the whole carcasses of goats, sheep and pigs,'[23] into a hole in the ground and force Dagda to eat the lot. The mixture is eaten with a spoon large enough to seat two people in the middle of it.

This massive meal has never to my knowledge been adequately explained, only commented on as an amusing incident to perhaps demonstrate Dagda's vast size. But clearly it has a meaning. It is plain that this is a reference to the stealing of the ambrosia from the demons. The Irish tales state how after the meal the Dagda is sexually aroused and takes one of the Fomhoiré women, who is so impressed with his lovemaking that she promises to help him in the battle the next day by using her magic against her own people.[24] She is undoubtedly the equivalent of the 'demon's daughter' who aids the gods in the battle by giving them the secret of the ambrosia of rebirth. That the eating of the porridge represents the drinking of the soma is made clear by the following incident: the Dagda returns to his own land, but is so full of porridge that he vomits up the whole lot – exactly as Sarama did in the Indian version of this story. Soma, then, as in the Indian myth, is held in the stomach or throat, and then disgorged.

To me Dagda's drinking and then vomiting of the porridge make sense only if seen as a soma theft in the Indo-European tradition. Unquestionably, the 'porridge' found along with the ergot in the stomachs of Tollund and Graubelle man is physical proof that the Dagda's meal was no simple bowl of oats. It was the ritual drink of the British Mysteries.

The meaning of the cauldron/cattle theft myth is far more fundamental than the justification to go pillaging. It is obvious that behind the change in religion lay a fundamental shift in the psychological make-up of pre-historic man. After all, the new religion did not offer just a chance to raid neighbouring farms; it also offered a new way of perceiving the world – and, importantly, a very necessary one.

At the end of the third millennium BC, in contrast to his predecessor's relatively peaceful existence, man lived in what was becoming an increasingly dangerous world, in which concentration and attention needed to be focused on the here and now (as evidence of augmented weaponry and warfare shows). Indeed, it might be argued, to continue to hold onto ego-negating beliefs fostered by a communal drug-cult was tantamount to suicide in those times. Populations were growing and were on the move: the old divisions of territory looked over by the ancestral tomb were increasingly under threat, and land for farming was growing scarce. Could it be that the old religion under a god king obsessed with cosmic order had in fact become a dangerous luxury? To preserve the life of the tribe, men had to be warriors under a war leader; they had to be able to protect their families from attack, and so it was necessary to develop a strong, rational, decisive ego. It is easy to imagine how the old gods of rapture and release could be personified as harmful, as demons, and how, having been freed from communality and given a taste of personal power and wealth, some would be unwilling to return to the old ways.

In this manner the conflict between the gods of the old and new religions became symbols, the outer manifestation of a more important change that was occurring within the mind of prehistoric man – a war between the twin aspects of his soul.

Notes

1. Matthews, J and C (1996) p. 8.
2. Hutton, R (1993) pp. 103–7.
3. Glob, P V (1983) pp. 101–3.
4. Campbell, J (1962) pp. 182–3.
5. See Doniger O'Flaherty, W (trans.) (1975) p. 84.
6. The Hebrew word for the waters that God divides on the second day of creation is *Tehom* – a derivative of Tiamat. See Campbell, J (1964) p. 85.
7. See Markale, J (1993) p. 238.
8. Lincoln, B (1991) p. 10.
9. Lincoln, B (1991) p. 12.
10. *Rig Veda* 10.8.8–9, quoted in Lincoln, B (1991) p. 10.
11. A modern translation of this tale can be found in Gantz, J (1986).
12. This version of the tale is taken from the paraphrased one found in Matthews, C (1987) pp. 84–5.
13. For a discussion of soma see Rudgley, R (1993) pp. 43–55; Rudgley, R (1999) pp. 226–9 and McKenna, T (1992) pp. 97–120.
14. McKenna, T (1992) p. 101.
15. In fact the image created by this myth is, perhaps coincidentally, suggestive of the layout of Avebury itself – with the River Kennet as the ocean, Avebury itself as Vasuki, and Silbury as Mount Mandara.
16. These quotes are taken from the translation of episodes in the *Mahabharata*, found in Doniger O'Flaherty, W (trans.) (1975) pp. 274–80.
17. Doniger O'Flaherty, W (trans.) (1975) p. 278.
18. Doniger O'Flaherty, W (trans.) (1975) p. 128.
19. Doniger O'Flaherty, W (trans.) (1975) p. 289.
20. Doniger O'Flaherty, W (trans.) (1975) p. 72.
21. Dixon Kennedy, M (1996) p. 258.
22. 'Lord' or 'Red' of 'Perfect Knowledge'.
23. Dixon Kennedy, M (1996) p. 100.
24. Doniger O'Flaherty, W (trans.) (1975) p. 100.

Chapter 16

THE WAR
OF THE TWINS

According to Joseph Campbell:

> *The battle ... of gods against Titans at the beginning of the world,*
> *actually was of two aspects of the human psyche at a critical moment*
> *in human history, when the light and rational, divisive functions,*
> *under the sign of the Heroic Male, overcame ... the fascination of the*
> *dark mystery of the deeper layers of the soul.*[1]

On one level this was the triumph of the individual over the collective – on another the change from a kind of prehistoric communism to one of prehistoric capitalism – and it signalled the birth of the 'rational', non-mystical mindset that endures today in the West. It truly was a change of psychology.

Some scholars have attempted to find a physiological base for such a change, arguing that monumental changes in the nature of society caused developments in the human brain. For instance psychologist Julian Jaynes argues that living in larger communities (such as cities) where there was a marked increase in warfare, led to development of the left hemisphere of the brain (which houses the ego and displays analytical thinking, reason and logic) at the expense of the right hemisphere (which displays a more artistic bent, being more intuitive, mystical and receptive).[2] The development of the ego, he argues, 'severed' the once free-flowing communication between hemispheres; thus the Persephone side of the psyche, emphasised in the drug cults of the Neolithic, was split from the Demeter side and thus became the unconscious. Stan Gooch, on the other hand, argues that the ego is in the cerebrum and the unconscious in the cerebellum. Both scholars were looking for a mechanical biological answer to this split in the prehistoric psyche.[3]

Jaynes gives the specific date of 1250 BC for the emergence of the ego, but the dominance of ego (the 'left brain' or the cerebrum) may have begun as soon as man began to talk and make tools.[4] This dominance, however, could have been tempered by civilisations more open to the 'unconscious' – to the 'right' – who actively engaged in 'right-brain' activities induced by drugs or shamanic trance. Thus the drug cults of Neolithic man, like the initiations at Eleusis, enabled him to restore the balance and live in an undivided Eden.

Although Neolithic man attempted to bridge the gap between right- and left-brain activity, the moment he encountered a more extreme left-brain culture – such as that of the Beaker Folk – he was at a disadvantage, in much the same way that in a fight between a stoned hippie and a drunken lager lout, the latter, by his very nature, has the advantage.

If the narrowing of consciousness, acquired to promote the 'ruthlessness and efficiency needed to survive', was indeed the core of the Arya religion I can fully understand why the old tombs were blocked. The old world, in which the living and the dead mingled, had ceased. Man was no longer in tune with his 'right brain', no longer in communication with the deeper cosmic dance of life and death that was aped by his rapturous Neolithic predecessors, for it had been closed off to his conscious mind – as if a psychological Berlin Wall had divided his psyche. The doors to Eden had been sealed for good. Mankind had emerged from the twilight world – the spinning castle of the underworld god – into the clear light of day.

For the solar Arya the moment of victory over the forces of darkness was the point of sunrise. Had not Re killed the underworld serpent Apophis at this moment, signalling his victory over night? This is the reason why the victory of the Arya marked the end of the nocturnal lunar rites of the serpentine god of the ever-dying moon, and the beginning of the rites of sunrise.

Before this point man had sought to identify himself as an aspect of that god who was both dead and living – periodically a lord of the abyss and then a lord of life – the universal *daemon*. This was the 'secret of the two partners' given to the pharaoh after the completion of the Heb Sed. The revelation that the two parts of the god (Shiva and Shava, if you will: the lord of life and the lord of the abyss) were one was symbolised by the wearing of the double crown; and in Eleusis it was the re-uniting of mother and daughter which revealed that Persephone and Demeter, *eidolon* and *daemon*, were one. But in the new religion of the Indo-Europeans these dual aspects were irreparably split – like the brain postulated by Jaynes – and man began to identify with the *eidolon*, the limited ego-driven god of light, and the *daemon* was shut away in the underworld. Fundamentally this meant that the perception of the 'cosmic game', that 'dance of death' which had so enraptured his predecessors, had ended.[5]

The Arya's mythology was not entirely new, more a refashioning of the old myth, adapted to meet their own means. They specifically altered the emphasis of the myths, which were at base the same vegetal myths as those of their Neolithic predecessors, to support a system in which war, individual power and plunder were the new virtues.[6]

This refashioning of the older rites included an altered use for the Neolithic *kykeon* drink, which became their soma, for the Indo-Europeans used these narcotics to swell their egos, not to dissolve them. Soma seemed to offer them a sense of immortality in the continuation after death of the *eidolon*; for them the idea of immortality came not from the realisation that man was a splinter of an undying god but from the belief that the mortal personality could survive death. This engendered a new horror – an intoxicated warrior unafraid of death.[7] Their ideal was a warrior – like Achilles or Cú Chulainn – whose aim in life was to make a name for himself, the very antithesis of the mysteries that sought to kill off the *eidolon*. These warriors are reminiscent of the medieval Assassins, a word derived from 'hashish', who used this drug to nullify their fear of death in battle. This is why Cú Chulainn – he of the wolfish *fearg* – had stolen it from Cú Roí. The Arya used the drug to foster not a sense of the one being part of the many, but the exact opposite. It enabled them to become a *hoamawergaz* ('soma-wolf') or *Ulfhednar* ('Wolf-head') – an intoxicated warrior. 'We have drunk the soma: we have become immortal', they sing in the *Rig Veda*, praising this miraculous liquid for its ability to give courage and strength.[8]

The cup of rebirth was no longer a vessel of initiation; it was the narcotic contents that were now important, not the symbol of the vessel itself that had once sought to dissolve the ego through rebirth. In time soma was replaced by mead, for the Indo-Europeans were not so much interested in the psychotropic effects of the drug but wanted something that would give them bravado in battle – and this is what alcohol offered.

If the real meaning behind these myths was psychological rather than vegetal, what did the dragon slaying represent? To Jung, the slaying of the dragon symbolised what he called the 'Battle for deliverance from the Mother' – the emergence of a strong independent ego and self-consciousness from out of a state of relative instinctual unconsciousness.[9]

Jung sees the dragon as a symbol of unconsciousness (seen in a negative light from the viewpoint of consciousness), from which the individual is to be 'rescued', and this is a theme that recurs with striking frequency in the initiation ceremonies of young men in many tribes. Such puberty initiations aim to sever their ties to the family, and to turn them from boys, clinging to their mothers' apron strings, into men. Taken from their mothers they are often secluded in a shelter or cave that represents the inside of a monster's or serpent's belly – it is both stomach and womb.[10]

The boys are 'rescued' by the male elders and initiated into their mysteries – freed from the serpent's jaws, reborn like the sun. Might not the practitioners of the Beaker cult have 'liberated' themselves from the dominance of Nghi, casting him down (as Yahweh did Lucifer) and thus severing the apron strings of the Great Mother herself? If this is so – and if Jung is correct in linking the stages of growth in the consciousness of the individual with the stages of growth in the consciousness of mankind – then the level of psychological maturity exemplified by the Arya was no longer that of the childlike 'unconscious' Neolithic (albeit a self-induced state) but that of the teenager, with all the self-aggrandised angst and joie de vivre that goes with it. They were triumphant with new-found power and independence, casting down the bugbears of childhood and achieving independence from the ever-living ever-dying serpentine view of the cosmos. And with the emergence of the ego, the one god (the god of death and rebirth) had become separated into two parts – a light and a dark aspect.

The arrival of these two gods is shown on a number of Bronze Age ceremonial boats from Denmark that depict a pair of horned warriors – and other rock carvings show a couple in connubium and a second male figure behind them with an axe ready to strike.[11] The two brothers had appeared on the scene: 'Man' and 'Twin', the light and the dark.

'Twin' is a humanised version of the demonic (originally *daemonic*) serpentine god of the Neolithic – Nghi – whose body, once freely given to form the cosmos, is now offered by his solar brother, 'Man'. Twin, as his name suggests, is the original unity made dual by the axe-strike of the solar hero; he is sky and ground split by the sun at the horizon. Again, it is Bruce Lincoln who reconstructs this primal myth for us:

> At the beginning of time – so the Proto-Indo-European cosmology held – there were two brothers, a priest whose name was 'Man' (*Manu) and a king, whose name was 'Twin' (*Yemo), who travelled together accompanied by an ox. For reasons that are not specified, they took it upon themselves to create the world, and towards that end the priest offered up his brother and the ox in what was to be the first ritual sacrifice. Dismembering their bodies, he used the various parts to create the material universe and human society as well, taking all three classes from the body of the first king who ... combined within himself the social unity.[12]

Reading this passage I was immediately struck by two things: firstly, that the slaughtering of the ox was, of course, the same as the slaying of 'Twin', bringing to mind the ritual substitutions of the Cretan bull court and the Apis bull; and secondly, that the triple division of the first king (reflecting his origin in the three-headed serpent Nghi) into the three classes (druides, equites and plebes in Gaul) was the ultimate origin of the three blows dealt to the Bachlach and the bog men! The bog men were certainly playing the role of 'Twin' – *Yemo, the serpent lord, whose murder by his twin brother had led to the creation of the universe. It seemed as if the sacrificed men of the Iron Age were re-enacting the creation of the cosmos. It was an act that also made *Yemo the lord of the dead.

With sudden renewed interest I picked up my notes on the Celtic myths, in search of the warring brothers. The tale, of course, is oft repeated. Lleu is defeated in a triple murder at the hands of Goronw 'Pebr' – the 'fiery', a name hinting at a solar aspect to his character. Cú Chulainn, whose strength waxes and wanes with the strength of the sun, defeats Cú Roí, whose ever-spinning fort in the tale of Bricriu's feast, is guarded by an immense serpent – which, originally, I thought, was Cú Roí himself as Nghi.

But the most illuminating parallels are to the Grail King, who, like Bran, Shiva, Tammuz, Attis and Osiris, was wounded in the thigh – not, however, by the boar, but by Balin, a reflex of the defeat of Bran by Beli, or of Brennius by his brother Belinus. This Indo-European myth, which delights in the split of *eidolon* and *daemon*, is thus the ancestor of the motif of the dolorous stroke of the Grail.

The defeated brother from Irish tradition appears in one form as a figure known as Eber Donn – Eber the 'dark one' – who appears mostly in folklore as a kind of lord of the dead. He appears as Donn Cuailnge – the great 'black bull' who fights against Findbennach Ai, 'the white horned bull of Ai', in the epic 'Cattle Raid of Cooley'. This battle results in the death of both beasts and the formation of natural landscape features from their remains; in other words, the cosmos was created through death and dismemberment.

In this light the Battles of the Moytura in the Irish Book of Invasions, in which the *Tuatha* defeat demonic the one-eyed Fomhoiré, repeat this cosmic struggle between 'Man' and 'Twin', Trito and Nghi, Arya and non-Arya, beaker user and grooved-ware user. The same plot is told when the Gaels defeat the *Tuatha* at Teltow and force them to abide under the earth – closing off the doors of their fairy hills so only poets and heroes could enter them in search of the cauldron of immortality. These tales all replay the same theme – a new division in man's psyche rather than invasions and holy war.

In the old mystery cults this dismemberment had symbolised the dispersal of the original god into every aspect of creation, so that each man and woman possessed part of the divine spark; each person, through his or her *daemon*, was literally part of god. But the myth of *Yemo turned this creation into purely a material event.

*Yemo appears in Norse myth as Ymir– the frost giant whose vast mountainous body is carved up by *three* deities – Odin, Vili and Ve – to create the world:

Of Ymir's flesh
The earth was shaped
From his sweat the sea,
Mountains from his bones,
Trees from his hair,
And from his skull the sky[13]

From this it can be seen that he is akin to the Greek Atlas, who is in fact –
unlike the common depiction of him as a man holding the world on his
shoulders – a primal giant, described in the same way as Ymir, whose very
body was the earth. The Welsh Bran, described in no uncertain terms as
mountainous, is clearly related to these others. Perhaps the mountainous
giant's body parts became the cosmos itself, just as the head of Rahu
became a mountain.

A similar fate, as the *Táin* has shown, awaited the cosmic ox:

The Bull jerked back his hoof. His leg broke, but the other bull's horn
was sent flying to the mountain nearby. It is called Sliab nAdarca, the
Mountain of the horn, ever since … He stopped to drink in Finnlethe
on the way, he left Finnbennach's shoulder blade there – from which
comes Finnlethe, the White One's shoulder blade, as the name of that
district. He drank again at Ath Luain, and left Finnbennach's loins
there – that is how the place was named Ath Luain, the Ford of the
Loins …[14]

This passage recalls Plutarch's list of the sites formed by the distribution of
the god Osiris's body parts.

The head was buried at Abydos, his left eye in Lower Egypt, his
eyebrows at Pelusium, his jaw-bones at Faket, parts of his head at
Het-Gar … his phallus at Het-Bennu.[15]

And in Roman myth a similar fate befalls the divine twins Romulus and
Remus, who were suckled by a wolf. Remus is killed during the foundation
of Rome by his brother (or by senators, according to Plutarch) and his
body parts are distributed around the capital.[16] The name of the slain

brother, it has been suggested, derived from Yemos ('twin'), with the initial changed to an 'R' to alliterate with his brother in later times. And the water-dragon Vritra is termed a gelded bull, whose body is 'scattered in many places'. In Persian tradition the bull killed by the god Mithras plays such a role: from its body came vegetation; from its backbone, wheat; and from its blood, wine.[17]

And then there is the base of the Gundestrup Cauldron, which depicts the *taurobolion* – the bull sacrifice – with a man lunging at the beasts, accompanied by a dog. This sacrificed bull is obviously a reflex of the self-sacrificed bull-lord, Shiva, Dionysos or Osiris – 'the Bull of his mother' – and so forms a parallel to the god's death.

In time the slaying of the bull was replaced by the slaying of the horse, a much documented Indo-European rite. The killing of the horse, in place of the killing of the bull by 'Man', is found in many myths and rites. But the Irish tale of the 'Curse of Macha' contains the clearest Indo-European elements. Macha is the other-worldly wife of an Ulster warrior named Crundchu, who unwisely boasts of her swiftness in running to the king, Conchobar mac Nessa, who forces her to run publicly against his horses. Macha gives birth to twins during her run, and dies from exhaustion. With her dying breath she curses the men of Ulster so that in times of distress and need they will be 'as weak as a woman in labour'.[18]

Here the birth of twins from the death of the horse goddess is clear. It is after Macha that the site of Emhain Macha is named – meaning the 'twins of Macha'. Interestingly, it also means 'twin battle', a fact that has resonance with my theme. But it is the death of the old maternal religion that yields power to her matricidal sons.

The twelfth-century Welsh chronicler, Giraldus Cambrensis, in his account of his journey through Ireland, talks of a bizarre kingship ceremony he witnessed in Donegal:

> *Once all the people had been assembled together, a white mare was led into the middle of the crowd. Then, in full view of everybody, this person of highest rank [the king] approached the mare bestially, not like a prince but like a wild beast, not like a king but like an outlaw, and behaved just like an animal, without shame or prudence.*

Immediately afterwards the mare was killed, carved up into pieces and thrown in boiling water.[19]

The king then bathed in a cauldron of its broth. 'Once this ritual had been performed, his rule and authority were assured.' This could be taken as a traveller's tale were it not for the fact that other examples occurred around the Indo-European world. In Rome at the October horse feast, or Equus, horses were dismembered,[20] and, more strikingly, in India, in order to renew her husband's power, the queen performed in a rite known as Asva Medha – literally, 'horse-drunk'. A stallion was chosen and tethered to a post, symbolic of the centre of the cosmos. It was then driven into a stream, while a dog was clubbed to death and placed in the water so that it floated downstream beneath the horse to the land of the dead. After this the spotless stallion was let loose for a year. The lands it entered became the territory of the stallion's counterpart, the king.[21] On the horse's return the king's wives anointed it, and decked it with garlands. The priest then suffocated it. The chief queen lay beside the dead horse and simulated intercourse with it. The horse, whose body was associated with the creation of the cosmos, was then dismembered and the king drank the broth of its flesh and was purified.

Might such a rite have once been practised in the windy Vale of the White Horse, whose skeletal body, like the bones of a giant monster littering the hill, was perhaps once thought to be the foundation of those very hills, his blood forming the rivers and his hair becoming trees, bushes and grass.

But the original sacrifice was neither a bull nor a horse, but a man – and in later times it would be so again. For instance, according to Tacitus, the Iron Age Germanic Semnones tribe met together at an appointed time in a sacred grove to perform 'the sacrificial dismemberment of a man for the public good'.[22] This act Alby Stone regards as 'a dramatised repetition of the cosmic dismemberment'.[23]

Tacitus, in his *Germania*, provides evidence that it was the same 'Twin' and 'Man' who the Germans regarded as their ancestors. He records that in traditional songs the people claim descent from the three sons of Mannus son of Tuisto.[24] Here is a variant, with Mannus becoming the son, not the twin, of Tuisto ('twisted, dual, entwined – twin'), just as in Greek myth Zeus is Cronos's son, not his brother, but the meaning remains the same.

Given the similarities between the German and Celtic bog finds, I was left in no doubt that a similar rite of dismemberment or triple wounding in Celtic lands was also a re-enactment of the cosmic sacrifice of 'Dis Pater', the god Caesar claimed was the ancestor of the Gauls – the serpent twin, the universal *daemon* of the Mysteries.

I could now say with some surety that the old man with the arrow in his throat at West Kennet (a man affected with spina bifida, with a supernumerary toe – surely a lame king!), the man riddled with arrows at Stonehenge and the missing skeleton of the man from the central axis of this site, were all unfortunate 'aboriginals' chosen to play the role of the defeated native god 'twin' or 'serpent'. Their world-creating sacrifice would form a new cosmos ruled by the sun kings, in which the old order was usurped. Its holy sacrament – the drink of vision – would be abused so as to give these newcomers an even greater sense of victorious ego.

And they were not alone. Near the base of 'Adam', one of the pair of remaining stones in the Beckhampton avenue that leads westwards from the Avebury henge, was found a skeleton (a foundation sacrifice, perhaps), and in the Sanctuary an adolescent, and still more bodies within the circles themselves and along the West Kennet avenue. Before the coming of the Beakers no burials took place at Avebury, so perhaps these bodies, like the man from West Kennet and the two from Stonehenge, are evidence for the usurpation of 'Twin' by 'Man'. But how could I be sure that these unfortunates were playing the role of *Yemo, that such a battle between Twin and Man had taken place in the henges of prehistoric Wessex? I knew, in fact, because *the very sites were named after them.*

Notes

1. Campbell, J (1964) p. 80.
2. Jaynes, J (1993) pp. 205–22.
3. His theories offer a fascinating view on this subject – perhaps revealing that this 'battle of the two brains' has been going on since the earliest times. Indeed, his ideas complement those expressed here, revealing that the conflict that occurred between the Neolithic populations and the bronze age Arya was but a repetition of a conflict dating back tens of thousands of years between two opposing parts of the brain. See Gooch, S (1975) and (1995).
4. Jaynes, J (1993) pp. 205–22.
5. Campbell, J (1962) p. 181.
6. Campbell, J (1962) pp. 178–9.
7. Campbell, J (1962) p.181.
8. Doniger O'Flaherty, W (trans.) (1981) p. 135.
9. Jung, C G (1986) p. 329.
10. Eliade, M (1995) p. 40.
11. Glob, P V (1988) p. 157 and Glob, P V (1983) p. 164.
12. Lincoln, B (1991) p. 7.
13. Grimnismal 40–1, quoted in Stone, A (1997) p. 91.
14. Kinsella, T (1990) p. 252.
15. Quoted in Stone, A (1997) p. 127.
16. Stone, A (1997) p. 115.
17. Cumont, F (1903) pp. 136–7.
18. Matthews, C (1987) pp. 31–3.
19. Giraldus Cambrensis (trans. O'Meara) (1951) p. 93.
20. Mallory, J P (1991) p. 136.
21. Campbell, J (1962) pp. 190–7.
22. Stone, A (1997) p. 112.
23. Stone, A (1997) p. 112.
24. Stone, A (1997) p. 113.

Chapter 17

DINAS EMRYS

In the Welsh language the sound 'm' is often mutated to 'v', so the names *Ave*bury and *Ames*bury (the nearest settlement to Stonehenge, but arguably the name originally given to the monument) are clearly related. The only person, so far as I know, to have commented on this is Count Nikolai Tolstoy, who argues that instead of being named, as popularly thought, after the historical Dark Age warlord Ambrosius Aurelianus, the sites were named after a Celtic figure named Emrys – a name that may have stemmed from a word meaning 'divine' or 'immortal', from the same Indo-European source as the Latin *ambrosia*.[1]

It is not difficult, however, to take the next step and see 'Ave'/'Ame' as connected to the Indo-European *Yemo ('twin'), which in Irish becomes 'Emhain' (pronounced 'Em-in' or 'Ev-in'). If the initial 'Y' had been dropped in the Irish and the 'm' could mutate to a 'v', an original Yemobury or Yemo'sbury[2] could easily in time become both Emo'sbury and Evobury – both pronounced like the modern placenames. If these literary games were correct it seems possible that the defeat of 'Twin' has been remembered at these places for 4,000 years.

But it is not only the name that has been remembered. If the great religious war of prehistoric Wessex had been preserved in legend then I would expect to see evidence of a victory by the incoming Arya over the native population, perhaps linked with the taking of the bluestones from another site and their incorporation at Stonehenge – or, in the case of Avebury, a myth to account for the presence of foundation sacrifices to cement the foundations of the avenue and sanctuary. And I was not disappointed.

Geoffrey of Monmouth, in his *History of the Kings of Britain*, tells the story of the early sixth-century British ruler Vortigern, who invites the Saxons under their leaders Hengist and Horsa ('Stallion' and 'Horse')[3] to come to Britain and help him defend his throne. Vortigern[4] falls in love with the daughter of Hengist. As part of the marriage deal he allows the Saxons to occupy land in Kent, but, treacherously, they bring many men to invade the land. Vortigern hosts a meeting between Britons and Saxons at 'Mons Ambrius', close to 'the Cloister of Ambrius' on Salisbury Plain, to negotiate a truce, but the Saxons conceal knives in their boots and, on a given signal, massacre the Britons.

Later in the tale, after establishing himself as the new British king, Ambrosius Aurelianus wishes to construct a monument fit for the Britons slaughtered at Mons Ambrius. He asks Merlin for advice, and the wizard tells him to bring the fabled 'Giant's Dance' from the mountain of Killaraus in Ireland.[5]

Ambrosius Aurelianus sends his brother Uther Pendragon with 15,000 men to Ireland, where they win a battle over the stones, which are then dismantled and transported to Salisbury Plain by Merlin. The stones are re-erected around the grave of the slain Britons in the same formation as they had lain at Killaurus.[6] This monument is, of course, Stonehenge.

The fate of Vortigern provides a clue to the Avebury deaths: having fled to Mount Erith (Snowdonia, North Wales), Vortigern attempts to construct a fort that might protect him from Saxon threat. But the building will not stand. Vortigern's magicians advise him to:

> *look for a lad without a father, and that, when he had found one, he should kill him, so that the mortar and the stones could be sprinkled with the lad's blood. According to them the result of this would be that the foundations would hold firm.*[7]

Vortigern's scouts manage to find a boy whose mother was visited, it was said, by the Prince of Darkness. The lad is Merlin, also called Merlin *Ambrosius* or Emrys. Merlin Emrys, however, persuades Vortigern that his magicians are wrong, and orders a pool beneath the foundations of Mount Erith to be drained, stating that at its bottom are two hollow stones containing two dragons – a white and a red one. When the pool is drained the dragons fight; first the white has the upper hand, but eventually the red proves victorious.[8]

Merlin Emrys interprets this strange vision to Vortigern propheti-cally as the defeat of the Britons (the red dragon) by the Saxons (the white dragon), and the eventual recovery of the Britons under the exiled sons of Constantine – Ambrosius Aurelianus and Uther Pendragon. The fort is thereafter known as Dinas Emrys – 'The Fort of Ambrosius'. The next day Merlin's prophecy is proved correct. The sons of Constantine return and rally the Britons. Vortigern is eventually found and burned to death in his tower.

After reading Bruce Lincoln on the subject, I couldn't help but read between the lines and see this whole drama as nothing less than a memory of the war between Twin and Man, with the Britons playing the role of the defeated aboriginals and the Saxons that of the Arya (with their totemic horse). Vortigern, the British leader, who falls for the Saxon princess and thus invites the Saxons in, is the equivalent of Tarpeia inviting the Gauls into Rome, or Blathnat betraying her husband and allowing Cú Chulainn to enter Cú Roí's spinning fort. Interpreted in this light, the mention of the building of Stonehenge as a memorial is indeed highly suggestive of the refashioning of Stonehenge by the Beaker Folk, who possibly seized the Preseli bluestones from the mountains of Wales and incorporated them into the monument, which Pitts calls a 'symbolic tomb'. And this is also the conclusion reached by Tolstoy, who sees in Geoffrey's tale of Stonehenge the fragment of a native Bronze Age literature.[9]

Tolstoy argues, too, that the building of the Giant's Dance at Amesbury and the building of Vortigern's tower at Dinas Emrys are two versions of the *same incident*.[10] Dinas Emrys means the 'Fort of Ambrosius' in Welsh, just as Amesbury means the 'Fort of Ambrosius' in English. Tolstoy is thus arguing that the legend associated with Dinas Emrys was originally set not in the North Wales fort of the same name, as had been assumed, but at either Stonehenge or Avebury, for as Lewis Thorpe, in his translation of Geoffrey's *History*, states:

By Mount Ambrius ... Geoffrey may be thinking of Avebury and muddling it with Amesbury. Geoffrey repeatedly treats Stonehenge and Avebury/Amesbury as if they were one place.[11,12]

I thought of the individuals set beneath the stones, no doubt as 'foundation sacrifices', and I realised that they were playing the role of Emrys in the tale. What's more, Merlin Emrys's vision of the fighting dragons is highly reminiscent of a sketch made by the eighteenth-century antiquarian William Stukeley of Avebury. This shows a giant serpent – with the two avenues snaking from the main circle, and with the 'head' of the dragon at the sanctuary, near Hackpen Hill (hac-pen being Welsh for 'serpent's head'). Stukeley's serpent temple has been much ridiculed, especially given the imaginative nature of his reconstruction,[13] but for how long, I wondered, had that hill born its strange Celtic name? Might Geoffrey have seized on a local tradition?[14] And as the myth says, the youth sacrificed at this megalithic circle associated with the serpent was to be killed and placed under the stones as a foundation sacrifice – which is precisely what exists archaeologically.

Though the temple was no doubt the production of Stukeley's over-active imagination, the Avebury complex, seen from the air, seems remarkably similar to the scene portrayed in the Churning of the Milky Ocean myth, which tells of the battle between the gods and demons over soma – ambrosia. If the River Kennet were the Milky Ocean, and Silbury Hill with its spiral pathway, the spinning Mount Mandara, then the serpentine Avebury would be Vasuki, who spins around Mandara, the pole, to churn up the sea into butter and soma. Of course, Avebury had never 'spun around' Silbury (though it would have appeared to do so by the celebrant spiralling up the path on Silbury Hill), but from the south of the site at the time of its construction, if one had looked up at the pole the constellation of Draco (the serpent) would have been seen to spin around it, for in 2600 BC the pole lay not at Polaris, but within the coils of Draco, while the Milky Way lay close by. Perhaps it was this stellar dragon that Merlin Emrys had seen at Dinas Emrys – and then I remembered that according to Geoffrey he had seen a fiery dragon in the sky that appeared from out of a bright star after the death of Ambrosius Aurelianus. All perhaps, a coincidence, but adding to the mystery that surrounds these ancient sites.[15]

PLATES

Plate 1. *The mysterious medieval legend of the Holy Grail tells of the grievous wounding of the Fisher King that blasts the fertility of the land. Do the ultimate roots of this legend lie in the sacrificial rites of the pagan Celts? (© John Grigsby, adapted from medieval illuminated manuscript)*

Plate 2. *The existence of a sacrificial tradition amongst the Celts is evidenced by the discovery of many Iron Age victims preserved in peat bogs throughout north-west Europe. This man was found at Lindow Moss in Cheshire. (© The British Museum)*

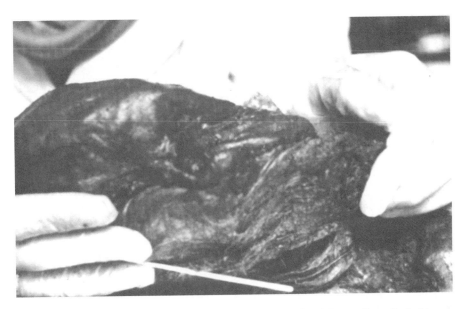

Plate 3. *The killing of Lindow Man (who was garrotted, stabbed and drowned) recalls the bizarre rituals of folklore and Celtic myth. Such a death was normally reserved for heroes or gods. (© The British Museum)*

Plate 4. *Celtic myth reveals that the bog victims were playing the role of a deity associated with magic and the underworld – a 'lord of the animals' or divine shaman. Such a figure is probably depicted here, accompanied by a stag, serpent and wolf, on the Gundestrup Cauldron, found in a sacrificial bog in Denmark. (© National Museum of Denmark, Copenhagen)*

Plate 5. *The Indian reflex of this deity, known as Shiva-Pasupati, is seen here on a seal from the Indus Valley culture. This god – who possessed a magical drink called soma that granted immortality – was, like the Fisher King, emasculated in an act that blasted the cosmos. (© John Grigsby)*

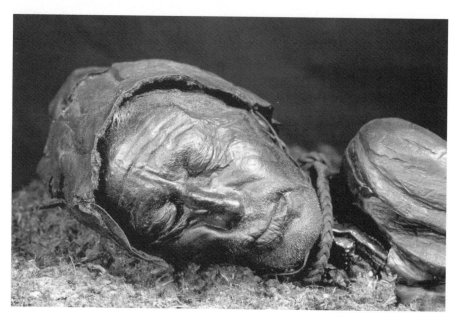

Plate 6. *Analysis of the stomach contents of the sacrificed Tollund Man (above) revealed that he had ingested large quantities of ergot, a hallucinogenic fungus, prior to his sacrificial death, strengthening the likelihood that he was a shaman. (© Silkeborg Museum)*

Plate 7. *Welsh myth tells of a hero named Bran who received a fatal wound to the thigh and possessed a cauldron of rebirth that could bring the dead back to life (as echoed in this scene from the Gundestrup Cauldron). Is Bran the ancestor of the Fisher King or do his origins lie even further back in time? (© National Museum of Denmark, Copenhagen)*

Plate 8. *The Neolithic peoples of Britain, who worshipped a magical, underground deity, buried their dismembered dead in great communal tombs such as Wayland's Smithy, Berkshire, above, perhaps in the hope that, like their god, their departed would be reborn from the earth. (© Rob Speight – Ancient Sites Ltd)*

Plate 9. *It is probable that the wounded god of the Celts originated from an earlier Neolithic fertility deity (typified by the Egyptian Osiris, above) and was brought to Britain with the introduction of farming from the Near East. This husband of the great goddess was associated with the bull, the serpent and the moon. He underwent a yearly death, dismemberment and rebirth, mirroring the life of the crops. (© John Grigsby, adapted from the Papyrus of Ani)*

Plate 10. *In Irish myth the Neolithic passage grave at Newgrange (above) was said to be the dwelling of a cauldron-owning deity named the Dagda, thus providing a link between the god of the Neolithic farmers and that of the Celts. (© Martin Byrne – www.carrowkeel.com)*

Plate 11. *Within the chambers of Newgrange (above) and nearby Knowth, archaeologists discovered large stone basins. Were such objects remembered in Celtic myth as the magical cauldrons of rebirth that could revive the dead? (© Martin Byrne – www.carrowkeel.com)*

Plate 12. *The 'cauldron' at Knowth. Such cauldrons were perhaps symbolic of the revivifying womb of the earth goddess, and it is possible that the bones of the dead were placed within them in hope of rebirth. (© Martin Byrne – www.carrowkeel.com)*

Plate 13. *On the morning of the winter solstice the fertilising rays of the rising sun penetrate the internal chambers of Newgrange through a specially constructed 'lightbox' above the doorway. It is possible that the dead were thought to be reborn at this magical time, when heaven met earth, though there is evidence to suggest that such rebirth rites were not limited to the departed. (© Martin Byrne – www.carrowkeel.com)*

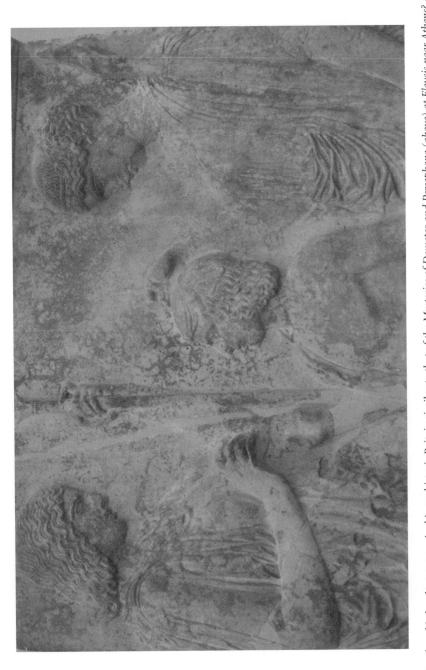

Plate 14. *Was the rebirth cult once practised in prehistoric Britain similar to that of the Mysteries of Demeter and Persephone (above) at Eleusis near Athens? At the centre of the Mysteries, a cult based on the Near Eastern model, was the ritual ingestion of ergot, which granted the initiate a sense of immortality. (© Paul Grigsby)*

Plate 15. *Traces of a hallucinogenic drink from within distinctive Neolithic 'grooved ware' pottery vessels (a shard of which is depicted above) suggest that the Neolithic Britons included the use of mind-altering substances in their rituals. (© John Grigsby)*

Plate 16. *The use of 'grooved ware' pottery spread south from its place of origin in the Orkneys, accompanied by a new tradition of monumental building – that of the henge. Such sites appear to be oriented to celestial events. At Callanish (above), for example, once every 18.6 years the moon was seen to rise from a nearby hill known as the 'sleeping beauty'. It then disappeared and reappeared within the circle, thus aping the death and rebirth of the lunar god. (© Rob Speight – Ancient Sites Ltd)*

Plate 17. *It is possible that in Neolithic Britain rebirth rites were accompanied by the sacrifice of an individual playing the role of the dying god, a practice carried out in other agrarian societies. In ancient Egypt, for instance, it is believed that the pharaoh was once beheaded in the Sed ritual at Saqqara (above). (© Rob Speight – Ancient Sites Ltd)*

Plate 18. *Silbury Hill, the largest man-made mound in prehistoric Europe, seems to share a common ancestry, both symbolic and architectural, with the 'sacred hills' – the pyramids and ziggurats – of the Near East. (© Rob Speight – Ancient Sites Ltd)*

Plate 19. *Indo-European myth tells of the battle between the old god (the lunar/serpent) and the new solar warrior god (typified by the Greek Zeus, above), who casts the former into the underworld. Is this myth the true origin of the 'dolorous stroke' of the Grail legends? (© John Grigsby)*

Plate 20. *Legend states that the conical hill on the slopes below the ancient white horse at Uffington was where St George slew the dragon; but the origin of this myth lies in a great conflict in prehistory between the older 'communal' religion and a new individualistic faith adopted from the continent at the end of the Neolithic. (© Rob Speight – Ancient Sites Ltd)*

Plate 21. *The dragon-slaying motif reflects a great change in the mindset of prehistoric man, evidenced in the move away from communal society and burial traditions towards the adoption of a warrior aristocracy and single burials, often accompanied by metalwork and weapons, and so-called Beaker pottery, above. (© Dover Museum)*

Plate 22. *With the advent of social change the old communal tombs were sealed forever, and the great stone circles (such as Avebury, above) became the burial grounds for the 'beaker' users. Does the name of this site preserve a memory of the great religious conflict that took place here 4000 years ago? (© Rob Speight – Ancient Sites Ltd)*

Plate 23. *Stonehenge, aligned on the midsummer sunrise, became the focal point for the new religion. But before long it fell out of use as the heaven-gazing religion was replaced by rites focusing on water and the underworld. Was the latter cult an attempt to re-establish contact with the old deity with his cauldron of immortality, cast into the underworld by the solar victor of the Indo-Europeans? (© Peter Chow)*

Plate 24. *Welsh myth links the quest for the cauldron with the release of a prisoner from the underworld. This prisoner – in one myth named Mabon, the divine son, who escapes from his prison on the back of a salmon – can be explicitly linked to both the god of the Neolithic and the Fisher King of the Grail legends. (© National Museum of Denmark, Copenhagen)*

Plate 25. *In the Grail legends the asking of a specific question is instrumental in the healing of the Wasteland. Did oracular rites, like those performed by the priestess of Apollo at Delphi (above), once accompany the sacrificial death of the bog men? (© Paul Grigsby)*

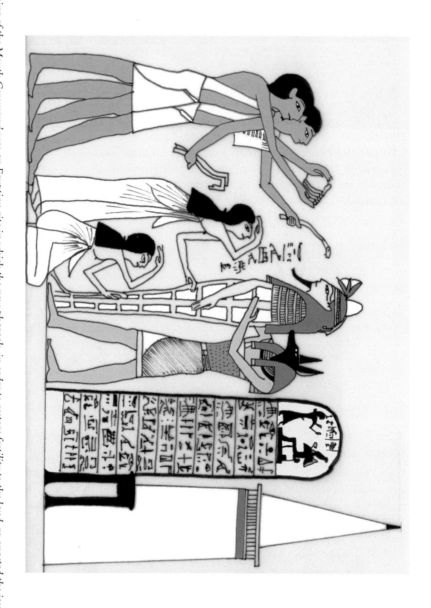

Plate 26. *The 'Opening of the Mouth Ceremony' was an Egyptian rite in which the new pharaoh, in order to restore fertility to the land, re-enacted the journey of Horus to the nether world to heal the emasculated god, Osiris. Was the Grail quest a remembrance of an equivalent rite performed in Celtic Britain involving the sacrificed bog men, a rite that was thought to heal the Wasteland by re-establishing contact with the slain underworld god? (© John Grigsby, adapted from the Papyrus of Ani)*

The work of Bruce Lincoln finally allowed me to piece together some of the more obscure elements of the Grail traditions. The 'brother battle' that had given me such problems in the early days of my quest had now been revealed as an Indo-European reforging of the motif for the death and rebirth of the vegetal lunar god of Neolithic times – a reforging based on a psychological change, but one which finally explains the roots of the triple death motif.

Looking back on what I had learned about the Wounded King from my brief foray into the myths and rites of the Neolithic and Bronze Age, I jotted down what I now knew of his origins:

1   He was ultimately derived from a Neolithic god, possessing a cup containing a sacred narcotic, who as the ever-living and dying son and lover of the mother was periodically slain or castrated and reborn.

2   His brother Beli ('Bright/light'), who caused the dolorous blow, was the solar 'Man' of Indo-European myth, killing his brother 'Twin' in a re-forging of the castration motif.

3   The name of this 'Twin', *Yemo, was remembered in the name of both Avebury and Amesbury, where it fitted in with the archaeological evidence for a conflict of religion at these, and other sites.

4   The triple death had its origin in the severing of the three heads of Nghi ('Serpent'), the old Neolithic lunar serpent whose body formed the three classes of Indo-European society.

5   This was also an act of creation, forming the cosmos.

6   It was also portrayed as an act that 'released the waters' after drought, tying it in with the legends of the Celtic saints in which their decapitation causes holy waters to appear.

7   From its roots in the motif of the boar wound inflicted on the vegetal king, the wounding of the god became a symbol for a change in psychology, a battle between the emerging ego and the more mystical communal side of the personality. On a mystical level the new individualism meant an affirmation of the *eidolon* and a neglect of the universal *daemon* within.

My discoveries may have brought me nearer to understanding the motifs that had surrounded the killing of the bog men, but as far as the Grail legends were concerned the wounding of the king was just the prologue to the quest for the vessel itself. I had to the best of my knowledge uncovered the origin of the dolorous stroke, but the whole *raison d'être* of the Grail myth was an attempt to *heal* this wounded king, to undo the enchantment that his wounding had caused – something that was anathema to the Arya myth and more in keeping with the earlier Neolithic form of the myth in which the death of the god was mourned.

It was slowly dawning on me that by the time the legends of the Grail were written a reversal of sympathy had taken place – as fundamental as the change from Neolithic to Indo-European had been a millennium earlier – and that although they were rooted in the Indo-European tradition, they reflected a state of mind more on a par with the mystery traditions of the ancient world.

It was time to return to the Iron Age Celts.

Notes

1. Tolstoy, N (1988) p. 140.
2. The 'bury', of course, being a Saxon translation of the Celtic *dun* or *dinas*, meaning 'fort' or 'settlement'.
3. 'Stallion' and 'Horse', perhaps totemic ancestor deities, not historical personages.
4. Whose name is in fact a title, meaning 'Great Ruler'.
5. Geoffrey of Monmouth (trans. Thorpe, L) (1986) p. 196.
6. Geoffrey of Monmouth (trans. Thorpe, L) (1986) p. 198.
7. Geoffrey of Monmouth (trans. Thorpe, L) (1986) p. 167.
8. Geoffrey of Monmouth (trans. Thorpe, L) (1986) p. 169.
9. Tolstoy, N (1985) p. 137.
10. Tolstoy, N (1985) p. 134.
11. Lewis's footnotes to Geoffrey of Monmouth, p. 195.
12. Tolstoy's arguments are convincing: he recounts that Killaraus – where the Giant's Dance came from – is actually the site of Uisnecht, and that there is a 'collapsing castle' tale surrounding the megalithic stones found there. Cursed by Saint Patrick, no structure could be built upon the stones without toppling to destruction. 'This,' he states 'is a common folktale motif attempting to explain the dilapidated state of *megalithic monuments*.' (Tolstoy, N (1985) p. 134.) The appearance of it at Dinas Emrys indicates that the real location of the events is a megalithic stone circle.
13. Malone, C (1989) p. 90.
14. Having seen how such omphalloi typify the pole, is it a coincidence that the pole at the time of the building of Avebury was not Polaris in Ursa Minor, as it is today, but, due to a phenomenon known as precession (a slight wobble in the earth's axis) lay in the heart of the coils of Draco, the serpent?
15. Geoffrey of Monmouth (trans. Thorpe, L) (1986) pp. 200–1.

Chapter 18

SECRET RITES

My discovery of the Indo-European background to the motifs of the Grail legends had followed closely after my return from a trip to Egypt in the November of 1998. Until this time the whole 'brother-battle' question had been a stumbling block in my quest. In Egypt my mind had been brought back to it repeatedly in the form of the figure of Osiris, the god slain and dismembered by his fiery brother Seth. It was easy, in that wonderful land, under the intense blaze of the sun, to see how Seth, the god of the dry desert, had been seen as the enemy of the lush vegetal Osiris. But unlike the Aryan reflex of this myth, Seth's act was seen as ultimately destructive – Seth, the blasting heat of the day, who could therefore be linked to the solar gods of the Arya, was the embodiment of chaos, and it was his brother, the god of the underworld, the *Yemo of the Egyptian pantheon, who was the more honoured and respected deity.

What had most impressed me on my travels was the stepped pyramid of Djoser and the Heb Sed court at its feet, for in the rites that had once been performed there I could recognise many motifs from the material I had been researching over the previous few years concerning the death of kings and the severed head. On the edge of the desert in Saqqara, my thoughts were hundreds of miles away, with the bog men of north-west Europe.

Within a few months of my return home, however, my mind was once again preoccupied with the world of the Beaker Folk and the rise of the individual in prehistoric society, and my Egyptian vacation was pushed to the back of my mind. But in the spring of 1999 – while vainly attempting to put my theories into some kind of order – my thoughts returned again and again to the Heb Sed court, as if there were something of importance there to my quest which I had failed to see.

The Heb Sed, as I had discovered, had been a mummery based on the death and rebirth of the god in which he symbolically lost his head and his kingship was renewed – an act that would confer on him the title King of Two Lands. It was a rite that I had seen as akin to the rebirth rites of Eleusis, in which it was intended that the pharaoh, through a rebirth experience, would become aware of both the upper- and underworld aspects of his nature; or at least he would symbolise these aspects for the people, whether he actually underwent any psychologically transforming experience or not.

When I eventually dragged my thoughts back to beakers and dragon slayings I realised why it was the Heb Sed had continued to bother me: it seemed to possess an uncanny similarity to some of the Irish tales I had read that talked of the death of kings. And in investigating this at first tenuous link, I came to a stunning conclusion concerning the nature of Iron Age Celtic religion – that it had seen a readoption of many of the tenets of the earlier religion of the dying and living lunar bull of the Neolithic.

The most memorable example of the ritual death of a king in Celtic myth was that of the Irish Conaire Mor. Conaire, the legend states, is chosen as king in a ceremony known as Tarbh-feis ('the bull-feast'), a divinatory rite in which a bull is killed and a druid drinks of its broth and dons its hide.[1] Four other druids chant over him, so that he may see a vision. In this particular tale the visionary dreams that the next king is to be found walking naked along the road to Tara, and this turns out to be Conaire Mor, son of Mess Buachala ('the cowherd's fosterling'). The druids foresee that his reign will be distinguished, yet, according to custom, impose a series of *gessa* (magical restrictions – a kind of taboo) on him. Conaire is fated to die on the day that they are broken.[2] His death is told in the epic 'Destruction of Da Derga's [the Red God's] Hostel', which begins with the king settling a quarrel between two of his servants, thus breaking one of his *gessa*. Once the quarrel is settled he heads back to his capital at Tara, but rides 'rightwise' around its bounds, breaking yet another taboo (in fact, by the end of the day he has broken them all).

Fear overcomes Conaire so he seeks shelter at Da Derga's hostel, asking his companion Mac Cecht if he knows of it. He does – it has seven doors and seven apartments between each door – and the very road that they are travelling on goes through the midst of it.³ A strange hostel indeed! On the way there three red horsemen precede the king (another one of his taboos), and despite his best efforts he cannot bribe them to stop. These are men from the *sídhe* – from the house of Donn, i.e. the land of the dead:

> *Behold, lad, great tidings! Weary the horses we ride. We ride the horses of Dond Tetscorach of the Side. Although we are alive, we are dead. Great omens! Cutting off of lives, satisfaction of crows, sustenance of ravens, din of slaughter, whetting of blades, shields with broken bosses after sunset. Behold!*⁴

The chilling quality of their words sums up the feeling of the entire oeuvre.

Once everyone is seated in the hall, the Bachlach Fer Caille and his ugly wife (the red-haired lake dwellers) arrive with a squealing pig, and then the Mórrígan appears, seeking shelter. She is a lone woman entering the hostel after dark – an occurrence that breaks yet another of Conaire's *gessa* – but his sense of hospitality overrides his common sense, and she is allowed within.

The hall is then attacked by a group of plunderers headed by the one-eyed Ingcel and a man named Fer Roigan. There is great slaughter, and the hall is set alight and extinguished three times.⁵ The attackers' druids magically cause Conaire to thirst, and so the king asks Mac Cecht to fetch him water. Mac Cecht suggests that he asks a servant, for he is not prepared to leave the king's side. The servants, however, can find no water because it has all been used to extinguish the fire, so Mac Cecht is forced to leave the king to search for it.

The rivers of Ireland dry up before him, and he travels the entirety of the land until finally one stream allows him to take water. But on returning to Da Derga's hostel he finds Conaire being beheaded; Mac Cecht pours the water into the mouth of the severed head – and the head thanks him:

> *A good man Mac Cecht!*
> *Welcome, Mac Cecht!*
> *He brings drink to a King.*
> *He does well.*⁶

Mac Cecht returns to the rout, but can feel a slight pain, so he asks a passing woman if it is an ant that has bitten him. She says yes, an ant of the ancient earth (i.e. a wolf), and with those words Mac Cecht dies.[7]

On the surface the tale is simply the record of the death of a king within a hostel – but there are clear hints that this was a ritual death, similar to the beheading of the pharaoh in the original, literally enacted, version of the Heb Sed.

I knew from many Irish legends that the death of a king usually took place within such a feasting hall rather than on the battlefield. Da Derga's hostel in the tale of Conaire seems to have been a bizarre building consisting of a number of doorways and a road going through its middle – not a warm place to stay the night! However, archaeologist Rob Loveday has stated that the double-entrances of henge monuments reveal that sacred paths or trading routes might once have gone right through them.[8] Was the 'feasting hall' a henge, or at least the later Iron Age equivalent? This would, after all, explain the seven doors, if these 'doors' were, in fact the gaps between stones or posts – for did not the Stonehenge trilithons form doorways? Looking at other 'feasting halls' it is clear that they, too, were not simple alehouses; for example, the hall of Bricriu, in which Cú Chulainn played 'the beheading game', was built in the likeness of the 'red branch' hall at Emhain Macha, with nine apartments between the hearth and the wall. Round the central apartment were *12* others, one for each of the *12* chief Ulster warriors. It took *7* strong men to erect the pillars of the hall, and 30 seers to advise on the plan.[9]

Evidently this site incorporated numerical symbolism relating to the months, weeks and days – it had a calendrical function. The feasting hall built for Bran in the second branch of the *Mabinogion* was also a 'special' type of hall; Bran, it was said, could not be contained in a 'normal house' because he was a giant. Might this special construction have been open to the sky – in short, was it an outdoor sacred grove or ritual enclosure rather than a beer hall? The idea must have some merit, but why had such buildings not been recorded as ritual structures? The answer is simple: if the early medieval scribes who first recorded the Irish myths had no knowledge of such sacred enclosures (these having been destroyed with the advent of Christianity), they could easily have assumed – given the references to doorways, pillars, central hearths and sacred feasts in the tales –

that they were the equivalent of the contemporary hostel. The clinching piece of evidence is archaeological: in most cases where a feasting hall has been mentioned in the tales, subsequent excavation of the relevant site has revealed no such building, but an Iron Age ritual enclosure.

At the site of Emhain Macha, for example, where the mead hall of Conchobar mac Nessa and his Ulster heroes was supposedly situated, excavation revealed no feasting hall but a circular structure 140 feet/43 metres in diameter, formed within a ditch inside a bank and built in around 100 BC.[10] This familiar arrangement of bank and ditch proves that the site was not used for defensive purposes, but was a religious site. Within its boundaries were concentric rings of timbers, the outer ring linked by planks reminiscent of the lintelled sarsen stones at Stonehenge.

Also, KnockAulin, or Dun Ailinne, the royal site of Leinster in the tales, does not appear to be a defensive fortress or feasting hall, for it too is set out with its ditch inside its bank. There is evidence that there had been occupation on this site since Neolithic times. This magnificent site had a 70-foot/22-metre-diameter palisade – again, consisting of upright posts. Three concentric rings of posts were built some time after 250 BC, then two further rings were added at a later date. This was no feasting hall – for in all probability it was never roofed.

What's more, both Emhain Macha and Dun Ailinne were *ceremonially burned* then placed under a huge ceremonial mound. These conflagrations were neither accidental nor the result of war, but systematic and orderly.[11] There was little doubt in my mind that the motif of the burning of the feasting hall that accompanied the death of the king in the Irish tales was based on actual occurrences.

These sites were not feasting halls or chieftains' houses but great ritual buildings highly suggestive of the Neolithic and Bronze Age henges that had been seen as the centre of the cosmos – and the killing fields of the murdered twin. The problem with linking the two classes of site is the fact that the building of henges ceased around 1,500 years before the Iron Age ritual enclosures were built. The possible connection between the sites, then, seems to indicate that the Celts for some reason readopted the use of hengiform ritual used by their Neolithic forefathers.[12]

These Iron Age henges, symbolic of cosmos, were to my mind highly suggestive of the Heb Sed court, whose four sides represented the limits of

Egypt. It was possible that Conaire, by going the wrong way around Tara, had been 'unmaking' the bounds of the cosmos, just as the pharaoh, when he emerged reborn, re-established them by firing an arrow into each wall of the Heb Sed enclosure and walking its perimeter. The breaking of Conaire's *gessa*, I surmised, had been a ritual act to dissolve order and return the land to chaos – a necessary step before rebirth could take place. In Irish myth the death of the king occurred at Samhain, a date seen as the crack between summer and winter, a time of in-between-ness when the dead walked with the living and chaos reigned. It also seems possible to link the dry desert heat of Seth that caused Osiris's death to the magical thirst placed on Conaire by his attackers' druids and dried up the very rivers of the land – clearly a Wasteland motif. When finally Conaire does receive water, it is as a severed head, a head that is able to talk. Perhaps the 'secret rites' performed over the head of the dead pharaoh had been connected to the talking of the head. For now this was just speculation, but later I would have to look seriously at this question.

The burning of the hall, associated with triple deaths, is a common theme in Irish myth. King Diarmuid son of Fergus is stabbed with a spear at the doorway of the house of Banban the hospitaller, which is surrounded by enemy troops and then set alight. The king subsequently hides in a vat of ale, but the burning central pillar of the house crashes down on his head.[13] One Muirchertach dies a similar death: trapped within a house, surrounded by his opponents (the sons of the one-eyed Cormac), he hides in a vat of wine to escape the fire, but the house falls on him and he is either burned to death or drowned. Diarmuid's death follows an invitation into the bed of the host's daughter; and Muirchertach's demise coincides with the meeting of an other-worldly woman when he is seated on his hunting-mound.[14] It is obvious that these women were to play the role of Kali/Mórrígan in the death of the kings.

The appearance of a one-eyed attacker in both the tale of Muirchertach and Conaire is an unmistakable link to the deaths of St Alban (slain by the executioner whose eyes fell out) and Balder (slain by the *blind* Hodr). Like the lunar god of the Neolithic, Balder was sent into the underworld, after the fiery Loki had tricked Hodr into killing him. His wife Nanna (once Inanna?), in grief, throws herself on the funeral pyre (an act suggestive of the rite of suttee), from where it was said they would emerge after the fiery battle of Ragnarok at the end of time – when the hall of Valhalla would be *burned to the ground* – to rule the new world.

Mention in this myth of Ragnarok – the final battle of the Germanic gods in which the entire cosmos is destroyed by fire[15] – is interesting. The burning of the halls in Celtic myth hints at a lost Celtic Ragnarok-type myth that has not been passed down in the surviving literature.

At this point in my quest I was too engrossed in the thought of a Celtic Ragnarok to notice that in the Germanic myth of Balder the slaying of the god by the blind Hodr at the instigation of the *fiery* Loki was seen as a heinous crime. Instead of celebrating the victory of the solar god over the old Tammuz-like deity and his Inanna, the myth relates how Balder's death causes a Wasteland. The gods decree that he can be brought back to life if every creature mourns for him. All do save one, a giantess named Thokk, who is Loki in disguise. So Balder is left to languish in Hel until after the twilight of the gods – Götterdammerung – when he will rule the three worlds. Earlier in my quest I had linked Balder to the Wounded King, slain by his fiery brother, and whose death from a spear wound blights the land, just as the death of Conaire at the hands of the druids of the one-eyed Ingcel seems to be linked with the drying up of the rivers.

But for the moment my mind was on the burning halls ...

Notes

1. Matthews, J and C (1996) pp. 242–3.
2. Gantz, J (trans.) (1986) pp. 66–7.
3. Gantz, J (trans.) (1986) p. 69.
4. Gantz, J (trans.) (1986) p. 71.
5. Gantz, J (trans.) (1986) p. 103.
6. Gantz, J (trans.) (1986) pp. 104–5.
7. Gantz, J (trans.) (1986) p. 105.
8. Gibson and Simpson (eds.) (1998) p. 31.
9. Gantz, J (trans.) (1986) p. 221.
10. Harbison, P (1989) pp. 156–8.
11. Harbison, P (1989) p. 157.
12. The Roman writer Strabo, talking of a Gallic ceremony held on an island at the mouth of the Loire, is able to shed a little light on the destruction of temples and its link to sacrifice: 'It is their custom once a year to remove the roof from their temple and to roof it again the same day before sunset, each woman carrying a part of the burden; but the woman whose load falls from her is torn to pieces by the others; and they carry the pieces around the temple crying out "euoi", and do not cease until their madness passes away; and it always happens that someone pushes against the woman who is destined to suffer this fate.' (*Geographia* IV, 4, 6.)
13. Rees, A and B (1961) pp. 333–5.
14. Rees, A and B (1961) pp. 338–41.
15. Crossley Holland, K (1980) pp. 173–6.

Chapter 19

RAGNAROK

The Norse myth of the final battle and the all-consuming cosmic conflagration known as Ragnarok was the northern equivalent of the Day of
Judgement, except that, unlike its Christian counterpart, even the gods
(save Balder) would be destroyed. It does not make easy reading.

Originally, it can be assumed, Ragnarok had been a yearly event, in
which the cosmos was dissolved with the death and rebirth of the god-king;
but in time the event was seen to fit into an escalating series of vast ages:

*An axe-age, a sword-age, shields will be gashed: there will be a wind-
age and a wolf-age before the world is wrecked.*[1]

At the end of time, so the Norse myth states, Fimbulvetr, the winter of
winters, will descend, and there will be three years without summer. The
wolf Skoll will swallow the sun; his brother Hati, the moon. The earth will
shake, as Fenrir, the great wolf, is set free from his underworld prison. The
seas will break their banks as the Midgard serpent writhes in turmoil – and
Loki will escape his chains. Fenrir, flames gushing from his jaws, his lower
jaw scraping the ground, his upper, the sky, will advance towards the home
of the gods.

From each of Valhalla's 540 doors will issue 800 men, led by Odin,
holding his spear, Gungnir, in his hand. On the plain of Vigrid the gods will
fall – though taking their enemies with them. Thor will slay the serpent
Jormungand, but die of his venom. The wolf will swallow Odin whole, but
Vidar, Odin's son, will rip his jaws in twain (reminiscent of what Marduk
did to Tiamat), avenging the one-eyed god's death. Then Surt, the giant
who has guarded Muspell, the realm of fire, since the first day, will spray

fire in all directions. The great hall at Valhalla will be destroyed. The nine worlds will burn to ashes, and the world sink into the sea. But it will rise again – a primal green mound from out of the water, like the cosmic mountain Silbury or the Egyptian Nun, the primordial mound in the marshes of the Nile. Here, Balder, released from Hel, will begin to rebuild the race of the gods, and Lif and Lifthrasir, who hid within the world tree Yggdrasil, will emerge into the new world to begin the human race again.[2]

Although no Ragnarok theme has been preserved in Celtic myth, some Classical authors reported that the Celts feared nothing save that 'the sea should rise and drown them, or the sky fall and crush them, or that the earth open up and swallow them' – all suggestive of such a cosmic upheaval.

A clear parallel to the Germanic Ragnarok is found in Hindu tradition. Here the cosmos is created and destroyed by a great conflagration, and on a truly massive timescale. But the figures involved show a debt to the great cosmic order of the Neolithic. According to Indian lore, the length in years of our cosmos is divided into four ages or *yugas*, each declining in holiness as time continues, with the present Kali Yuga being a time of great sin and evil – the 'wolf age' of the Viking myth. In the *Mahabharata* the four yugas last 12,000 x 360 years; that is, of course, 4,320,000 years. The Kali Yuga, being a tenth of the total time, is therefore *432,000* years. Returning to Ragnarok, the number of warriors issuing from Valhalla (540 x 800) is, coincidentally, *432,000*. This figure is also found in Babylonian writings, in connection with the period of the reigns of the kings before the great flood – yet another reference to a cataclysmic end of civilisation.[3]

Quite clearly these numbers reveal a continued adherence to the great cosmic order of the Neolithic world (*Me, Maat, Dharma* and *Tao*), in which the king gave up his life at the appointed time, dictated by the motion of the heavens – a system that had in all probability originated in the Near East and spread with farming. From the evidence I had gathered on the subject, the death of the king in Germania and in Celtic lands was part of this cosmic dissolution.

But, like the murder of Balder, this sense of cosmic order was a totally pre-Arya concept; it was a return to the earliest rites of the stone circles where the kings aped the heavenly deaths and rebirths. Might the fact that these early monuments were seemingly being built again in Iron Age times hint that this was indeed the case, that the Celtic religion was somehow a readoption of some of the elements of the ancient ousted Neolithic religion – or the continuation of a cult that, like the mysteries at Eleusis, had continued to exist perhaps in secret since the earliest times?

The occurrence of the wolf was also important. I thought of Mac Cecht who was killed by a wolf – and the pharaoh who was led into the chapel to be beheaded by the wolf god Wepwawet – the opener of the way. I also thought of Rudra, the scorching 'howler' who annihilated the cosmos in the Indian tradition; surely he was the equivalent of the Germanic Fenris, whose blistering heat dries the waters. The fire was but the prelude to rebirth, however, as the tale of Demophoön at Eleusis shows. But was the burning sensation of the 'tooth of the wolf', which through its lysergic (from Lycos, 'wolf') acid granted the experience of immortality, indicative of Ragnarok, or was the idea of Ragnarok derived from the burning sensation caused by the drug? This was a question to which I did not – and did not expect to – find the answer.

In Indo-European myth the killing of Vritra, a reflex of twin and Nghi, releases the water, but in the Grail legends it is the opposite – the wounding of the lunar king causes the drying up of the waters, and the healing of his wound then allows them to flow again. Perhaps the best symbol for this fiery death and rebirth is that of the phoenix – derived from the Egyptian 'Bennu bird', who after its fiery immolation and rebirth lands on the cosmic mound of Nun and through its cry ushers in the new creation.[4]

The Heb Sed had enacted this death and rebirth in a symbolic court, and I had associated the feasting halls in Irish myth with such a court, yet there was more evidence of the ritual nature of this game of death and rebirth – the fact that it was played out on a gaming board.

This game was known as Fidchell, a kind of chess, and it was said to have been the invention of the god Lugh. After researching the symbolism of the game, Celtic scholars Alwyn and Brinley Rees found that the board was often seen as the microcosm of Ireland, or of Tara, its capital. The board consisted of a grid of 7 x 7 squares, with five pieces at its centre – representing the king at Tara and his four supporters, the kings of the four provinces. At Samhain – that uncanny break in the order of the year – the kings would sit within the feasting hall in a manner suggestive of the board game, and battle over the forces of chaos that had been unleashed on the land.[5] That the land and the board were one is clearly demonstrated in an old poem by Tadhg Dall Ó hUiginn, which states:

> *The centre of the plain of Fal is Tara's castle, delightful hill; on the exact centre of the plain, like a mark on a parti-coloured Brandubh board.*[6]

The word used for Fidchell here is Brandubh ('black Bran'), perhaps a link to the Bran of Welsh legend and his defeat in a similar ritual battle inside a specially constructed hall. According to the Rees brothers the purpose of the gaming boards was possibly akin to that of the Tibetan dice contest in which the Dalai Lama played against a commoner who assumed the role of the King of the Demons.[7] But whereas the Dalai Lama won his battle over the demons, it seems clear that in Fidchell, from what I had uncovered about the rites of the feasting halls, the king would die before order was re-established.

This magical chess game is also found in Welsh myth. Gwenddolau, Merlin's patron, was said to have had a board with pieces of gold and silver which played themselves – but it is a late tale from the *Mabinogi* which reveals more of the battle. In 'The Dream of Rhonabwy' the eponymous hero seeks shelter in a hag's domicile, but, unable to get to sleep under the paltry blankets, borrows a yellow ox-hide. Under the hide, like a druid enacting the 'Tarbh feis', he dreams of the battle of Badon, in which Arthur defeated the Saxons, but this is a re-enactment of the battle that is carried out daily in the other world. It is a battle out of time – reminiscent of Odin's warriors who fight each day in Valhalla, but the next day awake whole to fight again. The conflict is played out on a Gwyddbwyll ('wood wisdom') board. Rhonabwy watches as Arthur plays the game with his nephew Owein, whose troops are able to transform into ravens (Bran). The opposing forces act out the moves that are played on the board. First Arthur takes the lead, then Owein, until Arthur crushes the gold pieces and a truce is called.

It is entirely possible that Lindow Man had played such a ritual game before being dealt his triple blows.

My investigation of the evidence for a Celtic Heb Sed had come up with many interesting and relevant points, but the tales that I had drawn on had not gone beyond the decapitation of the victim, after which the head was seen to speak. Bran may have entertained his guests for 87 mystical years, but so far the tales had not hinted at a rebirth as such, or a renewed connection to that underworld god as evidenced in the Egyptian rite. But the myth of Pwyll, whose tale formed the first branch of the *Mabinogi*, was such an account.

Pwyll, whose name means 'wisdom', meets Arawn, the King of Annwn (the Welsh other world) while hunting. Arawn appears as a huntsman himself, and is evidently related to the Bachlach of Irish myth, the god of the underworld. But instead of killing him, as a good solar-victor would, Pwyll swaps places with the king and lives for a year and a day in his underworld court, *in the semblance of Arawn* yet remaining faithful to his new friend by shunning the advances of Arawn's wife. At the end of the allotted time, after a combat at a ford with a figure named Hafgan ('summer song'), he is awarded the title Pen Annwn ('the Head of Annwn') and returns to his people with the seven magical swine of Annwn as a gift:

> *And by reason of his sojourn that year in Annwn, and his having ruled there so prosperously and united the two kingdoms in one by his valour and his prowess, the name of Pwyll prince of Dyfed fell into disuse, and he was called Pwyll Head of Annwn from that time forth.*[8]

The image of Pwyll as head of the other world, leading the seven magical swine back to Dyfed, is highly reminiscent of the end of the Heb Sed, where the pharaoh emerges with both the tall white skittle-shaped crown of Upper Egypt and the shorter red crown of the north, with its serpentine coil. Pwyll wears no crowns, but his title proclaims him to be king of two lands – Upper and Lower Dyfed, that he, like the pharaoh, had united through his sojourn in the land of the dead. After his 'initiation' he marries Rhiannon – 'Great Queen', a horse goddess and sovereignty figure, equivalent to the figure of Mert in the Egyptian rite – who accompanies him after his rebirth.

The tale of Pwyll is obviously reminiscent too of the uniting of the Demeter and Persephone aspects of the personality, something highly suggestive of the mystery religions. His sense of identification with the underworld god is so clear that he even takes on his physical appearance; this is because the underworld god – the *daemon* of the Classical mysteries – was first experienced as another before being revealed as an aspect of his own self. Pwyll and Arawn are one, and while Pwyll is in Annwn he remains chaste. Possibly this was where the Gawain poet got the idea of making Gawain spurn the advances of Lady Bertilak, but it also made me think again about the beheading game. Might it be possible that this motif was a memory of a *symbolic* beheading – that the three blows dealt to the hero to discover if he was a worthy champion were the symbolic blows dealt to the pharaoh as an initiation into the mysteries of the god of the deep in the Heb Sed?

Pomponius Mela said of the druids, 'although they refrain from taking the life of those men whom they consecrate to their divinities, they still lead them onto their altars and wound them slightly'.⁹ This was no sacrifice, but an initiation rite that killed-off the *eidolon*, revealing the eternal twin within. Both literal and symbolic enactments of the myth were present in Celtic times, it would seem.

My examination of Celtic myth had revealed many examples of a ritual combat between the underworld powers and the fiery solar principle. However, as opposed to the earlier Bronze Age system, in Celtic tales the heroes were generally not the figures with fire or light but the defeated gods themselves. For instance, Goronw Pebr ('Goronw the fiery') kills the Welsh hero Lleu; Pwyll, in the first branch of the *Mabinogi* fights Hafgan ('Summer Song'), and Beli ('bright') originally is the killer of Bran – although it is with Bran that our consideration lies. What has changed is that in all of these examples our sympathy is with the opponent of the solar figure. The victory of the sun is no longer, it seems, cause for celebration. And, indeed, in the tale of Lleu, after he is killed and brought back to life, he murders Goronw in return, just as Horus, the son of Osiris, overcomes Seth.

Such a reversal of sympathy is clearly demonstrated in the myth of the taking of Ireland by the Celts. In Classic Indo-European myth, the conquered aboriginal people of a land are associated with serpentine demonic powers and are crushed and cast into the underworld, as Cronos is by Zeus. However, in Ireland, the land is divided and the conquered peoples, the divine *Tuatha Dé Danann*, far from being subjugated and despised, become the very gods of the Celts. The *Tuatha* are given the subterranean part of

Ireland – the burial mounds of the Neolithic dead, which become the gateways to the paradisal land of youth. Their abode is no dark Hades crammed with the tormented bat-like souls of Classical tradition; it is no longer demonised, but is a fair land of plenty, where beneath the apple trees man and god mingle like Adam and Yahweh in Eden before the fall.

Joseph Campbell had been aware that somehow Celtic myth differed considerably from its Indo-European roots, but his explanation of why was now out of date:

> *The Celts, like the Germans were patriarchal Aryans; however, with their westward drive into Gaul and the British isles in the first millennium BC, they entered the old Bronze Age sphere of the Great Goddess and her killed and resurrected son, whose cults of the seasonal round and rebirth were soon combined with their own.*[10]

I had learned that the Celtic culture was in the main an indigenous product, and thus the Celts were not strictly 'Aryans' but a Neolithic population who had become Aryanised, either through acculturation or through the anathema idea of some kind of small-scale infiltration. Therefore the adoption of the rites of the goddess and her killed and resurrected consort was not so much a borrowing as a readoption of beliefs once held – and which, in certain parts of the province, may never have been completely forgotten.

This adoption was evidenced not just in a new regard for cosmic order and kingly sacrifice, but also in the refeminisation of myth. For the Arya woman had been booty taken in war, and even the sovereignty of the land was to be stolen from its previous 'owner'. But although strong elements of this patriarchal Aryanism continued to dominate much of Celtic society, Celtic myths reveal that to some extent a reversal in this attitude had begun to take place. The fact that the mysterious *Tuatha* were descended from a goddess is highly relevant. Danu's role as matriarch is reminiscent of the Great Mother of the Neolithic – and in the Celtic world the goddess was of primal importance. She was Mórrígan 'Great Queen', the seductress, the war goddess; she was Brighid, patroness of the arts, and often appeared in triple form. Shrines in Roman Britain were set up to a myriad of divine females and local spirits – goddesses of water, healing, fertility, horses and the underworld, to name but a few. In legend the Celtic other world teamed with beauteous, wise and powerful women; and who could ignore the mythical Irish Queen Medb, whose husband Ailill only bore the title 'King' because of his marriage to her. She was no 'prize', but a powerful, independent, highly sexual woman – whose very name meant 'the intoxicator'. I had only to think of the flame-haired Boudicca who led the revolt against the Romans in AD 60 to realise that women such as Medb were not restricted to myth.

Looking back at the myths of the Neolithic, it seems that the dying and reborn divinities could be either male or female, Tammuz or Kore; but for both sexes it was the goddess who was instrumental in bringing about their rebirth. In the Indo-European religion, however, woman played little or no part. If anything she was identified with the serpent: the snake Pythia slain by Apollo was female, so was the gorgon Medusa slain by Perseus, and the Tiamat slain by Bel-Marduk. The myths were patriarchal, possibly gynophobic. The reappearance of the regard for the divine feminine that countered the misogynistic outlook of the Bronze Age was one of the major aspects of Celtic religion. The cauldron stolen by the Arya had been merely the container of a drug, but for the Celts its meaning was the same as that held by the initiates of the Classical Mysteries – it was the womb of the goddess in which rebirth would be found.

I was able to imagine such a drastic turn around (or *enantiodromia*, as the Greek sophist Heraclitus called it) occurring in the religion of prehistoric Britain because there was good evidence of it happening elsewhere in the Indo-European world – namely, in India. Joseph Campbell states that the Hindu religion of India today, although more recent than that of the Indo-European Vedas, owes its spirit to the pre-Vedic world-view. In time the will of the warrior-god Indra became subsumed beneath the cosmic order that he had so valiantly struggled against, and his killing of the water dragon Vritra, once the victory stroke, became deemed an awful crime, for the dragon, as later tales state, had been a Brahmin.[11]

This was precisely what I had envisaged occurring in Britain – a return to the sense of cosmic order that rises above the autonomous will of the solar Aryan gods, and the conception that the slaying of the dragon and the murder of *Yemo were events that had blighted the cosmos, that had caused the Wasteland.

This is not to say the deed could be completely undone, for the sacrifice of the god had created the world; the sacrifice still had to take place, or, thinking mystically, the divinity still had to be dismembered so that the divine spark could be present in all of us. But there was a return to the older myths where the god, instead of lying inert in the depths, as had always been the case before the rise of the Arya complex, would have to be rescued from his prison. Persephone had to be sought once more in Hades to bring back the fertility of the land, though the healing of the Wasteland was now more to do with psychology than with seasons or vegetation. It was this re-establishment of the rites of a pre-Indo-European past that held the key to the rites of the Grail – for the whole legend was an attempt to reverse the splitting of the god in the brother battle.

The quest for that which had been lost is nowhere better shown in Hindu myth than in the search for Agni – the personification of the sacrificial fire onto which soma was poured. Agni and soma are often combined, and in a version of the theft of soma, Indra often saves Agni from the stomach or throat of Vritra. Agni is described as a bull, or a firebird, whose fiery immolation is the same as the self-sacrifice of the Bennu bird in Egypt. But what intrigued me was that he was seen to be 'lost', like Persephone, and the gods had to search for him.[12] And where was he found?

Agni is living in the subterranean waters ... the blessed oblation bearer is asleep in the waters.[13]

As time passed and the pre-Vedic sympathies rose to the fore, the theme of the rescue of this self-immolated bull became more and more like a game of 'hide-and-seek', as Wendy Doniger O'Flaherty calls it, 'with Agni sometimes seeking but more often hiding, moving sometimes from earth to heaven but more often from heaven to earth'.[14] Can a similar move be glimpsed archaeologically in what happened in Britain? Did the Celts begin to seek for something lost under the water – a something that cannot be other than the defeated god of the Neolithic Age, the fiery divine spark?

Three hundred years after the completion of Stonehenge the ceremonial centres of the Bronze Age were mysteriously abandoned. After 1500 BC no more monuments were built, and by 1000 BC evidence begins to mount for the adoption of a new cult – ritual depositions in sacred lakes, bogs and rivers. The splendid solar-horse-cult wagons of Denmark were thrown into bogs, revealing a possible reversal in fortune for the sun, or a change in allegiance on behalf of the worshippers.

The twin gods no longer adorned great solar barges – instead, Danish artefacts began to show a new deity, a woman in a corded skirt holding a vessel in her outstretched hands.[15] It is hard not to see in her the ancestress of the Grail maidens of medieval romance, holding the *cista mystica* of Eleusis – the female symbol of the container that offered rebirth, the womb of the goddess through which the old wounded god would be reborn.

Part of the reason for this change may have been the dramatic change in climate that began around 1800 BC and lasted until around 400 BC.[16] The average temperature fell by many degrees and led to the formation of blanket bog on formerly fertile farmland. Increase in demand for land led to an escalation in war. Larger defensive settlements – hill forts – began to be built. Might this period of change have been remembered as the Wasteland? Could it be that the readoption of pre-Aryan cults demonstrated a belief that the optimistic, rational solar religion had somehow 'failed'? Had there been some kind of re-evaluation of beliefs and an attempt to reintegrate the side of the psyche that solar rationalist religion had 'demonised'?

The deterioration of the climate was escalated by other natural disasters. In 1159 the volcanic eruption of Hekla in Iceland sent huge clouds of dust into the atmosphere, blocking off the sun in the north of Britain for many days.[17] During the same century in the Mediterranean, the eruption of Thera led to the partial destruction of the island of Santorini. This disaster destroyed the Minoan civilisation and also disenfranchised many coastal settlers, leading to mass migrations and ensuing wars over land in southern Europe.

The fact that the Celtic calendar was based on the pastoral year, as opposed to the solar Bronze Age calendar, is suggestive of an abandonment of the solar religion due to climate changes. Perhaps the circles were abandoned because the skies above were no longer clear. But if the brother battle was a myth of psychology, then surely the *enantiodromia* was psychological in origin, too – a psychic backlash. Turning to the underworld may have had as much to do with psychology as with a change in the climate.

The Wasteland of the Grail myth, I reasoned, resulted from a drying out of the land, turning a once lush land into a barren desert (the Grail knight is in some cases known as the 'freer of the waters'). In the Late Bronze Age the slaying of the dragon Vritra had been seen to bring forth water, but in the new religion the opposite happened; it was the *healing* of the wounded lunar-serpent king that restored the moisture. If the Wasteland was all about climate, then surely it would be a dark, wet place rather than a desert, and the restoration would be of the sun's power, not the waters.

The desert-like nature of the Wasteland reveals its origins in the Near East – for there it was dryness that caused the barren land, and the god who had to be rescued from below was the lush green spirit of vegetation. Clearly such a myth had no relevance to the vegetal cycle of Britain, where the winter was cold and damp. The change in climate that occurred may well have been the catalyst for this change of religion – for the productivity of the land would have been effected – but the symbols used hint that the turnaround had more to do with the mind than the land.

And what convinced me of that was what I subsequently read in the world's earliest recorded epic – that of Gilgamesh – for in this marvellous and tragic tale the reason for the return to the waters is plain to see.

Notes

1. Crossley Holland, K (1980) p. 173.
2. Crossley Holland, K (1980) p. 175.
3. The origin of these numbers is a puzzle. It may derive from Mesopotamia where the soss of base 60, multiplied by itself four times, yields the very same number. Therefore the great cosmic clock ticked along at base 60. But there is another explanation – precession. Due to a slight wobble in the earth's axis – as mentioned earlier when stating that the pole star lay in Draco in ancient times – the sun rises in a slightly different place against the background of the zodiac each year. This is a very slow process, with each shift by 1 degree taking 72 years. It has been suggested that observation brought this to the attention of the Mesopotamians – and this number represents a double turn in the zodiac, a return to the start. Both explanations are plausible, but Campbell says a numerical system seemingly derived from the heavens '… might indeed have been the result only of a sheer (but then how really wonderful!) accident'. (Campbell, J (1962) pp. 118–9.
4. See Bauval, R and Gilbert, A (1995) pp. 206–21, and Hancock, G; Grigsby, J and Bauval, R (1998) pp.184–8.
5. Rees, A and B (1961) p. 154.
6. Rees, A and B (1961) p. 155.
7. Rees, A and B (1961) pp. 155–6.
8. Jones, G and T (1974) p. 9.
9. Markale, J (1986) p.186.
10. Campbell, J (1968) p. 124.
11. Campbell, J (1962) p. 184.
12. A good introduction to Agni can be found in Doniger O'Flaherty, W (trans.) (1981) pp. 97–118 and Doniger O'Flaherty, W (trans.) (1975) pp. 97–115.
13. Doniger O'Flaherty, W (trans.) (1975) p. 102.
14. Doniger O'Flaherty, W (trans.) (1975) p. 97.
15. Glob, P V (1983) p. 158.
16. Darvill, T (1987) p. 127 and Parker Pearson, M (1993) p. 95.
17. Parker Pearson, M (1993) p. 100.

Part Four

THE FISHER KING

Chapter 20

MAN OF JOY
AND SORROW

In the Sumerian king lists, Gilgamesh – 'the man of joy and sorrow', two parts god and one part man – is named as the fifth king of the dynasty of Uruk, founded after the flood, and his reign a mere 126 years.[1] After him his son reigns for but 30 years, and here regal longevity ceases. Gilgamesh is the last of the god-kings, his reign a turning point between immortal and human kingship. And this is the importance of that tale, for it tells of the ending of the cosmic game and the dawn of the individual. But it does so not with the victorious zeal of the dragon-slaying Arya, but with the realisation that in cutting himself off from the immortals, the king is doomed to die.

Gilgamesh is too proud, so the gods create a hairy wild man named Enkidu to fight him. But instead of one killing the other they become friends, setting off on a number of adventures that smack of the killing of 'twin'. They come across the forest-dwelling Humbaba, whose 'breath is like fire, and his jaws are death itself'. He guards the cedars so well that 'when the wild heifer stirs in the forest, though she is sixty leagues distant, he hears her'. In other words he is the wild herdsman. Together they kill him:

Gilgamesh … took the axe in his hand, he drew the sword from his belt, and he struck Humbaba with a thrust of the sword to the neck, and Enkidu his comrade struck the second blow. At the third blow Humbaba fell.[2]

A triple death, it would seem, of the primal forest dweller. Gilgamesh the proud wields the wonder-stroke of Indra. Gilgamesh is triumphant – he is full of fire and pride, and in this state the goddess Ishtar seeks him for a lover.

Gilgamesh spurns her advances, saying how she turned the herdsman into a wolf, so that his dogs bit his thighs. Gilgamesh is unwilling to die in connubium with her in the temple, as the old cosmic order dictates.

When she hears his response Ishtar falls into a rage and begs her father Anu to help her destroy him – asking that the 'Bull of Heaven' be given to her to let loose on Uruk. The earth cracks open and many die at the on-slaught of this celestial beast, yet the two heroes play the bull like the bull dancers on frescoes at ancient Knossos in Crete, the tauromachy of Mithras or the killing of the Apis bull by the pharaoh. Enkidu cried to Gilgamesh, 'My friend, we boasted that we would leave enduring names behind us. Now thrust your sword between the nape and the horns.'[3] And so, in matador style, the bull is slain.

Gilgamesh and Enkidu have now totally alienated themselves from that other part of their being – the bull is dead, the forest dweller is slain by triple blows. But their victory is pyrrhic. It is the dolorous stroke.

Enkidu dreams that the gods take counsel; they decide that since the pair have killed both Humbaba and the bull of heaven, one of them must die. And it is the dreamer who is to suffer this fate. The death of Enkidu reiterates the severance of man from nature. It is the hairy wild man, the natural side of Gilgamesh, that is to die. But this also sees the end of the brash bravado of Gilgamesh. He becomes suddenly frail and human – he mourns, weeping for seven days 'until the worm fastened' on Enkidu.[4]

After this time kings are mortal men with human reigns. Gilgamesh is the first to realise what mortality is. Is this not what was going on in late Bronze Age Britain? Severed from the Neolithic communal existence by the 'splitting of the primal brain', as Jaynes puts it, Gilgamesh is no longer a puppet of god, a fleshly apparel of a cosmic force, a scale on the great world serpent. Gilgamesh is an individual, an entity of the here and now, an *eidolon*, and thus finite. And this is the poignant bittersweet tragedy of Western man; Gilgamesh is a hero in his ephemeral condition.

The realisation of personal death in prehistoric Britain, I concluded, lay in an adoption of a cult of the underworld – a water cult in which the people sought below what the gods above had not only failed to deliver, but had actively separated them from. It is obvious that they wanted to find immortality again – and where better to look than in the depths where they had imprisoned it in the first place, in the waters that were part of the water dragon of old – the abyss.

The Grail myth – that quest to find the court of the wounded king, the rich fisher, as he was sometimes known – seems to speak of this. But the Grail myth was written down 2,000 or so years after this crisis. Gilgamesh, however, offers a contemporary view of this Bronze Age crisis, for the man of joy and sorrow, like the Grail knights, was to set off on a quest ...

He seeks the great ancestor Ut-na-Pishtim who lives in the 'land of Dilmun, in the garden of the sun; and to him alone of men they gave everlasting life'. The journey, however, is to take place not on mortal soil, but in the underworld, which Gilgamesh reaches by boarding the serpent-prowed boat of Urshanabi, the ferryman of the dead. When he at last reaches his goal, he finds Ut-na-Pishtim reclining on his back, like the Wounded King himself. He questions him about the living and the dead, and asks him how to find the life he is searching for, but Ut-na-Pishtim is stern in his answer:

> *There is no permanence. Do we build a house to stand forever; do we seal a contract to hold for all time? From the days of old there is no permanence...the sleeping and the dead, how alike they are ...* [6]

The words jolted me back to Glob's use of this phrase to describe the countenances of the bog men, who were the wounded kings of north-west Europe. They, like Ut-na-Pishtim, dwelt without ageing in their watery underworld abode. Had they been killed and forgotten, or had some Celtic Gilgamesh journeyed to meet with them after their deaths – like the pharaoh entering the chapel of the slain Osiris in the Heb Sed?

Gilgamesh asks another question: 'Tell me truly, how was it that you came to enter the company of the gods and to possess everlasting life?' Ut-na-Pishtim replies, 'I will reveal to you a mystery, I will tell you a secret of the gods.' [7]

The secret he tells is what made the discovery and subsequent translation of the epic of Gilgamesh such an important find in the nineteenth century. It is an account of the biblical flood, with Ut-na-Pishtim playing the role of Noah. He is warned by the god of wisdom Ea (or Enki) that the gods are to destroy mankind, and he alone will escape unharmed.

But Ut-na-Pishtim has another secret. 'There is a plant that grows under the water, it has a prickle like a thorn, like a rose; it will wound your hands, but if you succeed in taking it, then your hands will hold that which restores his lost youth to a man.'[8] Diving to the bottom of the ocean, Gilgamesh seizes the wonder herb. His intention is not to swallow it whole in victory, as Indra did the soma, but to take it home to Uruk and share it with his people. While on his way home Gilgamesh decides to bathe in a pool, but a serpent lying in the water detects the sweet aroma of the plant. 'It rose out of the water and snatched it away, and immediately it sloughed its skin and returned to the well.'[9] And Gilgamesh would die a mortal.

Gilgamesh's quest failed. But I knew from my readings of Celtic myth that the knowledge gained from the watery depths had not been allowed to slip away so easily. The Grail quest, after all, was achievable. But how exactly was this 'reintegration' achieved? How did the ancient Celtic initiates heal the split between the two realms, between *eidolon* and *daemon*?

This answer, too, lay in the depths of the water – with a flood-surviving great ancestor who would in time be known as the Fisher King ...

Notes

1. Scholars believe that a king named Gilgamesh actually existed – probably around 2700 BC – and that he reigned at Uruk, the biblical Erech. He strengthened the walls of this city, probably with cedar wood from the great forests of the Amanus mountains in north Syria, and at Nippur he rebuilt the shrine of the goddess Ninlil. See Sanders, N K (trans.) (1972).
2. Sanders, N K (trans.) (1972) p. 82.
3. Sanders, N K (trans.) (1972) p. 88.
4. Sanders, N K (trans.) (1972) p. 96.
5. Sanders, N K (trans.) (1972) p. 97.
6. Sanders, N K (trans.) (1972) pp. 106–7.
7. Sanders, N K (trans.) (1972) p. 107.
8. Sanders, N K (trans.) (1972) p. 116.
9. Sanders, N K (trans.) (1972) p. 117.

Chapter 21

THE SALMON
OF WISDOM

The epic of Gilgamesh provided a clue to the *raison d'être* of the Celtic water cults. I could see now that the increase of ritual deposition began at the time of the abandonment of the solar circles, when, perhaps catalysed by climatic decline, an *enantiodromia* of belief occurred.

The appearance of the water cult is puzzling if looked at, as many scholars did, in connection with the decline in temperature and an increase in overcast skies. It would seem likely that instead of offering objects to the gods below, prehistoric man would have built better shrines to the sun gods to placate them and beg them to return. But no; if any deities were being 'placated' they were the water divinities. Were the people begging the water gods to cease their relentless advance, offering precious objects to buy their favour? I doubt it.

It was, I believe, more a question of honouring a deity who was perceived as dwelling under the water – i.e. in the underworld. Carl Jung has argued that water was a symbol for the 'unconscious' – the depths of the mind – so perhaps the renewal of the underworld cult was an attempt to gain favour or to re-establish contact with the maternal depths and the god who had been relegated to the watery abyss. In other words, they were honouring the dying and rising moon bull of the Neolithic, the universal *daemon*, imprisoned there by his brother, the demiurge, or – to use split-brain terminology – the right brain, the part that allowed for the experience of immortality and from which man had become alienated.

From the earliest times the death of this god had formed the cosmos itself, and therefore, when this drama was enacted in Celtic times, the victim would still die and be placed in the water, following his cosmosgonic triple death, because creation still had to take place. But the rites did not end there, for the god now had to be reawakened so that the contact between the upper- and underworld could take place. And this was the Grail quest – a heroic dive into those depths to heal the Wounded King (or the Fisher King as he was sometimes known). And I would soon discover why he was so called.

I had already stumbled on a fishy connection to the murdered god at the start of my quest, in the figure of the wounded Nuada/Nodens the 'fisher', and also in the tale of Cú Roí, whose soul was said to reside in an apple within a salmon that could only be caught once every seven years.[1] The salmon was possibly an aspect of this underworld god, but there was an even greater clue in Celtic myths from both Ireland and Wales to link the fish to both the rescue of the slain god and the obtaining of other-worldly knowledge – and this was the existence of a figure known as the 'Salmon of Wisdom or Knowledge'.

According to Irish lore the miraculous Salmon of Wisdom lived at Conla's well. At the side of the well grew magical hazel trees, whose nuts, when eaten, granted wisdom; it was said that these trees blossomed and produced fruit in the same hour, which then fell into the well, to be eaten by the fish, into whose flesh the wisdom-giving properties were transferred.[2] This symbolism may well have been present in the killing of Lindow III, whose last meal had consisted entirely of hazelnuts.[3] Tollund and Grauballe Man, it could be argued, had received 'other-worldly knowledge' by taking ergot. Perhaps the presence of these 'nuts of wisdom' in the British finds indicates a shared tradition of ingesting wisdom-granting foods, whether they were psychotropic or not. But there was another link between Lindow III and the hazel-eating Salmon of myth.

The distinguishing feature of Lindow III, the hazelnut chewer, was his polydactylism – he had two thumbs on each hand. I had already noted that his deformity might have marked him out as special, but the thumb appears in Celtic myth specifically connected to the hazel-eating Salmon of Wisdom. A legend concerning the poet warlord Fionn mac Cumhal tells how he gained great wisdom from this miraculous fish. The creature, like the salmon-soul of Cú Roí, emerged every seven years at Fec's pool. After seven years of waiting, a druid named Finneces managed to hook the fish, asking the young Fionn – then named Demne ('Deer') – to cook it for him, making sure he did not touch a morsel in the process. During the cooking, however, Demne burned his thumb and automatically put it in his mouth to cool – thus unwittingly obtaining the magical wisdom for himself. From then on, his name now changed to Fionn (meaning 'fair' or 'bright') he had only to suck his thumb again to receive any knowledge that he desired.[4] It might all be a huge coincidence, but surely to a people for whom the thumb and the hazel were linked with shamanic or other-worldly knowledge, the figure of Lindow III would have stood out.

Other tales give differing accounts of how Fionn acquired knowledge. Some say he drank it from a well in the other world, others that he trapped his thumb in the door of a *sídhe* (a fairy mound), and that as the door slammed a goddess carrying a vessel containing *don lionn iomhas* (the liquid of inspiration) stumbled so that its contents splashed his thumb.[5]

So the inspiration could come in the form of both salmon flesh and liquid in a golden vessel. The latter had to be the same narcotic brew that I had come across many times already on my quest: a brew that once again had been taken to elicit a transpersonal experience, not to increase the martial valour of the imbiber.

The lack of ergotised grains in the stomachs of the British bog men indicated that if they had been given a drug, as had their Germanic cousins, it had not been administered in their food. Maybe they had been given a filtered brew so that the water-soluble acids would remain but not the grains themselves. Perhaps, because the skin easily absorbs lysergic acid, the substance had been applied externally (on the thumb?). But it was also possible that the druid-shamans had used other methods of trance-induction, and that the eating of a wisdom-giving food or drink had in time become a symbolic process. Clearly the image of gaining wisdom through the eating of the flesh of the fish is wholly symbolic – akin to the Christian Communion in which the eating of the 'body' and 'blood' of Christ offers 'eternal life' – for, as a Welsh myth clarifies, the salmon and the god are one.

The Welsh Fionn (literally as well as mythologically, because the two names are etymologically related) was one 'Gwion' Bach, who would in time be known as Taliesin. Gwion Bach is the helper of a 'witch' named Ceridwen and her husband Tegid the Bald, who live at the bottom of Lake Bala in North Wales, and who possess a miraculous cauldron. Immediately the tale calls to mind the primal cauldron-bearing lake-dwellers of Irish mythology; the couple are the primal divine pair of Celtic religion. It is assumed that Ceridwen, through whom Gwion Bach achieved rebirth and illumination, was in origin none other than the Great Goddess, who had ever been the lover and mother of the transforming, resurrecting god, and whose distant avatar would be the beauteous Grail maiden. Ceridwen prepares a brew of *awen* ('inspiration') for her ugly son Afagddu ('utter darkness'), but on stirring the cauldron, *three* drops fly onto Gwion's *thumb*. He puts it in his mouth to soothe the burn, whereon the knowledge reserved for Afagddu becomes his.

Ceridwen, in her anger, pursues the boy – first as a greyhound, for Gwion has transformed himself into a hare, then as an otter when he becomes a fish, and as a hawk when he turns into a bird. Gwion finally becomes a grain of wheat, and is eaten by Ceridwen as a hen. Nine months later she gives birth to him and sets him adrift on the waters in a basket on the eve of Beltane. Gwion, Moses-like, sails down the river, to be found in a salmon trap by a man named Elphin mab Gwyddno, on May Day. On seeing the babe Elphin cries, 'Behold the radiant brow!' so naming the boy ('Tal-iesin': 'radiant brow').

Taliesin had been a historical poet of the Dark Ages, a bard in the court of Urien of Rheged, but the tale of Taliesin and the vast number of poems attributed to him were actually written during the period of the Welsh Gogynfeirdd (the 'fairly early poets'), i.e. between 1080 and 1350, when a Celtic renaissance was taking place, led by the bards. Much as the Renaissance artists of Italy did with old Classical legends, the bards probably drew on fragments of ancient lore and myths from an oral tradition that have not survived to the present day. It is often thought that the tale and poems of Taliesin are purely inventions of the Middle Ages, but I was willing to accept that some of the material contained within them was of pagan origin; after all, much the same has been said of the tale of Bran, whose wounding, beheading and cauldron quest matched stories from the *Rig Veda* point for point.

Taliesin boasts that his imbibing of the three magical drops has given him knowledge beyond measure; it is suddenly as if he has knowledge of all of history: 'I have attained the muse from the cauldron of Ceridwen … I am able to instruct the whole universe.'[6]

I was with my king
In the heavens
When Lucifer fell
Into the depths of Hell ...

I carried the banner
Before Alexander ...

I was in the Ark
With Noah and Alpha ...

I was instructor to the whole universe.
I shall be until the Judgement
On the face of the Earth.

The boy Gwion has been made aware of an immortal side of his nature. Clearly Ceridwen's brew contains the same properties as Fionn's magical salmon. But the salmon connection is also present in Taliesin's poetic boasts, for he says, 'it is not known whether my body is of flesh or fish'.

Taliesin, found in a salmon trap, is himself the Salmon of Wisdom, he who is eaten and reborn from the goddess's body. He is the fish and Ceridwen the vessel in which he is transformed and reborn. But who is this salmon? In an older translation of Taliesin's poem 'Hanes Taliesin', quoted in Robert Graves's *The White Goddess*, among his many boasts, he claims:

Johannes the Diviner
I was called by Merlin.[7]

This Johannes is John the Baptist – a hairy John, associated not only with baptism (i.e. rebirth through water) but with decapitation, his head having being borne into the feast on a dish for the dancing girl Salome, just as the head was borne on a silver salver before Peredur. Joseph Campbell has remarked how John had seemingly got both his name and his water rite from the Sumerian 'God of the House of Water' Ea, also known as *Oannes* (from which comes the English *John*),[8] who was depicted as *half-man, half-fish*.

181

The Greek Berossus described Oannes, the being who brought wisdom to mankind after the flood, as having the body and head of a fish (with the man's head below that of the fish), and alongside its tail were the feet of a man. Oannes taught man wisdom and science before once again disappearing into the sea.[9] It is clear that this Near Eastern fish man possesses knowledge beyond that of an ordinary mortal.

The depiction is not of a monster but of a man in a fish suit – a priest enacting the bringing of knowledge to mankind after the deluge. Indian myth tells a similar tale: Vishnu, as a fish, dives into the sea (as did Gilgamesh) to gain the lost wisdom of the Vedas. The fish man was privy to all knowledge from the earliest times, and Taliesin is clearly part of this tradition, achieving knowledge through rebirth from the female vessel – the cauldron and the goddess.

It is surely no coincidence that the French *gradale*, the serving platter from which the word Grail is derived, was usually reserved for the serving of *fish*, and that in Robert de Boron's version of the legend the Grail was served accompanying a meal of fish that had been caught by Bron, the Fisher King. So the Grail is depicted as either a platter containing the wisdom-giving salmon or, as in the case with Peredur, the severed head of the primal ancestral water god whose body was both flesh and fish – the Fisher King.

The reason why the Wounded King is given this name in the legends is the rather lame explanation that this is how he passed his time – fishing on the lake of Brumbane when the moon was changing and his pain great. But when compared with the half-man half-fish Oannes, who is depicted holding a pail of immortality, another explanation springs to mind: he is the salmon itself, the primal divinity in his aquatic abode. (Many Celtic wells, in addition to housing severed heads, contained sacred fish.) The symbol of the fish – an alternate symbol for the god of the deep – had a specific shamanic meaning beyond simply 'a dweller in the water', for fish were the oldest animals, alive from the start of time, and that is why their knowledge of history was unsurpassed.

The Irish folk story 'The Hawk of Achill' tells of the age of this salmon. On a freezing night the hawk of Achill steals into an eagle's nest, kills her chick and takes its place. The eagle complains of the coldness of the night, but the hawk says he has known one colder. When the eagle questions her 'chick' on this seeming impossibility, the hawk bids her seek the blackbird to discover the answer to this quandary. The blackbird cannot remember a colder night, nor can the stag, who has lived for 4,000 years, but he directs the eagle to an ancient salmon named the Goll (blind one) of Asseroe. He can remember a colder night – one Beltane near the start of time. On that night he had become stuck in the ice and the hawk had taken one of his eyes. Your chick, the salmon tells the eagle, can be none other than the Hawk of Achill. The mother eagle flies back to her nest, but the cunning hawk has long since fled.

In other tales the oldest animal is a salmon named Fintan.[10] He was said to be the great-grandson of Noah, who alone of all the Irish *survived the flood*, and who told the men of Ireland the history of their land.

Fintan's myth is paralleled in the Irish tale of Tuan mac Cairell, a sixth-century chieftain who told a local saint, St Finnen, how he had been born thousands of years earlier as the nephew of Partholan, the first of the men to settle in Ireland.[11] Tuan alone escapes the pestilence that kills these first settlers, and he roams wild in the hills, naked and covered in long hair.[12] One evening he falls into a deep sleep, and awakes to find himself transformed into a stag.

Tuan stays in this form for countless years until, standing at the mouth of his cave in old age, he becomes a boar – and is young again. After a boar he becomes an eagle, and then, finally, a salmon. And so he exists until the sixth century, when he is caught by fishermen and served to Cairell's wife at supper, and so enters her womb and is born again as a man, as was Taliesin from Ceridwen.[13]

Salmon of Wisdom seems to be a title possessed by those initiates who had tasted immortality from the cauldron; it was as if each initiate who entered into the cauldron of rebirth, the womb of the goddess, was reborn as the salmon itself. What this reminded me of was the fact that the Grail knight ascended to the role of Fisher King when the quest was achieved: he who sought the salmon became the salmon, just as in the Classical Mysteries he who sought the *daemon* within realised his identity with the universal *daemon*, the dying and resurrecting god Adonis who had been known to his Syrian initiates as Icthys (the fish).

As a reborn youth the initiate Taliesin is set adrift into life in the basket – surely the same image as the basket or winnowing fan of the Eleusinian and Dionysian Mysteries that held the phallus, symbol of the dismembered god who would be reborn as Liknites. This was the same phallus that had been swallowed by the fish in the mysteries of Osiris – the 'soul' of Cú Roí in the salmon – the seed entering the maternal underworld to be reborn. It was therefore no coincidence that Ceridwen had swallowed Taliesin as a grain. Thus the *eidolon*, Gwion, was cast off in favour of the daemon, which as a fragment of the divine was aware of the totality of the cosmos, of past and future.

The Grail quest, then, was nothing less than a dive into the waters of the primal condition to gain the knowledge of the god of the house of water, whose head was processed at the feast, in the *gradale*.

If this was the case, then the bog bodies definitely had not lain undisturbed in their crystal prisons. The killing of the victim – enacting the brother battle and thus creating the world through a rending of the watery chaos – *was just the first part in the mystery*. This is what the archaeologists and historians had missed all along. These weren't simple offerings for good harvests; the killing of the victim merely paved the way for the most important part of the rite, the part not preserved in archaeology – the attempt to contact the dead god, to win from him, in his watery depths, the secret of immortality possessed by the ancients. In other words, what was important was the secret part of the Heb Sed, in which the two lands were reunited through unspoken rites involving this drowned and dismembered god.

To further support the theory that the salmon and the wounded god were one, was the fact that Fintan the salmon was also known as the Goll of Asseroe (who had only one eye, the other having been taken by the hawk – a feature that linked him to the 'Wild Herdsman'). I had already explored the symbolism of the one eye in relation to shamanism, and it clearly was connected to other-worldly knowledge. The Irish goddess Boinn (the 'white cow', mate of the Dagda) visits an other-worldly well, and walks around it thrice anti-clockwise. A great wall of water emerges and deprives her of a thigh, a hand, and an eye.[14] The wisdom she receives from the well turns her into a 'Goll'.

'One-eyedness' is also a quality assumed by the 'demons' in Indo-European myth; it was shorthand, if you will, for the aboriginal Neolithic knowledge – to be one-eyed was to be in the unity of the wild state, before the birth of duality. When Lugh closed an eye in battle, or the druids stood on one leg to cast spells, they were assuming a powerful aspect, that of the primal god who existed before duality – i.e. before the split between the ego and the unconscious.[15]

Returning to the shamanic theme, I began to wonder whether the journeys to the land of the ancestors, such as those in the *Epic of Gilgamesh*, were depictions of shamanic journeys. Was the Grail quest a shamanic journey?

Might the 'knowledge' gained by these heroes in their quest for the wisdom of the ancestors represent the shaman's journey into the other world (or Jung's 'collective unconscious'), and thus effect a re-establishing of contact with the parts of the mind repressed when the ego separates from the unconscious, or with the mystical knowledge of the divinity within – the Persephone aspect? Did such experiences 'recomplete the partial mind' and thus heal what Jung called the 'self-division' of modern man, which causes a sense of 'loss of instinct and rootlessness'? Seemingly so. The cult of the Salmon of Wisdom – of which Lindow III was no doubt a part – was a native mystery tradition based on a shamanic initiation using the same symbols (the fish and rebirth through the mother, with the winnowing fan) as the Classical Mysteries. And the one-eyed god, the monopod, was obviously the phallus of Dionysos that would be found in the basket. Taliesin's story highlights the core of this religion.

Shamanic myths tell of a time when the land of the mortals and the land of the gods were joined and man could commune with his ancestors without the aid of a shaman. After these lands separated, shamans were needed to bridge the gap. Shamans themselves thought their modus operandi had somehow degenerated from a once-natural ability. The affinity to the split psyche is undeniable. The experience they rendered, of being beyond the duality of the brain, of conscious and unconscious, is amply symbolised by the loss of an eye – it is the giving up of duality in return for the original unity. Reconnection with the mystical side would grant access to supra-personal knowledge; as Holger Kalweit says:

The shaman is part of the age-old tradition of the Perennial Philosophy
– the mystical teaching of unity of all things and all being ... This level
of consciousness, like a giant telephone exchange, affords awareness to

all other realms of awareness ... Those that have returned from this world [the shamanic other world] say that present, past and future exist simultaneously, and that to enter this world is tantamount to enlightenment. Many people felt that in some inexplicable way they had gained total knowledge ... One person who returned said: 'It seemed that all of a sudden, all knowledge – all that had started from the very beginning, that would go on without end – that for a second I knew all the secrets of the ages, all the meaning of the universe, the stars, the moon – of everything.'[16]

There is in this last statement a feeling akin to that expressed by Taliesin in his poems:

I have been in many shapes before I achieved congenial form
I have journeyed as an eagle
I have been a roebuck on the mountain
I have been three periods in the prison of Arianrhod
I am a wonder whose origin is not known ...

Or:

I know the names of the stars from north to south ...

In which case this is not just some reintegration of parts of the personality – it is a revelation of something far beyond the human mind. These myths of the gaining of ancestral knowledge point to a very real pivot in psychology in prehistoric times – a re-embracing of the instinctive and intuitive 'wisdom' of the Neolithic (the time before the apocalyptic flood, seen a divine punishment). But the important point is that this is not a return to a state of unconsciousness; it is very much a conscious return, and as such has much in common with the fate of the shaman, who does not degenerate into psychosis but strengthens his own personality through his experiences, achieving a uniting of the 'bicameral mind' – or, in modern Jungian terms, the 'ego' and the 'unconscious'.

Might the return to the underworld and rejection of the rational solar cult at the end of the Bronze Age be seen as some kind of cultural 'shamanic crisis', and the essence of Celtic religion that replaced it as shamanic in nature, searching within to re-establish contact with the ancestral wisdom lost to man through his self-division?

To Jung this unconscious repressed side of the psyche is the 'more universal, truer, more eternal man dwelling in the darkness or primordial night. There he is still whole, and the whole is in him, indistinguishable from nature and bare of all ego-hood.'[17]

It is clearly this aspect of the personality, the *daemon*, that the initiates of Eleusis had become identified with, not the fleeting ego – and in becoming aware of this new depth to their beings, achieving that state of undivided self-hood Jung calls 'individuation'. And the bog man, housed in the darkness of the primordial waters – a hairy shamanic figure that could speak the language of the animals – was this self-same 'more eternal man' who needed to be rescued after his world- (and ego-) creating self-sacrifice.

Stanislav Grof states that such an experience opened the mind to what he termed 'transpersonal' states of consciousness, involving 'an expansion of consciousness beyond conventional boundaries of the organism, and, correspondingly, a larger sense of identity' – i.e. the other world of the shaman. He says:

> *People, who have during their lifetime experientially confronted birth and death and connected with the transpersonal dimension, have good reasons to believe that their physical demise will not mean the end of their existence. They have personally experienced in a very convincing way that their consciousness transcends the boundaries of their physical body and is capable of functioning independently from it.*[18]

Or, as Abraham of Santa Clara, an Augustine monk puts it: 'Someone who dies before he dies does not die when he dies.'[19]

And according to John Matthews:

> *The descent of the initiate into the natures of each created species is an essential learning process. Divinity is implicit in all life – to discover and appreciate that divine nature is not accorded to many. The initiate seer-poet goes into the hide, the feather, the scale, the atom, the DNA of all life-forms and reassembles them as a totality of knowledge.*[20]

Matthews is saying that the whole history of evolution is open to the shaman. And by achieving this vision (whether through drugs or other means), the bog bodies had become, through this change in consciousness, aware of the entirety of organic life; they had become the 'master of the animals', aware of their own evolution from fish in the primal oceans, through reptiles and mammals, to human being. After all, there is an unbroken chain going back linking each of us to not just our human forefathers but also, through millions of years of evolution – back through apes, rodents and reptiles – to the first fish. If we could learn all that each of those millions of lives has known, just think how wise we would be. Perhaps the shaman had gained that knowledge; he had identified with that Being behind his own present being, a Being who, like Tuan mac Cairell, had been man, boar, stag and fish.

Such a figure, at one with the animals, appears to Fionn mac Cumhal:

> *One morning when Fionn was in the wood seeking Derg, he saw a man in the top of the tree, a blackbird on his shoulder and in his left hand a white vessel of bronze, filled with water in which was a skittish trout, and a stag at the foot of the tree. And this was the practice of the man: cracking nuts; and he would give half the kernel of a nut to the blackbird that was on his right shoulder while he would himself eat the other half ...*[21]

He ate half an apple, threw the rest to the stag, and poured water from the cauldron into his hand so that both he and the bird could drink. The man is depicted wearing a hood – perhaps like that of Tollund Man, and he eats nuts like Lindow III. His position at the top of the tree hints at his shamanic nature.

The evidence that I had accumulated certainly hinted that shamanism was at the heart of these ancient myths and experiences. The Grail myth was a quest for lost knowledge – not knowledge in the sense of something to be learned like a list, but an experience of totality that initiated the individual into what Jung terms 'individuation' (the making conscious of the totality of the psyche, the totality of being, and even beyond – the realisation of one's unity with the whole cosmos).[22] The Grail knight achieved the realisation that the Fisher King was actually a part of himself, his own latent divinity – trapped in the underworld since the end of the Neolithic. And as the Celtic myths make clear, the Wasteland would be healed by the rescue of that prisoner.

Notes

1. A woodcut by Breughel depicts a medieval custom in which a 'wild-man' clad in *fish scales* is mock-drowned in a lake. See Bly, R (1990) pp. 245–6.
2. Matthews, J and C (1996) p. 21.
3. For polydactylism see Turner, R C and Scaife, R G (1995) pp. 56–7, and for hazelnuts see pp. 80–1.
4. Matthews, J and C (1996) p. 138.
5. O'Farrel, P (1995) p. 56.
6. Quoted in Graves, R (1961) pp. 81–2.
7. Graves, R (1961) p. 89.
8. Campbell, J (1964) pp. 349–50.
9. Quoted in Hancock, G (1996) p. 85.
10. Matthews, C (1987) p. 135.
11. Matthews, J and C (1996) p. 94.
12. Matthews, J and C (1996) p. 94.
13. Matthews, J and C (1996) p. 97.
14. Matthews, J and C (1996) p. 17.
15. Of course there is also the connection to the 'third eye' of Hindu lore; and no doubt Stan Gooch would interpret the symbol as a reference to the 'inner eye' of the brain – the pineal gland. See Gooch, S (1975) p. 263.
16. Quoted in Matthews, J (1991) p. 39.
17. Quoted in Jung, C G (1989) p. 53.
18. Grof, S (1998) p. 16.
19. Grof, S (1998) p. 151.
20. Matthews, J (1991) pp. 176–7.
21. Ross, A (1996) p. 421.
22. This realisation is described in the Sanskrit phrase *Tat tvam asi* ('thou art that'), or in the Christian 'I and the father are one'. For a discussion of these higher states of realisation see Wilber, K (1996) pp. 253–71.

Chapter 22

MABON

During my quest I had traced the development of one myth through a number of transformations. This myth, which began with the simple death and rebirth of the god of the seasonal round, had entranced the first astronomer farmers in its incarnation as the rescue of Tammuz by Inanna, and in the Aryan age had been perverted into the theft of a vessel containing soma, the narcotic brew that had once afforded man an initiation into the supra-individual, but became the instrument for battle. Around the middle of the second millennium BC, however, an *enantiodromia* had occurred and man, now aware of his mortality, was set to embark on a quest like that of Gilgamesh, a journey to recover the secret of the old religion that granted immortality to the initiate of the Celtic mysteries.

During this reversal of sympathy the myth regained its original slant, though it became coloured by the intervening Arya myth. The soma quest had now become an attempt to undo the self-division caused by the killing of the old god, by journeying into his realm and drinking from the cauldron or releasing the prisoner – an act that would summon in a golden age.

Just as Isis sought the drowned Osiris after his death at the hands of his brother in the marshes of the Nile, and Demeter sought Persephone – in whose rites, after the *kykeon* had been drunk, the celebrants would see her rise from the abyss – so did the Celtic shamans seek to rescue the prisoner known as Mabon ('the Son'), the child of the great Mother herself, whose tale appears in the story of Culhwch and Olwen in the *Mabinogion*.

This early tale – possibly dating from the ninth century AD – tells of the winning of the beautiful Olwen, daughter of the giant Yspaddaden ('hawthorn') by the hero Culhwch ('pig-run', after the place he was found as a child). He can win her only if the giant is beheaded, which can be done only if he fulfils a number of *anoetheu* ('impossible tasks'). The motifs found in this tale are clear: Olwen ('white track', so named because of the trefoils that spring up where she walks, and also, of course, connected to the Milky Way and the River of Milk in the tale of Cú Roí) is the Blathnat of the tale, and her father is the Cú Roí. But in this tale, unlike in the Aryan myths, Yspaddaden dies willingly once the tasks are completed. One of the *anoetheu* set by Yspaddaden is to hunt the boar Twrch trwyth, but this can be done only if Mabon, son of Modron ('mother') is released, for only he can hunt with the magical dog needed to capture the boar. And it is from the razors and comb to be found on the crest of the boar that Yspaddaden is to be shaved then beheaded.

However, unfortunately Mabon has been lost since the start of time, and no one knows his whereabouts.

He was taken from his mother when three nights old, and it is not known where he now is, nor whether he is living or dead.[1]

But Culhwch is nephew to Arthur, who enlists three of his knights who know the language of the birds and beasts – Cai, Bedwyr and Gwrhyr Gwastawd Ieithoedd – to find the boy. Their quest echoes that of the mother eagle in the tale of the Hawk of Achill, for first they seek out the blackbird, asking if she has heard anything of Mabon son of Modron who, when just three nights old, was taken from between his mother and the wall. She tells them that she has lived long enough to peck away a smith's anvil, but has never heard of Mabon, and directs them to the Stag of Rhedynfr. Though he has seen a mighty oak progress from an acorn to a withered stump, his answer is the same; he then sends them to the ancient Owl of Cawllwyd, who has lived as long as three forests. The owl cannot help, nor can the Eagle of Gwern Abwy, the oldest bird. Yet he knows of an animal who is even older. He says that at the start of time he fought with a salmon, the Salmon of Llyn Llyw, the oldest living creature, so he will surely know something of Mabon. They find the salmon and he takes Cai and Bedwyr on his back and ferries them to a castle in Gloucester, where he has heard a strange lamenting. Sure enough, the lament is that of Mabon, imprisoned here since the beginning of the world. Gwrhyr fetches Arthur's men while Cai and the Salmon break down the wall, freeing the youth.[2]

The rescue of Mabon can be linked with the quest for the Hindu god Agni – the sacrificial flame who either hides in the waters or is a prisoner in the underworld. O'Flaherty says of him:

> *The myth of the finding of Agni is an analogue to the myth of the finding of the stolen Soma, and is, in fact, a variant of it, for it is the golden liquid of fire that is the basis of the Indo-European myth of Agni and Soma together.*[3]

In the *Rig Veda*, Agni is found hiding within the body of Vritra, the serpent demon, and has to be rescued from him by Indra, much as the Greek form of Indra, Zeus, rescues his siblings who are swallowed by their father Cronos. When the time comes for Zeus to be swallowed, his mother Rhea replaces the baby with a stone. In later alchemical thought the Grail was believed to be this very stone vomited by Cronos.[4] It is the soma freed from the throat of Rahu, or the porridge vomited by the Dagda.

But Agni in time is more than the sacred narcotic to be stolen from the demons; Agni lives for ever, his body forms the cosmos: 'His bone became the pine tree, his fat and flesh became a sweet-smelling resin …'[5] What's more, he is sacrificed by a priest named Hotr ('the invoker'), related, perhaps, to the Norse Hodr.[6] Agni is thus akin to Balder – he is the old lunar god personified, and, as the Hindu myths make clear, he is associated with the bull above all other. He is called 'the strong bull with sharp horns and seed a thousandfold'. The rescue of Agni is nothing less than the same act performed by Inanna in the old religion: it facilitates the rebirth of the slain god.

Because Agni is the carrier of sacrifices, he fears he will perish through fire, so he hides: 'He entered the waters. The gods wished to find him. A fish reported him and was cursed by him …'[7] But gods make him immortal so he can burn without dying: he is symbolised by the fire sticks that create fire.

All this is reminiscent of ergot and the immortality conferred on Demophoön. But what is most impressive is the fact that Agni's hiding place was given away by a *fish* – as, similarly, Mabon's whereabouts was revealed to Cai and Bedwyr by the Salmon.

The prisoner and the soma were one and the same image, and nowhere is this made more explicit than in a poem credited to Taliesin, who, legend records, was one of the seven survivors of Bran's expedition to Ireland. 'Preiddeu Annwn' (The Spoils of the other world) tells of the descent through seven other-worldy castles to rescue a prisoner and a cauldron:

> *Perfect was the captivity of Gweir in Caer Sidi,*
> *According to the tale of Pwyll and Pryderi.*
> *None before him was sent into it*
> *Into the heavy blue chain which bound the youth*
> *From before the reeving of Annwn he has groaned*
> *Until the ending of the world this prayer of poets:*
> *Three shipburdens of Prydwen entered the spiral city*
> *Except seven, none returned from Caer Sidi*
> *[the castle of the sídhe, or spiral castle]*

> *Is not my song worthily to be heard*
> *In the four-square caer four-times revolving?*
> *I draw my knowledge from the famous cauldron,*
> *The breath of nine maidens keeps it boiling*
> *Is not the head of Annwn's cauldron so shaped:*
> *Ridged with enamel, ridged with pearl?*
> *It will not boil the cowardly traitor's portion.*
> *The sword of Llwch Lleawc flashed before it*
> *And in the hands of Lleminiawc was it wielded*
> *Before hell's gates the lights were lifted (or a light was burning)*
> *When with Arthur we went with the harrowing –*
> *Except seven, none returned from Caer Veddwit.*[8]

The Gweir of the tale is none other than Gwri, the childhood name for Pryderi, the son of Rhiannon and Pwyll, the Mabon of the *Mabinogion*, who in the third branch becomes stuck to a golden bowl in a mysterious castle after chasing a boar. His mother journeys there and attempts to rescue him. The seven *caer* of the other world bring to mind the seven gates of the 'Land of No return' through which Inanna passed, shedding her vestments, in her search for Tammuz; and the same theme crops up in the search for Agni. In the *Rig Veda* Agni is described as hiding within seven mystical boundaries:

'The poets fashioned seven boundaries; he who was trapped. Went to only one of them.'[9] Caer Sidi, the 'spiral castle' in which the youth lies trapped, is clearly akin to the spinning fort of Cú Roí, in which resides the cauldron – and reminiscent of Silbury Hill with its spiral pathway.

As it is probable that Gwri Gwallt Euryn ('of the golden hair') and Gweir ('hay') are aspects of Mabon, it is clear that his myth is hedged in the same grain-based metaphors as the vegetation gods of the Near East. He is like the grain in the earth, apparently dormant, and awaiting rebirth – the seed, Liknites in the winnowing basket.

Although highly enigmatic, the poems of the pseudo-Taliesin, it seems, have underlying parallels with the Agni-Inanna schema. The appearance of these themes within Prieddeu Annwn means that one of three possibilities has to be correct: 1) the poems of pseudo-Taliesin do provide real mythical motifs; 2) it is all pure coincidence; 3) Taliesin's knowledge was not second-hand and he was, as he boasted, an initiate of this cult himself and the mysteries of the Salmon of Wisdom and the Cauldron of 'awen' had persisted, unseen, into the Christian era – just as the Classical mysteries had existed, sometimes in secret, away from the state religions. Greece, for instance, had maintained a state religion with the Aryan Zeus as its figure-head – the rites of the mysteries of Dionysos were always underground matters, and were often seen as dangerous to the stability of the state. Perhaps the same had been true of the Celtic mysteries; maybe under the surface of a religion that included many Aryan myths – telling of rites, conquest and dragon slayings, in the mould of the *Rig Veda* – these mysteries had flourished since the Neolithic.

The journeying to the underworld to obtain 'the treasure hard to obtain' is an echo of the motif that Leo Frobenius calls the 'Night Sea Journey' – an event in the life of heroes when they travel to the underworld to achieve rebirth, sometimes after being swallowed, like Jonah, by a water monster. While in the 'belly of the whale' the hero usually lights a fire with his fire sticks, facilitating his release – an act that symbolises creative illumination. As well as the clear link to the finding of Agni (the sacrificial fire) in the depths, the image also contains sexual symbolism in the production of fire through interaction between the 'female' socket and the male 'spindle'. Might not the thrusting of Llwch Lleawc's sword into the cauldron, and the line 'before hell's gates a light was burning' from Prieddeu Annwn (alternative translations of which reveal that this was the lighting of a flame) similarly refer to a relic of such an act of symbolic creation? The lighting of a torch, I had read, formed the start of the rites of Liknites at Delphi.

Surely the 'belly of the whale, the cave of the dragon', was the land of the demonic serpentine twin, and by going there a person united the partial mind and received the treasure, facilitating a new birth by the making of the fire in the womb. The journey to the Grail castle was a descent into the belly of the whale, but it was also a journey back through evolutionary time, like the journey of Gilgamesh, to a point before the split of the brother battle, before the fall, when the gods and man were one – i.e. a journey into the timelessness of the void.

But this was also, of course, the womb of the Mother. Mabon in chains was the child in the womb awaiting delivery. By seeking out the oldest animals, the heroes in the tale of Mabon were travelling back in time, returning to the primal chaos – as happened at the Samhain feast – regressing to some earlier, primal point of the cosmos, to the point of creation where divinity pours into the world like a wellspring. Which well describes what happens in the womb. Here, suspended in the waters of its mother, the foetus – which in its earliest form has gills – experiences a virtual whistle-stop tour of evolution from fish to mammal. The foetus is nourished by the placenta and bound to that grail of nourishment by the umbilicus, a coiled blue cord, no less (like the heavy blue chain that kept the prisoner bound in the underworld). This serpentine cord that reaches back to unity with the mother might lie behind the image of the caduceus, or even Tao. Was it a coincidence that Grof's patients, when taking LSD, entered an expansive state of consciousness where they had experiences of birth and death – an act which seemed to open them to transpersonal sides of the personality?

The fish in the Grail was the embryo in the womb, the phallus in the winnowing basket, Taliesin in the basket, the god man imprisoned and released from his cave – all potent symbols of rebirth in a Celtic rebirth cult.

What they uncover is a youth – an image of this original untainted divinity. This child is the 'son of the abyss', Dummuzi-Absu, whom Ishtar went to rescue from the underworld; he is 'Son of the Mother' whom Rhiannon seeks to rescue from the magical castle of the golden bowl; his role is that of Persephone, stolen from Demeter and taken to Hades. He is the god gored by the boar (his twin) and taken to the lands below. We are not to see him as childish. He is a child only in that he is newly created – he is closer to creation than we are. The rescue is a journey inwards, into that impersonal realm of the psyche Jung called the collective unconscious – a term 'psychological' enough for those of a rational mind to swallow, but which Jung himself, in his later years, saw in no uncertain terms as the mystical realm of the shaman.

But how could I be sure that Mabon was the slain twin, gored by the boar – or, like Osiris, slain by Seth while hunting the boar, so causing a wasteland? The answer was to be found in his relation to Pryderi, who like Mabon was stolen from his mother Rhiannon not long after his birth. When Pryderi is trapped in the other-worldly castle after hunting the boar the land is laid waste under an enchantment until Manawyddan, his uncle, undoes it and he is freed.

But perhaps the clearest indication that the prisoner in Annwn is the god slain by his solar brother is the myth of the Greek Cronos. Cronos – whose name Robert Graves suggests means 'crow'[11] – is foiled in his attempt to eat his son Zeus, who defeats him and imprisons him in an 'isle in the West', an isle that many classical authors identify with Britain. Here he is guarded by the hundred-handed Briareus until his release, an act that will restore the fabled Golden Age, a theme, as Caitlin Matthews points out, that is found in Virgil's fourth eclogue:

> *Now has the last great age begun,*
> *By Cumae's seer foretold*
> *New born the mighty cycles run*
> *Their course, and quit the old.*
> *Now too, the Virgin reappears, and Saturn recontrols the spheres.*[12]

But Saturn, who is Cronos, imprisoned by Zeus, the serpent father overcome by the sun, reappears as a youth:

> *Now is a new race on the way*
> *From heaven: do thou befriend*
> *The infant, all but born, whose day*
> *The iron brood shall end*
> *And with the golden fill the earth.*[13]

But this is only to be expected. As a vegetation god the lunar-serpent had died only to reappear youthful again. And what of the pharaoh at the Heb Sed, renewed after his decapitation and rebirth? Santillana and Von Dechend say:

> *Saturn/Cronos, he whom Zeus dethroned by throwing him off his chariot, and banished in chains to a blissful island, where he dwells in sleep, for being immortal he cannot die, but is thought to live a life-in-death wrapped in funerary linen, until his time, say some, shall come to awaken again, and he will be reborn to us as a child.*[14]

Mabon's chains are the blue chains of the watery abyss – the umbilicus that binds him to the mother.[15] And, like Cronos, he is the old slain god become young again, as Caitlin Matthews says:

> *The child is Mabon, the transformed Pen Annwn [head of the underworld], whose star rises once again.*[16]

If this is all correct, then the release of the prisoner is nothing less than the reintegration of the dark twin, foisted from power during the Bronze Age. The myth of Mabon lies at the heart of the British mysteries: he was the dying god of a Celtic Eleusis-type cult, the Wounded King in need of healing. His myth was a potent symbol for initiation into the druidic mysteries – a template for psychological transformation, which at certain points in history, as the bog men bore witness, had been enacted literally.

It is all very well talking about releasing prisoners and resurrecting dead gods, but in a ritual framework – like that which saw the death of the bog men – how was this to be enacted? I had seen how in the Egyptian Heb Sed the pharaoh, whose beheading was symbolic, acted out this rebirth, but what about in earlier times when the king had literally been killed? In this instance, clearly the rebirth was the enthronement of a new king – in which case the rites involving the severed head would have been of great importance.

The question that now had to be answered was what part did the severed heads of the bog men – like that of the dead pharaoh in the Heb Sed – play in such a rite of rebirth? What did the head actually do? One clue has already been given in the tale of Bran. The decapitated giant, whose head entertains his men in an 87-year-long other-worldly feast, says 'A fo bid Pen, bid pont' ('He who is chief, let him be a bridge').[17] The word he used for 'leader' was 'Pen' ('head'), so his words could be interpreted as meaning that the sacred decapitated heads, amongst which his own could be counted, *somehow acted as a bridge between the worlds*. And, once more, it is an Indian myth that illuminates this point.

It tells of the sage Dadhyanc, who taught the 'secret' of soma that he had obtained from the ambrosial udders of the cows of Tvastr, father of the god Indra. Tvastr ('Twin'!) had hidden his cows from his belligerent son, who in return had slain him in rage at being deprived of their gift of immortality. Only Dadhyanc knew the secret of their whereabouts, but would not divulge this to the god, who in his fury beheaded him. The head was hidden in the mountains and *fell into a lake from where it rose from the waters to answer questions*. It was from this oracular head that Indra learned, at last, the secret of soma.[18]

Were the severed heads and bog victims of Celtic religion playing a role similar to that of the sage Dadhyanc? From their watery abode were they offering the secret of immortality? In the Vedic myths soma was a drug that had to be stolen from the demon's throat, but here soma was not a narcotic liquid, but an initiating flow of words – a magic formula almost. Soma was the knowledge passed on through the speaking of the severed head, as if communication itself was the point: the passing on of occult knowledge from the realm of the dead.

On reading this myth I realised I'd heard this all before – in Norse myth.

The prime Norse god is Odin (Wotan), a warrior, huntsman and Lord of the Dead. He is a god of magic and a shaman, who sacrifices himself on the world tree Yggdrasil, on which he hangs for nine days and nights, with his spear Gungnir in his side, to grasp the other-worldly wisdom of the runes.[19] In one myth Odin, transformed into an eagle, swallows the magical blood of Kvasir – the divine mead of inspiration – and brings it to Asgard, the realm of the gods, and spits it into a bowl.[20] A soma theft if ever there was one!

Odin is able to converse with 'hanged men', a necromantic ability that will prove very useful because, after the decapitation of the giant Mimir,

Odin preserves his head with oils and spices and sets it in a well at the foot of Yggdrasil, where he gives him his eye in return for other-worldly knowledge![21] The imagery is clear: the other-worldly wisdom of immortality could be gained from the severed head kept in the well. And by receiving this knowledge, Odin becomes one-eyed – a primal Bachlach, the Salmon of Wisdom – and an initiate of the knowledge of the unity of all things, of the secret of the two partners. The head of Mimir consulted by Odin, like the head of Dadhyanc consulted by Indra, is that of the knowledgeable one, the twin (Mimir deriving, of course, from the Norse Ymir, a reflex of *Yemo).

In Classical myth this motif finds expression in the tale of Orpheus, who is ripped into pieces by the Maenads. His head is cast into the river Hebrus and floats to the island of Lesbos, where it is placed on a stone in a cave and becomes an oracle. Orpheus, like the Dagda and Shiva, possesses a magical lyre with which, like the Bachlach herdsman, he can enchant the animals. He is also a shaman, able to descend into Hades whilst alive in an attempt to rescue his beloved Eurydice (although this is ultimately unsuccessful). What's more, his name means 'fisher'.

Suddenly all became clear: the secret rites that had occurred at the Heb Sed were undoubtedly centred on the speaking of the severed head. Had not the head of Bran entertained his men at the other-worldly feast? Had not the head of Conaire Mor spoken when given water? Only the head on the dish seen by Peredur did not utter a word, and as a result the land remained waste, for he had failed to ask it a question! The head, of course, was oracular, like the severed head of Orpheus. This was the key to the Grail mystery – *the asking of a question.*

The land remained waste until the hero opened his mouth. Opened his mouth … In a flash I knew I had solved the mystery.

Mabon

Notes

1. Matthews, C (1987) p. 132.
2. Matthews, C (1987) pp.131–2.
3. Doniger O'Flaherty, W (trans.) (1981) p. 108.
4. Matthews, J (1997) p. 19.
5. Doniger O'Flaherty, W (trans.) (1975) p. 100.
6. Doniger O'Flaherty, W (trans.) (1975) p. 100.
7. Doniger O'Flaherty, W (trans.) (1975) p. 101.
8. Translated by C Matthews in Matthews, C (1987) pp. 107–8.
9. Doniger O'Flaherty, W (trans.) (1981) p. 118.
10. Campbell, J (1993) pp. 247–8.
11. Graves, R (1961) p. 66.
12. Quoted in Matthews, C (1987) p. 171.
13. Quoted in Matthews, C (1987) p. 171.
14. Santillana and Von Dechend (1977) p. 266.
15. In the Classical mysteries of the Persian god Mithras, such a figure – a lion-headed man entwined within a giant serpent, who holds the keys to the Underworld – is known as Cronos (or Aion), and represents eternity.
16. Matthews, C (1987) p. 172.
17. Jones, G and Jones, T (1974) p. 34.
18. Doniger O'Flaherty, W (trans.) (1975) pp. 56–9.
19. Crossley Holland, K (1980) pp. 15–17.
20. Crossley Holland, K (1980) pp. 26–32.
21. Crossley Holland, K (1980) pp. 184, 188.

Chapter 23

THE OPENING
OF THE MOUTH

It was the head of Dadhyanc rising from the lake that revealed to me the final solution to the mystery: the asking of a question. The soma pours out of his mouth as a flow of words revealing a great secret to Indra, words that were immortality. But how can words give life? I asked myself. It was the same as the Grail question; how could the asking of a question heal the Wasteland? And then it became obvious; it established communication with the wounded god. But this was all academic until I could prove that such a soma-filled head had healed a Wasteland in Celtic myth.

I would eventually discover that such an image existed in a myth I already knew – the tale of the curse of Macha. Macha, a horse goddess, dies giving birth to twins after being forced to run a race against the King of Ulster's horses. As she gives birth she curses the men of Ulster, saying that in their times of greatest need they, and their descendants for nine generations, will experience her birth pangs for five days and four nights, and have no more strength than a woman in labour.[1]

Surely the image of these men – who directly caused the death of Macha, who is no doubt the equivalent to Tiamat, the primal mother – is that of the wounded king, lying on his bier in agony. The pangs overtake them during the Táin, when only Cú Chulainn, who was immune to the pangs, was fighting the entirety of the Connacht army.

Cú Chulainn pleads with his earthly father Sualdamh to rouse the Ulstermen, but they lie prone in Emhain Macha. Sualdamh rides in to the rath (a circular enclosure) shouting 'Men murdered, cattle stolen, women plundered.'[2] He is ignored; the men just talk lethargically amongst themselves. Only after Sualdamh trips over his shield and his head is cut off on its sharpened rim (like the discus that cuts off the head of the soma-stealing Rahu) and brought into the hall upon the shield, do the men of Ulster finally listen to him.[3] Then the men are roused to action.

To me the symbol was clear – the pangs of labour, the punishment of Macha, was a Wasteland enchantment, undone by the words of the severed head, raising the Ulstermen from out of their torpor. Like the words from the mouth of Mimir or Dadhyanc, the words of the dead Sualdamh somehow end the lethargy, the curse. I had been happy with this reading of the myth until fortuitously I came upon a passage by Anne Ross in which she talks of the Ulster hero Conall Cernach – Conall the horned, he who in the cattle raid of Froech rescues the cows from the serpent, which he wraps around his waist. As 'Conall the horned', he was of course the wild herdsman Cernunnos, the shaman who was depicted holding the ram-horned serpent. Ross, speaking of the severed head of this hero, says:

> *Milk drunk from it was capable of removing from the Ulstermen their traditional weakness which came upon them in times of martial stress, and deprived them of their fighting powers.*[4]

Could it be more clearly stated than this? The milk is no doubt that of the three magic cows – it is soma, or the Dagda's porridge. It is to be drunk by the Ulstermen to end the Wasteland caused by the creative killing of the primal deity.

Now I knew what Peredur should have done – he should have picked up the severed head and drank from its mouth! But the flow from the mouth, like that from Dadhyanc, can be given as a formula, a magic word; it is the cry of the Bennu bird that ushers in the new creation after its immolation. This is why the Grail knight has to ask this wounded king a question – because a question promotes a dialogue. And only the head of a dead man can do this – for in death he becomes one with the lord of the underworld, just as the dead pharaoh in Egypt was to be identified with Osiris. The bog men, too, by their triple deaths had become one with this hidden deity; their wounded bodies or severed heads would be used by the living to communicate with the dead god, the dweller in the house of water, the primal fish of knowledge. They had literally become 'a bridge

204

for the people', linking the world of the living and the dead.

In the rites of Dionysos at Delphi, as the child Liknites was seen to stir in the winnowing basket – reborn on the site of the omphalos (the navel) – the priestess Pythia was performing a sacred rite involving a large cauldron on a tripod. She performed oracular rites, answering the questions posed to the god, acting as his mouthpiece. But to get an answer the questioners had to sacrifice a kid – a sacrifice that recreated the original sacrifice of Dionysos and his dismemberment and placing in the cauldron. Kerenyi states how this sacrifice stood for that of Dionysos, who had descended below and opened the knowledge of that realm to the questioner. Originally the sacrifice would have been that of a man – and this is clearly what was going on in Celtic times: men were dying, aping the god's death and dismemberment to provide oracular answers. This rite was seen to mirror that of the rebirth of the land in the coming back to life from a state of torpor of the god Liknites – the seed in the basket – Taliesin, the salmon in the stream. Pythia received her answers from oracular bones that flew into her hand, but in olden days the answer would no doubt have come from the god in the cauldron himself – like the prophesying head of Orpheus, whom Apollo apparently silenced after he drew the crowds away from his own shrine at Delphi. As either a head in the well or a wounded bog man, how was the oracular wisdom – that flow of milk from the mouth – to be elicited?

There is an Egyptian rite that shows how the king is to be woken; and it was this rite that had sprung to mind when I thought that the Wasteland would have been healed if only Peredur had opened his mouth. It is called the 'Opening of the Mouth' ceremony, and was performed on the dead pharaoh's mummy by his successor. In this ceremony, the would-be king, playing the role of the god Horus, son of Osiris, descends into the tomb, symbolic of the nether world, wearing a hawk mask (the soma-stealing fire-bird?). He 'rescues' his father Osiris (the old king, dead in his sarcophagus) from 'unconsciousness' – as the texts themselves put it – by opening the mouth of the dead man's mummy with an adze.[5]

Surely this was a form of the rite that was performed in secret at the Heb Sed, for the 'Opening of the Mouth' was the rite that transferred kingship to the dead man's successor, just as previously the Heb Sed had, although in later times when the death was symbolic it was a renewal of pharaonic power. The ceremony was a startling doppelganger of the Grail myth.

The dead pharaoh, as Osiris, is inert, dead, and passive: unconscious. He 'needs the care of his successor, his "beloved son", in order to achieve beatification and to function as a spirit.'[6] In other words, like the Wounded King, he cannot heal himself; he requires outside help.

These rites occur after the son Horus has been vanquished and has made peace with the evil Seth – with the fiery principle that had caused the wounding to begin with. The destructive dominance of the ego is thus curbed and, to use allusions from 'Hamlet' again, all that is 'rotten within the state of Denmark' is driven out by the victory over the murderous uncle, and the 'foul and most unnatural murder' is finally avenged. Horus immediately sets off to awake the soul of Osiris – to rouse him from un-consciousness.[7] This done, the New Year begins. This rite is not just about helping the crops grow again; it is about a spiritual rebirth. As Rundle Clark puts it, Osiris is:

> helpless, and the power he embodies is inert, asleep or listless, and completely passive ... the result of Horus' ministrations is that Osiris can 'send out his soul' or 'set himself in motion' ... they are the 'rescuing of the god' ... If the king carried out the required rites for his father, the latter could then become 'a soul', which meant that the powers of life and growth would begin again in nature.[8]

The Pyramid Texts reveal the words spoken in this ritual:

> May the god Ptah open my mouth, and may the god of my city loose the swathings which are over my mouth.

> Come loose the bandages, even the bandages of Seth.[9]

The bandages over the mummy's mouth are seen as the 'bonds of Seth', so by opening the mouth the dead god is freed from his bindings; they are the chains that keep Gweir in Caer Sidi, the chains of Zeus that hold Cronos in his island prison. They are his 'funerary bandages', as Santillana puts it, the unloosening of which will bring the Golden Age and the reappearance of the god on earth, just as the rebirth of Osiris would institute a golden age known as Zep Tepi (the 'First Time'). But only if his mouth is opened ...

The mouth of the mummy is literally clawed open with an iron instrument, releasing the 'soul' that flies to the heavens to be united with Osiris so that the dead king literally becomes one with the god, and awakes from the sleep of death. The Horus-Son is then crowned as pharaoh. The interesting point as far as Norse myth is concerned is that Horus can only wake his father (i.e. open his mouth) after presenting him with his eye![11] The ritual that takes place between the Horus-king and the mummy is identical to that between Odin and the mummified head of Mimir – especially the version practised at the Heb Sed where the pharaoh's head formed the integral part of the rites.

It now seems entirely probable that the remains of the bog men had been placed specifically in the uncorrupting tannin-stained waters of the peat bogs, so they, like the Egyptian mummy, or Mimir's head pickled in oils and spices, would be preserved for ever.

Unlike the earlier seasonal myths the Wasteland continues indefinitely if this 'opening of the mouth' is not performed. 'But if, after death, the deceased king were to remain for ever in this first Osiris form, the outlook for him and for the world would be grim and hapless.'[12] Until then the king waits lamenting in the prison. Arthur cannot rouse himself from the slumber of centuries. The Grail king remains sick until the pure fool asks the question. That which is unconscious cannot illuminate itself – it has to be searched for, redeemed.

I thought of the numerous local legends in which a simple country lad discovers Arthur and his knights sleeping in a cave, or under a hill. To wake the men he is required to perform a certain task, or to blow a horn and unsheathe a sword, but he normally flees in terror as the knights begin to move, and so the job is left undone. He hears a voice from the depths rebuking him for his cowardice that has kept the men imprisoned.[13]

That the awakening of Osiris is explicitly linked with the Grail legends is shown in the following esoteric hymn to Osiris, part of the god's mysteries in which the initiate undergoes a symbolic rite or shamanic journey equivalent to the 'opening of the mouth'. Its words could have come straight from the lips of one of the Grail knights:

I have come hither [into the mansion of the dead Osiris] to save myself
...
to sit in the room of Father Osiris
and to dispel the sickness of the suffering god, so that I can appear an
Osiris in strength,
that I may be reborn with him in his renewed vigour,
that I may reveal to you the matter of Osiris' thigh
and read to you from that sealed roll which lies beneath his side,
whereby the mouths of the gods are opened'.[14]

Rundle Clark says of this passage:

The affliction of the god is interpreted as a sickness which Horus will
cure. The thigh is an oblique reference to fertility; if the wound in the
thigh can be cured, the water and the male fluid will gush forth and
life begin again.[15]

This is the Grail quest, pure and simple. When the king revives, pharaonic power is transferred to the successor.[16] Thus the Grail knight often becomes the new Grail king; Pwyll becomes Pen Annwn; and the waters return to the land.

The relation between the wounded god and the waters is made clear in the so-called 'Elucidation' of Chrétien de Troyes' unfinished *Le Conte del Graal* (which is in fact a 484-line prologue tacked on by an anonymous author). Part of it reads:

In ancient times Logres [England] was a rich country but it was
turned into a Wasteland so that it was worth scarcely a couple of
hazelnuts. For the kingdom lost the voices of the wells and the damsels
that were in them. These damsels would offer food and drink to
wayfarers. A traveller had only to wish for food and seek out one of the
wells and a damsel would appear from out of the well with the food he
liked best, a cup of gold in her hand ...

But King Amangons broke this custom. Although it was his duty
to guard the damsels ... he raped one of them and took away her
golden cup for his own service. After that time no damsel was seen

issuing from the well. And so the service of the wells ceased. The land was laid waste: trees lost their leaves, meadows and plants withered and the waters were dried up so that no man might find the Court of the Rich Fisherman, he that once made the land bright with his treasures.

After this time, King Arthur instituted the Knights of the Round Table, who, were determined to recover the wells and protect the damsels. But though they made vows to God, they could never hear a voice from the well nor could they find any damsel, for these had been pierced by the swords of Amangon's followers or else hanged ...

On the day that the Court of the Rich Fisherman was found, and the correct answers received by the seeker, the waters flowed again; fountains, which had been dried up, ran into the meadows. Fields were green ... on the day that the Court of Joy was found.[17]

A wall of stakes, we learn from Chrétien in his *Erec and Enid*, surrounded this Court of Joy, on which were mounted severed heads. On coming to the court, if the magical horn were blown, the prisoner Mabinograin (derived from the child-god Mabon) would be released.[18]

The Elucidation, then, is rich in mythic symbolism. The rape of the maidens is akin to the rape of Persephone in Classical myth – and serves to sever the communication between the worlds, the 'voices' of the wells no longer being heard. In this instance it is clear that the rape of the female principle is behind the Wasteland, and is the equivalent to the wounding in the thigh of the maimed king. The king's wound renders him unable to keep the earth fertile – and the rape of the goddess is the rape of the land itself. However, the asking of the Grail question, it seems, regenerated these 'voices'. Here, explicitly, is the connection between the 'Opening of the Mouth' and the healing of the Wasteland – just as the waters that were dried up in the tale of Conaire Mor would have been restored once Mac Cecht performed his rite on the king's head and got it to speak.

To my mind the closest parallel to the 'Opening of the Mouth' rite in Celtic myth is found in the Irish tale 'The Phantom's Frenzy'. The would-be king, Conn of the Hundred Battles (a historic ruler of the second century AD), finds himself in the other-worldly court of the god Lug ('shining') – once the blazing victor of the demonic one-eyed Balor, but in the Celtic reversal of Bronze Age symbolism, now the god of the other world, who, like Odin, owns a pair of oracular ravens. A beautiful woman is in the underworld court, wearing a golden crown: she is the sovereignty of the land. Holding a golden cup she fills it with ale and asks the god 'to whom is this cup to be offered?' – which is nothing less than the Grail question itself: 'whom does the Grail serve?' On being asked this question the god enters a mantic fit of oracular ecstasy (the 'phantom's frenzy' of the title) and prophesies the future line of Irish kings – which is recorded on yew wands. Conn then becomes the king.[19]

Here the other-worldly descent of Horus, the transfer of kingship and the 'opening of the mouth' of the dead god are all apparent. And, of course, the golden cup in the hands of the goddess is the Grail itself.

In all probability such a ceremony lay behind the magical druidic technique known as Teinm Lada ('Song of Inspiration'). In this rite a freshly severed head was placed on a stone pillar before a fire within a 'feasting hall'. After a sacred meal of *salmon*, the head was touched with 'ogham' sticks (yew wands inscribed with a magical Celtic alphabet), whereon it begins to speak – and prophesy.[20] Such a rite could be used, so the texts say, by a druid wishing to discover the identity of a man's killer.

Irish myths preserve a tradition of the use of such yew wands for divination. In the Welsh poem 'The Battle of the Trees', Bran is thought to be the victim, because of the twigs he is holding in his hand. Odin undergoes self-sacrifice at the world tree to gain the knowledge of the 'runes' – inscribed wooden wands – from the underworld. Interestingly, twigs are often found in the hands of bog bodies – in the three from Borre Fen in Denmark, for example.[21] The runes were the native form of the bones in the cauldron used by Pythia at Delphi, and were the means by which the prophetic utterances of the god were communicated.

After over a decade of searching, I finally had an answer to the questions that Lindow Man had posed in the British Museum one winter's day long before. The bog men were the remains of kings, (or their surrogates), or druidic shamans (of both sexes) who in a literal re-enactment of the death and rebirth of the god underwent a ritual death to renew the creation of the cosmos – after which they were consulted as oracular severed heads to renew the communication between this and the other world, an act which granted to the participants a sense of immortality. In favour of this theory was the fact that Lindow Man had not been immediately dumped in the water, but kept on land for a matter of hours – during which time divinatory practices no doubt would have taken place. Even when placed in the water the dead man would have been preserved for eternity, like a mummy. Possibly he would be visited again and again to be questioned further or asked for blessings or magical assistance – the sinister origin of the wishing well.

I am not saying that the head literally spoke, that in some necromantic rite the spirit of the deceased spoke through his body; rather, the presence of the head itself, symbolising the god, had a psychological effect on the participant. The oracular use of severed heads was not unique to the Celtic realm; it appeared as a minor cult in Greece and Etruria in the centuries before Christ, for instance.[22] Julian Jaynes is adamant that such practices were grounded in the attempt to evoke aural hallucinations stemming from the subjugated right brain – in other words, the unconscious. It seems as if the Celts were following a similar pattern; the severed head acted as a symbol for their own unconscious divinity. By establishing a dialogue with the 'head' they opened themselves to this suppressed stream of knowledge – knowledge of a supra-personal nature, of realities beyond normal consciousness – and thus achieved apotheosis with the divinity within, the Persephone side of their being. But this was not a return to the original unconsciousness; it was a bringing into the light of that which had been lost. The ego did not dive into the depths to be dissolved again into the maternal abyss; it lit a fire in the whale's belly and escaped with the ultimate treasure – the conscious awareness of the totality of being, what the ancients had termed the *daemon* and what Jung called the 'Self'.

But the words of the head did more than prophesy. The Egyptian mummy god Ptah (a form of Osiris) created the world through his speech.[23] The cry of the Bennu bird ushered in a new world. It was an act of cosmogony. Similarly, the songs of the druid initiates such as Amergin and Taliesin formed the cosmos. As the Old Irish text Senchus Mor says: 'The druids claimed they made the sky, the earth, the sea and so forth, the sun and moon and so forth.'[24] In the beginning, I thought, was the Word ...

This rebirth cult no doubt existed as a mystery tradition, like that of Eleusis, initiating many into the knowledge of the deep. For most the dismemberment of the god was experienced as a killing off of the old personality and not as a literal death, but in some places at certain times the myth had been enacted in physical reality – perhaps in times of crisis when there seemed to be a special need to re-establish harmony with the hidden source of being. Celtic religion had many regional cults and variations, so possibly in some areas the tradition was interpreted more literally than in others. But to see the act of sacrifice as unholy and abhorrent is to misunderstand it. Christianity, after all, is based on the actual sacrifice of a man for the public good.

Two questions had beset me at the start of my quest, and now they had been answered. The first asked why an Iron Age man had been ritually slain and deposited in a peat marsh in prehistoric Cheshire. The second concerned the meaning of the legends of the Grail in which the wounding of a king in the thigh (perhaps by his brother) blasted the fertility of the land – an enchantment that could be undone only by journeying to a magical castle and asking a specific question (which would 'release the waters'). In time I had discovered that the two questions were in fact one.

At least I felt that I could go back to the British Museum with something to offer that man in the glass tomb. I now knew he had not died as an offering for fertility, not on such a materialistic level, anyway. His death was an attempt to forge a new way in the world – to heal a split in the Western mind. He died to become Pen Annwn, and the druids drinking from his cup would rebuild that bridge with the underworld that had been broken when the horse lords came – at least until Christianity arrived.

Now that I had explored the meaning behind the Celtic Grail to its deepest roots, it was possible to reconstruct the last few moments of the life of such sacrificial victims.

Within the sacred grove, at the edge of the water (neither on land, then, nor on water) at the cusp of the seasons, the consecrated man (playing the role of 'Twin', the old horned lunar god with his serpents) mates with a priestess (embodying the earth goddess) whose noose is around his neck. At a given signal a vicious blow to the man's skull ends the act; the noose is tightened and his jugular slit so that his blood pumps out onto the muddy ground. The three deaths – a legacy of when he was the triple-headed Nghi – now recreate the cosmos, defining the tripartite society. His dying paroxysms are observed with care. A ritual fire is lit, perhaps destroying the concentric posts of a grove, and the onlookers are silent as the old year, the old cosmos, is burned away. In the pause between worlds, the still before creation, the man is decapitated and his head is placed on a pillar before either an intoxicated druid in a mantic trance or the successor of the slain king, whose body is racked with the burning sensations of ergot. He casts his yew wands, perhaps touching the mouth of the dead man, his body arching and writhing, his soul descending to the gates of the other world. Quietly at first he begins to speak, and his voice is the voice of the deceased god. The druid's prophetic frenzied utterances are noted, a gentle breeze stirs the branches of the grove, and somewhere a bird begins to sing. The land is reborn.

Lindow Man and his fellow victims, whatever their origin and status in life, were by their deaths attempting a redemption of the split cosmos through enacting the murder and 'awakening' of the decapitated god, whose world-creating voice offered immortality to those with ears to hear, and re-established the Golden Age. Looked at psychologically, this deed was the re-establishment of an inner dialogue with the hitherto repressed ancestral parts of the psyche; looked at with a more open mind it somehow put the victim in touch with a supra-personal realm that granted him immortality. To the entranced druid priests sitting before the head, their hands still sticky with the blood of sacrifice, it was in fact their own lost divinity that sang to them, though with the face of a recently dead man.

And those who witnessed the rite, like the pharaoh at the Heb Sed, would have emerged like Persephone and Demeter – Kings of Two Lands.

I am reminded of the story of the rainmaker, a true story told to Carl Jung by his friend the Sinologist Richard Wilhelm (as told here by Colin Wilson):

Wilhelm was in a remote Chinese village that was suffering from drought. A rainmaker was sent for from a distant village. He asked for a cottage on the outskirts of the village, and vanished into it for three days. Then there was a tremendous downpour, followed by snow – an unheard of occurrence at that time of year.

Wilhelm asked the old man how he had done it; the old man replied that he hadn't. 'You see', said the old man, 'I come from a region where everything is in order. It rains when it should rain and is fine when that is needed. The people are themselves in order. But the people in this village are out of Tao and out of themselves, so I asked for a cottage on the edge of the village, so I could be alone. When I was once more in Tao, it rained.[25]

His Tao is the undivided mind that heals the Wasteland. The Celts, in their own way, were trying to re-establish Tao – a balance of the dark and the light and knowledge of the unity behind them. In the tale of Peredur the hero sees a vision of this cosmic harmony the maintenance of which was the *raison d'être* of the Grail quest:

Peredur rode on towards a river valley whose edges were forested, with level meadows on both sides of the river; on one bank there was a flock of white sheep, and on the other a flock of black sheep. When a white sheep bleated a black sheep would cross the river and turn white, and when a black sheep bleated a white sheep would cross the river and turn black. On the bank of the river he saw a tall tree; from roots to crown one half was aflame and the other green with leaves.[26]

Celtic religion was an attempt to maintain this state of cosmic equilibrium, and the sacrificial victim, in his death and rebirth, was the instrument through which that harmony would be achieved.

Notes

1. Kinsella, T (1990) pp. 7–8.
2. Kinsella, T (1990) p. 218.
3. Kinsella, T (1990) p. 219.
4. Ross, A (1996) p. 201.
5. Rundle Clark, R T (1959) p. 122.
6. Rundle Clark, R T (1959) p. 107.
7. Rundle Clark, R T (1959) p. 112.
8. Rundle Clark, R T (1959) p. 108.
9. Wallis Budge, E A (1989) p. 133.
10. Wallis Budge, E A (1989) p. 132.
11. Rundle Clark, R T (1959) p. 122.
12. Rundle Clark, R T (1959) pp. 121–2.
13. See Westwood, J (1987) pp. 6, 455–6.
14. Rundle Clark, R T (1959) p. 160.
15. Rundle Clark, R T (1959) pp. 160–1.
16. Rundle Clark, R T (1959) p. 161.
17. Quoted in Matthews, C (1989) pp. 250–2.
18. See Matthews, C (1987) p. 159.
19. This tale is told in Loomis, R S (1992) pp. 47–53.
20. See Matthews, J (1991) pp. 184–6.
21. Glob, P V (1988) pp. 86–93.
22. Jaynes, J (1993) p. 333.
23. Campbell, J (1962) p. 84.
24. Lincoln, B (1991) p. 182.
25. Wilson, C (1984) pp. 153–4.
26. Gantz, J (trans.) (1985) p. 243.

Epilogue

THE SPIRIT
IN THE BOTTLE

As I crouch down by the Chalice Well I mull over the last few years' thoughts that have brought me back here. And so my story of the Grail is told. And in my mind's eye I see Dion Fortune bending over the well, with the man bound within his niche – his face barely discernable, a pallid ivory moon in the bloodstained waters.

I lean over and see my own reflection staring up at me. This is all he ever was – the man in the depths, a reflection of those who would seek him and restore him to life. But the face below the water, if the Celts and the initiates of Eleusis were to be believed, was the enduring face, and what *I* saw as the reality was but a transient reflection, an *eidolon* in time and space of a timeless and enduring being. I have no doubt that Lindow Man went willingly to his death. He went to be a bridge for his people, perhaps in times of great stress when the way between the worlds had been lost. There are not enough remains to suggest that this rite was anything but a rare occurrence. For the most part, I believe, such ceremonies and initiations, like the later Heb Sed, would have been symbolic. The participant, like Sir Gawain, might have received the smallest of nicks on the neck, but his head would have remained firmly on his shoulders.

But perhaps when a person felt it was demanded of him or her, the great offering would be made. The shrivelled man in the British Museum was no hapless victim; he was a hero – a man sacrificed for his people; a redeemer; a prefiguration, dare I say, of Christ. Perhaps this is why, when Christianity arrived in the Celtic provinces, such sacrifices were deemed unnecessary – for had not Christ (whose symbol was the fish and whose disciples were

217

'fishers of men') undergone his self-sacrifice so that the cosmos would be redeemed *once and for all time*? Did not his flesh, consumed at the sacred feast, like that of the mystical salmon, confer life everlasting? Had he not harrowed hell and freed its prisoners? Christ bore all the hallmarks of a great Celtic hero or god. Celtic Christianity, it is clear, took over much of pagan Celtic belief. The transference was no doubt not a difficult matter: the priests even wore the druidic tonsure, and the legends of St Alban and St Winefrede, amongst others, show that some pagan beliefs were integrated into the new religion. A special place remained in the Celtic imagination for those magical wells and their grisly occupants, and the Christian veneer painted over them was extremely thin.

Paganism in Ireland came to an end after the death in 565 of Diarmait Mc Cearbaill, who six years earlier had celebrated the last ritual marriage with sovereignty at Tara. Similarly, in Britain, in 573, Rhydderch Hael at the battle of Arderydd on the river Esk wiped out the native paganism by defeating the heathen King Gwenddolau.[1] But Gwenddolau's bard, Myrddin, escaped to the wilds to prophesy and to compose poetry – and it is this man that lies behind the prophet Merlin, last of the druids.[2]

But did druidism die when that wolf-shaman finally perished in the crags of Celyddon?

Christianity offered a welcome message of love to a bloody world, yet the moral, masculine nature of this religion, like that of the Arya, came to be too one-sided. It rejected the world and the feminine in a manner not unlike the earlier Bronze Age cults, and once again relegated the instincts to a dark nether world, crowning the lord of that infernal realm with the horns of the pagan Celtic Cernunnos, the 'horned one'. For a second time the communal, shamanic culture was repressed by the domination of the sun: St Michael cast down the dark angel, and the realm of the old gods was once again a place of darkness and desolation. But bubbling under the left-brained dominance of Christianity an undercurrent of the old world continued to exist – including the Welsh revival of which the pseudo-Taliesin poet was part. Was it possible that a pagan mystery cult had continued to exist, hidden from the eyes of the Church? Absence of evidence, as they say, is not evidence of absence.

These were the new questions that were forming in my mind.

The druidic truths themselves had not been lost; the descendants of these pagan priests – the bards – had never forgotten the old myths, though their meanings may perhaps have faded. And when the bards became the raconteurs in the halls of the Norman nobility, their secular tales began to gain in popularity and underwent a renaissance. At the forefront of this rebirth were the tales of Arthur and his knights, which included the Quest for the Holy Grail – a legend that in the Christian Wasteland was still pregnant with meaning.

But now within this vessel of rebirth, the womb of the Mother, was to be found the blood of Christ, the Holy Sacrament that offered men life eternal. The contents of the cup in effect had not changed at all.

Whether or not the British mysteries continued to be celebrated, other hidden traditions certainly *did* exist, whose symbolism owed much to the earlier pagan traditions usurped by Christianity. Secret societies preserved the initiations of the mystery traditions, and continued the study of magic. But were these traditions a continuation of the pagan cults or spontaneous creations founded on the same archetypal symbolism?

Members of the mysterious military order, the Knights Templar, for instance, were said to worship an idol called Baphomet.[3] This idol was nothing less than a severed head, and its name, a coded form of the Greek 'Sophia' ('wisdom'), linked it at least nominally with the figure of Pwyll ('Wisdom'), the 'Head' of Annwn in Celtic myth. Many confessions, forced from the Templars by torture, revealed that the ability to bring *fertility to the land* was attributed to this head. Was it possible that the Templars had somehow managed to preserve some pagan Celtic lore in their rites, or was the evidence gleaned from so-called 'confessions' just hearsay, or blatant lies aimed at discrediting them? But if this was so, why had they struck on this particular image? Had someone invented a rite that by some miraculous coincidence aped the very Grail legend itself? Why did Wolfram von Eschenbach, in his take on the legends, make the Templars the guardians of the Grail? Here were questions I would like an answer to.

But it is in the symbols of alchemy that the best evidence for the continuation of the spirit of Celtic paganism is found. Alchemy was not just an early form of chemistry; it had a psychologically transforming side, and thus Jung relates it to the pagan mysteries. Alchemical symbolism, Jung argues, was undoubtedly rooted in pre-Christian, and evidently shamanic, tradition – a point of view echoed by master alchemist Albertus Magnus, the owner of a magical oracular gilded head, who states that alchemy was a continuation of the religion of the druids![4]

Certainly much alchemical symbolism – for example, the figure of the serpent/raven and its relation to the underworld power in need of redemption – had clear Celtic antecedents:

> *I am an infirm and weak old man, surnamed the dragon; therefore I am shut up in a cave, that I may be ransomed by the kingly crown …*
> *A fiery sword inflicts great torments upon me; death makes weak my flesh and bones … My soul and my spirit depart; a terrible poison, I am likened to a black Raven, for that is the wages of sin; in dust and earth I lie, that out of Three may come One. O soul and spirit, leave me not, that I may see again the light of day, and the hero of peace whom the whole world shall behold may arise from me.*[5]

The dragon and the raven hint at a connection to the serpentine lord chained in the abyss: Cronos, Odin, Bran and Lug are all underworld deities associated quite clearly with the raven (Cronos is related linguistically to the crow by Graves), and all are released from the unconscious state through either rebirth and rescue, or through other-worldly communication. The head of the crow was a particularly potent theme:

> *See that man in the shape of St Paul … He wishes to take the naked blade either to cut off his head or to do something else to that man who is kneeling at his feet … But do you wish to know the meaning of that man taking the sword? It means that the Head of the Crow must be cut off, the head must be cut off that man … who is kneeling … Take the head from that black man, cut off the Head of the Crow, and once it has been removed, the colour white will immediately come.*[6]

Jung is similarly of the opinion that alchemy had its origins in paganism, and as Nathan Schwartz-Salant says:

> *In a highly novel departure from Christianity's notion of the fall, Original Sin is depicted in an early alchemical myth as being the result of the castration of the original bisexual Great Goddess Cybele.*[7]

This, however, is no 'novel departure' but a return to the imagery of pagan mythology – the same imagery found in the Celtic creation myth of the death of the Irish goddess Macha, who is none other than the divided Tiamat. It is apparent that the 'purpose' of alchemy was identical to that of Celtic religion – to redeem the fallen cosmos. As Jung says:

> *The fundamental idea of alchemy points back to the Tehom, to Tiamat with her dragon attribute, and thus to the primordial matriarchal world which, in the theomachy of the Marduk myth, was overthrown by the masculine world of the father. This historical shift in the world's consciousness towards the masculine is compensated first by the chthonic femininity of the unconscious.*[8]

The word 'alchemy' could easily be replaced with 'druidism' – particularly where Jung says that the purpose of alchemy is to bridge the gulf between these worlds.[9] This was exactly the conclusion I had reached regarding druidic religion. Mercurius, the lapis or 'philosopher's stone', is created to compensate for this masculine light figure, the solar victor of the Bronze Age, just as the Celts turn to the worship of the underworld god, who is to be 'liberated' from the under-world where he is in chains, lamenting his lot. The releasing of this figure cures the Wasteland.

The pagan origins of the figure of Mercurius are clear; in alchemical lore he is shown as a three-headed snake.[10] Amazingly, he is the same 'Nghi', the three-headed 'cattle-stealing' serpent defeated by Trito in the Aryan victory myth par excellence. Had this image been rediscovered, or had it been bubbling away in the underground occult traditions from the earliest times?

The Mercurius of alchemy contains elements of the ecstatic god of pre-Bronze Age Europe, the serpentine divinity sacrificed by the Aryan solar hero to create the cosmos. The redemption and release of the spirit Mercurius are nothing but a continuation of the same impetus that had affected pagan religion. Indeed, woodcuts illustrating the death and rebirth of the king to form the Philosopher's Stone – from a manuscript entitled 'Rosarium Philosophorum' – could be used *in toto* to illustrate the ritual marriage, sacrifice and rebirth of the king in Celtic ritual.[11] They show the pair mating in a flowing stream before their death. It was Medb and Fergus in the lake all over again!

The Philosopher's Stone that turned base metal into gold is also depicted as a vessel – the *vas hermeticum* – and in Wolfram von Eschenbach's version of the *Grail Romance* the Grail is itself a stone, fallen from heaven during the war between God and Satan, and guarded by the Templars. In another tale, one recorded by the brothers Grimm, the spirit Mercurius is trapped within a bottle in the roots of a tree – like Osiris in the pillar at Byblos – and the alchemist Paracelsus releases him. The alchemist, it seems, had freed him from the glass prison.

Clearly, I think, looking into the depths of the well, there is still much work to be done here ...

I stroll down to the lion's head and take a drink of the bloody waters. I am not alone; many have come to the garden today. I glance at my watch – it is the first of February; I had forgotten the date. No wonder the gardens are full; it is the old Celtic festival of Imbolc, the end of winter – halfway between Samhain and Beltaine – and on the opposite side of the year from Lughnasadh, the feast of the god Lugh on 1 August (the date of Lindow Man's discovery). These festivals are once again being celebrated. Looking at the other pilgrims it occurs to me that the religion and culture of the Celts – the Celtic solution – has never been more relevant than it is today.

We stand at the same threshold where the first Celts stood nearly three millennia ago. Here in Avalon I can dream I am in Eden, but the fact is we are in as grave a Wasteland now as at any time in our history as a species. We continue to rape the earth, plundering her natural resources and burying our heads deeply in the sand and not thinking about the consequences of our actions. Perhaps the red-haired bog men hold the key. There can be no return to the religion of the past, but that is not to say that we cannot learn from them. What can they tell us – these wild men who were closer to the earth than we are, whose selfless lives could be given up for the good of the land? We too need to get in touch with that sense of unity with the cosmos that dwells within us – our own hidden twin.

In modern times the pagan undercurrent has exploded into the light of day, following the toppling from power of the Christian religion. God, as Nietzsche says, is dead, or at least in the form in which He dominated men's minds in the Middle Ages. And now in their droves people are re-embracing the 'Old Religion'. At the forefront of this renaissance lies Wicca, a modern religion crafted from old traditions that promotes a return to the pagan religion of the goddess. Some Wiccans model their rites on the psychology of Jung – who speaks of the wisdom to be found in the collective psyche and of the redemption of the god of the dark, whose active imagination was a psychological inner-journey that mirrored the visions of the alchemists and their predecessors, the shamans. Wicca is an eclectic mixture of pagan religion and ceremonial magic. It is not the religion of the Celts, but the spirit remains the same. As modern witch and Jungian psychologist Viviane Crowley states, it owes much to the Dionysian, and it is a paganism of 'ecstatic vision, of trance, of the loss of individual consciousness and its merging into Nature'.[12] In other words, it is equivalent to the drug cult of the Neolithic. History, it seems, is repeating itself.

And man is desperately in need of such a vision now – in this most heinous of Wastelands. I don't wish to launch into a diatribe against modern life, but how different might the world be if instead of raping nature we saw ourselves as part of it – if the vision of the Grail was ours? But here at least, at Glastonbury, there are the faintest glimmerings of a different way. The seeds have been sown, but whether they will grow to fruition before the land is blasted is another matter.

As I exit the gardens I glance up at the Tor, its tower dark against the racing clouds. Do I climb the summit again, or head back to the car? The spots of rain that appear on the pavement decide the issue for me. It is time to go home, time to leave Arthur's Avalon behind. But my mind stays with the Once and Future King – still sleeping under the land. When, I wonder, will he return?

I turn away from the Hill of Vision and mutter a silent prayer to whatever gods might be listening. I pray that we all may see Arthur awake from his slumber of centuries, not in the form of a national hero, but in our own being – for, ultimately, the healing of the Wasteland lies within.

Notes

1. Jones, P and Pennick, N (1997) pp. 100–2.
2. See Tolstoy, N (1988) pp. 65–79.
3. See Gooch, S (1995) pp. 185–6.
4. See Jung, C G (1968) *Alchemical Studies*, Collected Works Volume 13, Routledge.
5. Theatrum Chemicum, IV, pp. 569f, quoted in Jung, C G (1963) para. 733.
6. Quoted in Markale, J (1993) p. 79.
7. Jung, C G (ed. Schwartz Salant, N) (1995) p. 38.
8. Jung, C G (1963a) para. 26.
9. Jung, C G (1963a) para. 27.
10. Jung, C G (1963a) para. 31.
11. See Jung, C G (1983).
12. See Crowley, V (1996).

BIBLIOGRAPHY

Alcock, L (1989) *Arthur's Britain* Penguin Books

Ashe, Geoffrey (1957) *King Arthur's Avalon* Fontana

Ashe, Geoffrey (1990) *Mythology of the British Isles* Methuen

Bede (1955) *The Ecclesiastical History of the English People* Penguin Books

Benham, P (1993) *The Avalonians* Gothic Image

Beresford Ellis, P (1987) *A Dictionary of Irish Mythology* Constable

Bly, R (1990) *Iron John* Element Books

Bottéro, J (1992) *Mesopotamia* University of Chicago Press

Brennan, M (1994) *The Stones of Time* Inner Traditions

Brodie, N (1994) 'The Neolithic-Bronze Age Transition in Britain'
    British Archaeology Reports 238

Bromwich (trans.) (1985) *Selected Poems of Dafydd ap Gwilym* Penguin Books

Bauval, R and Gilbert, A (1995) *The Orion Mystery* Mandarin

Burl, A (1979) *Prehistoric Avebury* University of Yale Press

Burl, A (1999) *Circles of Stone* Harvill Press

Caesar (trans. Handford) (1982) *The Conquest of Gaul* Penguin Books

Campbell, Joseph (1959) *The Masks of God Volume 1: Primitive Mythology*
    Penguin Books

Campbell, Joseph (1962) *The Masks of God Volume 2: Oriental Mythology*
    Penguin Books

Campbell, Joseph (1964) *The Masks of God Volume 3: Occidental Mythology*
    Penguin Books

Campbell, Joseph (1968) *The Masks of God Volume 4: Creative Mythology*
    Penguin Books

Campbell, Joseph (1974) *The Mythic Image* Princeton/Bollingen

225

Campbell, Joseph (1993) *The Hero with a Thousand Faces* Fontana

Capra, F (1989) *Uncommon Wisdom* Flamingo

Castleden, R (2000) *Ancient British Hill Figures* S B Publications

Chadwick, N (1986) *The Celts* Penguin Books

Chrétien de Troyes (trans. D D R Owen) (1988) *Arthurian Romances* Everyman

Clarke, D and A Roberts (1996) *Twilight of the Celtic Gods* Blandford

Clarke, D V, Cowie, T G and Foxon, R (1985) *Symbols of Power at the time of Stonehenge* HMSO

Cooper, R (1977) *A Guide to British Psilocybin Mushrooms* Hassle Free Press

Cope, J (1998) *The Modern Antiquarian* Thorsons

Cotterell, A (1986) *A Dictionary of World Mythology* Oxford University Press

Crossley Holland, K (1980) *The Penguin Book of Norse Myths* Penguin Books

Crowley, V (1996) *Wicca* Thorsons

Cumont, F (1903) *The Mysteries of Mithra* New York

Cunliffe, B (1997) *The Ancient Celts* Penguin Books

Cunliffe, B (1988) *Greeks, Romans and Barbarians* Batsford Books

Cunliffe, B (2001) *Facing the Ocean* Oxford University Press

Darvill, T (1987) *Prehistoric Britain* Batsford Books

Delaney, F (1986) *The Celts* BBC Books

Dixon Kennedy, M (1996) *Celtic Myth and Legend* Blandford

Doniger O'Flaherty, W (trans.) (1975) *Hindu Myths* Penguin Books

Doniger O'Flaherty, W (trans.) (1981) *The Rig Veda* Penguin Books

Dronfield, J (1995) 'Migraine, Light and Hallucinogens: the neurocognitive basis of Irish Megalithic Art' *Oxford Journal of Archaeology* 14, pp. 241–75

Dronfield, J (1996) 'Entering Alternative Realities' Cambridge *Archaeological Journal* 6, pp. 37–72

Eliade, M (1995) *Rites and Symbols of Initiation* Spring

Eliade, M (1989) *Shamanism: Archaic Techniques of Ecstasy* Arkana

Ellis Davidson, H R (1988) *Myths and Symbols in Pagan Europe* Syracuse

Frazer, J G (1987) *The Golden Bough* (abridged single-volume edition) Papermac

Freke, T and Gandy, P (2000) *The Jesus Mysteries* Thorsons

Fortune, Dion (1986) *Glastonbury: Avalon of the Heart* Aquarian

Gantz, J (trans.) (1985) *The Mabinogion* Penguin Books

Gantz, J (trans.) (1986) *Early Irish Myths and Sagas* Penguin Books

Bibliography

Geoffrey of Monmouth (trans. Thorpe, L) (1986) T*he History of the Kings of Britain* Penguin Books

Gibson and Simpson (eds.) (1998) *Prehistoric Ritual and Religion* Sutton Publishing

Gilbert, R A (1991) *The Elements of Mysticism* Element Books

Giraldus Cambrensis (trans. O'Meara) (1951) *Topography of Ireland* Dundalk

Glob, P V (1983) *The Mound People* Paladin

Glob, P V (1988) *The Bog People* Faber & Faber

Gooch, S (1975) *Total Man* Abacus

Gooch, S (1995) *Cities of Dreams* Aulis

Graves, R (1960) *The Greek Myths* Penguin Books (2 vols.)

Graves, R (1961) *The White Goddess* Faber & Faber

Graves, R (1964) *Difficult Questions, Easy Answers* Doubleday

Gray, J (1988) *Near Eastern Mythology* Hamlyn

Green, M (1986) *The Gods of the Celts* Sutton Publishing

Green, M (1989) *Symbol and Image in Celtic Religious Art* Routledge

Green, M (2001) *Dying for the Gods* Tempus

Grigsby, John (1993) *Myth and the Mabinogi* (thesis available from University College of North Wales, Bangor)

Grimm, W and J (1993) *The Complete Grimm's Fairy Tales* Routledge

Grof, S (1998) *The Cosmic Game* New Leaf

Gwyn Griffiths, J (1960) *The Conflict of Horus and Seth* University of Liverpool Press

Hancock, G (1996) *Fingerprints of the Gods* Mandarin

Hancock, G (1998) *Heaven's Mirror* Penguin Books

Hancock, G and Bauval, R (1996) *Keeper of Genesis* Heinemann

Hancock, G; Grigsby, J and R Bauval (1998) *The Mars Mystery* Michael Joseph

Harbison, Peter (1988) *Prehistoric Ireland* Thames & Hudson

Herity, M and Eogan, G (1989) *Ireland in Prehistory* Routledge

Hooke, S H (1963) *Middle Eastern Mythology* Penguin Books

Hutton, R (1993) *The Pagan Religions of the Ancient British Isles* Blackwell

Hutton, R (1996) *The Stations of the Sun* Oxford University Press

Jaynes, J (1993) *The Origins of Consciousness in the Breakdown of the Bicameral Mind* Penguin Books

Jones, G and Jones, T (1974) *The Mabinogion* Everyman

Jones, P and Pennick, N (1997) *A History of Pagan Europe* Routledge

Jung, C G (1963) *Collected Works Volume 14: Mysterium Coniunctionis* Routledge

Jung, C G (1963a) *Collected Works Volume 12: Psychology and Alchemy* Routledge

Jung, C G (1968) *Collected Works Volume 13: Alchemical Studies* Routledge

Jung, C G (1983) *The Psychology of the Transference* Ark

Jung, C G (1986) *Collected Works Volume 5: Symbols of Transformation* Routledge

Jung, C G (1986a) *Analytical Psychology* Ark

Jung, C G (1989) *Psychological Reflections* Ark

Jung, C G (1990) *Memories, Dreams, Reflections* Flamingo

Jung, C G (ed. N Schwartz Salant) (1995) *Jung on Alchemy* Routledge

Jung, E and Von Franz, M. (1986) *The Grail Legend* Coventure

Kerenyi, K (1967) *Eleusis* Princeton/Bollingen

Kerenyi, K (1976) *Dionysos* Princeton/Bollingen

Kerenyi, K and Jung, C G (1985) *Science of Mythology* Ark Paperbacks

Keyte, H and Parrot, A (1993) *The Shorter New Oxford Book of Carols*
    Oxford University Press

Kinsella, T (1990) *The Táin* Oxford University Press

Lacy, N (ed.) (1988) *The Arthurian Encyclopedia* Boydell

Lethbridge, T C (1957) *Gogmagog: The Buried Gods* Routledge

Lincoln, B (1991) *Death, War and Sacrifice* University of Chicago Press

Loomis, R S (1992) *The Grail: From Celtic Myth to Christian Symbol* Constable

Lynch, F (1991) *Prehistoric Anglesey* Anglesey Antiquarian Society

Lynch, F (1997) *Megalithic Tombs and Long Barrows in Britain* Shire Archaeology

MacCana, P (1977) *The Mabinogi* University of Wales Press

Mallory, J P (1991) *In Search of the Indo-Europeans* Thames & Hudson

Malone, C (1989) *Avebury* Batsford Books

Malory, T (1969) *La Morte D'Arthur* Penguin Books

Mann, Nick (1986) *Glastonbury Tor* Annenterprise

Markale, J (1986) *Women of the Celts* Inner Traditions

Markale, J (1993) *The Celts* Inner Traditions

Markale, J (1995) *Merlin* Inner Traditions

Markale, J (1999) *The Druids* Inner Traditions

Matarasso (trans.) (1969) *The Quest for the Holy Grail* Penguin Books

Matthews, Caitlin (1987) *Mabon and the Mysteries of Britain* Arkana

Matthews, Caitlin (1989) *Arthur and the Sovereignty of Britain* Arkana

Bibliography

Matthews, John (1991) *Taliesin: Shamanism and the Bardic Mysteries of Britain and Ireland* Aquarian

Matthews, John (1992) *Gawain* Aquarian

Matthews, John (1993) *Robin Hood* Gothic Image Publications

Matthews, John (1997) *The Grail: Quest for the Eternal* Thames & Hudson

Matthews, J and C (1996) *Encyclopaedia of Celtic Wisdom* Element Books

McKenna, T (1992) *Food of the Gods* Rider

Megaw and Simpson (1988) *Introduction to British Prehistory* Leicester University Press

Meyer, K (trans.) (1993) *The Death Tales of the Ulster Heroes* Dublin Institute for Advanced Studies

Narby, J (1998) *The Cosmic Serpent* Phoenix

Neumann, E (1993) *The Origins and history of Consciousness* Princeton/Bollingen

Neumann, E (1996) *The Great Mother* Routledge

North, J (1996) *Stonehenge: Neolithic Man and the Cosmos* HarperCollins

O'Farrel, P (1995) *Ancient Irish Legends* Gill & MacMillan

O'Kelly, M J (1994) *Newgrange* Thames & Hudson

Parker Pearson, Michael (1993) *Bronze Age Britain* Batsford Books

Pennick, N (1996) *Celtic Sacred Landscapes* Thames & Hudson

Piggot, S (1965) *Ancient Europe* Edinburgh

Pitts, M (2000) *Hengeworld* Century

Pollard, J (1997) *Neolithic Britain* Shire publications

Powell, T G E (1987) *The Celts* Thames & Hudson

Rees, A and B (1961) *Celtic Heritage* Thames & Hudson

Renfrew, C (1998) *Archaeology and Language* Pimlico

Rhys Jones, T J (1977) *Teach Yourself Living* Welsh Teach Yourself Books

Richards, Julian (1991) *Stonehenge* Batsford Books

Richards, M (1996) 'First Farmers with no taste for Grain' *British Archaeology* 12 March 1996

Rohl, D (1998) *Legend* Century

Rolleston, T W (1987) *Myths and Legends of the Celtic Race* Constable

Ross, A (1996) *Pagan Celtic Britain* University of Chicago Press

Ross, A and Robbins, D (1989) *The Life and Death of a Druid Prince* Century Hutchinson

Rudgley, R (1993) *The Alchemy of Culture* British Museum Press

Rudgley, R (1999) *Encyclopaedia of Psychoactive Substances* Abacus

Rundle Clark, R T (1959) *Myth and Symbol in Ancient Egypt* Thames & Hudson

Sanders, N K (trans.) (1972) *The Epic of Gilgamesh* Penguin Books

Santillana, G and Von Dechend, H (1977) *Hamlet's Mill* Nonpareil Books

Sherratt, A (1996) 'Flying up with the souls of the dead'
    British Archaeology 15 June 1996

Sjoestedt, M (1982) *Gods and Heroes of the Celts* Berkeley

Stead, Bourke, Brothwell (1986) *Lindow Man* British Museum Press

Stevens, A (1990) *Archetype* Routledge

Stewart, R J (1986) *The Mystic Life of Merlin* Arkana

Stone, Alby (1994) 'Hellhounds, Werewolves and the Germanic Underworld'
    Mercian Mysteries 20

Stone, Alby (1997) *Ymir's Flesh* Heart of Albion Press

Stone, B (trans.) (1974) *Sir Gawain and the Green Knight* Penguin Books

Summers, Montague, (1934) *The Werewolf* E P Dutton, New York

Tacitus (trans. H Mattingley and S A Handford) (1986) *The Agricola
    and Germania* Penguin Books

Tolkien, J R R (1997) *The Monsters and the Critics and Other Essays* HarperCollins

Tolstoy, N (1988) *The Quest for Merlin* Sceptre

Turner, R C and Scaife, R G (1995) *Bog Bodies* British Museum Press

Wallis Budge, E A (1989) *The Book of the Dead* Arkana

Wasson, G; Hofmann, A and Ruck, C (1978) *The Road to Eleusis* New York

Wasson, S K; Ott, J; Ruck, C and Doniger O'Flaherty, W (1986) *Persephone's Quest:
    Entheogens and the Origins of Religion* Yale University Press

Weston, J L (1920) *From Ritual to Romance*

Westwood, J (1987) *Albion – A Guide to Legendary Britain* Paladin

Wilber, K (1996) *Up From Eden* Quest Books

Wilson, C (1984) *C G Jung – Lord of the Underworld* Aquarian

Wilson, C (1996) *From Atlantis to the Sphinx* Virgin Publishing

Wilson, C (1998) *Alien Dawn* Virgin Publishing

Wolfram von Eschenbach (trans. A T Hatto) (1980) *Parzival* Penguin Books

Zimmer, H (1974) *Myths and Symbols in Indian Art and Civilisation*
    Princeton/Bollingen

INDEX

Donn, 136, 153

Dover Castle, xv, xvii, xx, 5, 19, 27

Draco, 146, 149, 169

dragon, xxv, 122, 123, 134, 138, 146,
    152, 166, 169, 173, 175, 195,
    196, 220, 221

druids, xvii, xviii, xxvii, 17, 18, 19, 21,
    22, 25, 27, 46, 47, 49, 88, 104,
    105, 152, 153, 156, 157, 164,
    185, 211, 212, 218, 220
  'groves', 17, 47
  origin of name, 18
  religion, xviii
  training of, 17

Duggleby Howe, 103, 104, 107, 114,
    115

Dyfed, 24, 58, 163

Eber Donn, 136

Eden, Garden of, 121, 132, 165, 222

Efnissien, 57, 58, 94

ego, 91, 95, 116, 122, 128, 131, 132,
    133, 134, 140, 147, 185, 186,
    187, 206, 211

Egypt, xviii, 75, 76, 98, 100, 105, 106,
    107, 137, 151, 156, 163, 167,
    204

eidolon, 93, 94, 95, 96, 99, 106, 133,
    136, 147, 164, 174, 176, 184,
    217

Eleusis, 79, 91, 94, 96, 106, 132, 133,
    161, 187, 211
  Mysteries of, 91, 93, 94, 95, 96, 107,
    152, 161, 168, 183, 198, 217

Elphin mab Gwyddno, 180

Emhain Macha, 138, 155

Emrys, 143, 144, 145, 146

enantiodromia, 166, 168, 177, 191

Enkidu, 173, 174

entoptic phenomena. *See* Phosphenes

ergot, 12, 54, 56, 94, 95, 128, 178, 193,
    213

Eschenbach, Wolfram von, 4, 219, 222

Esus, 22, 45

Eurydice, 200

Excalibur, 21

Excalibur (film), 3

farming, 71, 74, 75, 78, 114, 118, 128,
    160

fearg, 53

Fenrir, 159

Fer Caille, 42, 45, 153

Fer Roigan, 153

Fergus Mac Roich, 40, 41, 156, 221

fermentation, 86, 89

fertility cults, 6, 7, 12, 21, 42, 44, 64,
    75, 76, 79, 90, 165, 167, 208,
    212, 219

Fidchell, 161, 162

Fimbulvetr, 159

Fintan, 183, 184

Fionn mac Cumhaill (Finn mac Cool),
    23, 40, 62, 178, 179, 188

fish. *See* Fisher King
  symbol, xxvi, xxvii, 4, 28, 51, 62,
    178, 179, 180, 181, 182, 183,
    184, 185, 188, 189, 193, 196,
    204, 217

Fisher King, The, xxvi, xxvii, 3, 4, 55,
    58, 62, 79, 176, 178, 182, 183,
    188

flood myths, 23, 122, 160, 173, 175,
    176, 182, 183, 186

Fomhoiré, 44, 127, 136

Fortune, Dion (Mary Violet Firth),
    xxiii, xxv, xxvi, xxvii, xxx, 9,
    217
  Avalon of the Heart, xxiii

fox, 10, 14, 30, 31, 35, 51, 52, 56

Frazer, Sir J G, 6, 7, 56, 64, 75, 99

Frobenius, Leo, 101, 195

Froech, 124, 204

Fussel's lodge, 77, 99, 125

Index

Index

Teutates, 22, 45

Thera, 168

Theseus, 107, 124

thigh wound, 32, 46, 55, 58, 59, 62,
       75, 78, 103, 136, 184, 208,
       209, 212

Thunor, 44, 82. *See* Taranis

Tiamat, 122, 123, 129, 159, 166, 203,
       221

Tir Na N'Og, 85, 87

Titans, 126, 131

Tolkien, J R R, xv, 31

Tollund Man, 11, 12, 35, 39, 42, 43, 54,
       128, 178, 188

Tolosa (Toulouse), 21

Tolstoy, Count Nikolai, 37, 50, 84, 143,
       145, 149, 224

tombs (prehistoric), 70, 71, 72, 73, 74,
       77, 80, 81, 86, 87, 90, 95, 97,
       99, 100, 103, 105, 107, 114,
       115, 119, 125, 132
    orientation, 77
    origin of form, 80

Tooth of the Wolf, 53, 54. *See* ergot

torc, 42

triple death, the, xvii, 22, 31, 35, 36, 48,
       50, 122, 147, 173, 178

Tuan mac Cairell, 183, 188

Tuatha Dé Danann, 44, 87, 127, 136,
       164, 165

Tuetones, 21

Tuisto, 139. *See* 'Twin' and Yemo

Tvastr, 199

'Twin', 135, 136, 139, 140, 145, 147,
       199, 212. *See* Yemo

Twrch trwyth, 192

Uath Mac Immoman, 32, 42

Udagan, 49. *See* shamanism

Uffington White Horse, 108, 139

Ulster, 23, 31, 32, 33, 40, 43, 124, 138,
       154, 155, 203, 204

Ulster Cycle, The, 31, 124

unconscious, 132, 134, 177, 185, 186,
       187, 197, 206, 207, 211, 220,
       221

underworld, the, xxiv, 41, 42, 44, 45,
       46, 49, 61, 62, 75, 76, 79, 80,
       82, 83, 88, 92, 98, 99, 103, 106,
       108, 119, 122, 125, 126, 132,
       133, 152, 156, 159, 163, 164,
       165, 174, 175, 177, 178, 184,
       186, 189, 193, 195, 196, 198,
       201, 210, 212, 220, 221

Urshanabi, 175

Uruk, 173, 174, 176

Uther Pendragon, 144, 145

Ut-na-Pishtim, 175

Valhalla, 157, 159, 160, 162

Vasuki, 125, 129, 146

Venus, 84, 98, 99

vernacular literature, xx

Virgil, 197

Vishnu, 126, 182

vitrum, 14. *See* body painting and
    woad

Vortigern, 144, 145

Vritra, 122, 125, 138, 161, 166, 167,
       169, 193

Wales, xx, xxiv, xxv, 17, 21, 23, 27, 65,
       70, 117, 144, 145, 178, 179

Wasteland, the, 3, 4, 29, 55, 70, 106,
       156, 157, 166, 167, 168, 169,
       189, 197, 200, 203, 204, 205,
       207, 208, 209, 214, 219, 221,
       222, 223

water cults, xxiv, xxvi, 10, 11, 13, 20,
       21, 22, 28, 37, 40, 123, 129,
       147, 161, 167, 169, 175, 180,
       184, 187, 193, 196, 199, 207,
       208, 209, 212, 217, 222

Wayland's Smithy, 109

wells, xvii, xxvii, 19, 20, 22, 36, 182,
        208, 209, 218. *See* water cults
Wepwawet, 106, 161
werewolf, 51, 52, 53, 56
West Kennet longbarrow (Wiltshire),
        69, 70, 71, 72, 73, 83, 100, 101,
        109, 114, 117, 140
    elderly male buried in, 70, 71, 72,
        109, 114, 117, 140
Weston, Jessie L, 6, 7
    From Ritual to Romance, 6
White Horse Hill (Uffington), 108
Wild Herdsman, 47, 48, 49, 54, 184
Wild Hunt, the, xxiv, 48
Wilhelm, Richard, 56, 213
woad, xvii, 14
wolf, 48, 49, 50, 51, 52, 53, 54, 59, 95,
        106, 133, 137, 154, 159, 160,
        161, 174, 218

Woodhenge, 97, 116
    child sacrifice at, 97
Worsley Man, 13, 19, 42
Wotan, 48, 199. *See also* Odin
Wounded King, the, 3, 4, 5, 15, 55, 57,
        58, 71, 103, 147, 157, 175,
        178, 182, 198, 206

Yahweh, 122, 134, 165
Yemo, 135, 136, 140, 143, 147, 151,
        166, 200
Yggdrasil, 160, 199, 200
Ymir, 136, 137, 200
Yspaddaden, 191
yuga, 160

Zeus, 126, 139, 164, 193, 195, 197,
        198, 206